PRACTICING POSITIVE
Psychology Coaching

PRACTICING POSITIVE

Psychology Coaching

ASSESSMENT, ACTIVITIES, AND
STRATEGIES FOR SUCCESS

ROBERT BISWAS-DIENER

WILEY

JOHN WILEY & SONS, INC.

Library of Congress Cataloging-in-Publication Data:

Biswas-Diener, Robert.
Practicing positive psychology coaching : assessment, activities, and strategies for success / Robert Biswas-Diener.

    p. cm.
    Includes index.
    ISBN 978-0-470-53676-6 (pbk.); 978-0-470-88186-6 (ePDF); 978-0-470-88192-7 (eMobi);
    978-0-470-88193-4 (ePub)
    1. Personal coaching. 2. Positive psychology. I. Title.
    BF637.P36B563 2010
    158'.3—dc22

                        2010010870

Printed in the United States of America

10 9 8 7 6 5 4 3 2 1

Contents

Acknowledgments   vii

CHAPTER ONE   Education to Empowerment: An Introduction
to Applying Positive Psychology Coaching   1

CHAPTER TWO   Using Your Best to Make You Better   19

CHAPTER THREE Harnessing Positivity   39

CHAPTER FOUR   Making Molehills out of Mountains: Coaching Goals
and Hope for the Future   59

CHAPTER FIVE   Positive Diagnosis   75

CHAPTER SIX   Positive Assessment   99

CHAPTER SEVEN Gray Hairs and Gravestones: Positive Psychology
Coaching Across the Lifespan   125

CHAPTER EIGHT   The Practice of Positive Psychology Coaching   145

Endnotes   153

Author Index   163

Subject Index   165

Acknowledgments

I would like to thank my editor, Marquita Flemming, for her kind words and guidance; also, thanks to everyone at John Wiley & Sons who helped make this book possible. I am also indebted to a number of positive psychologists who helped inform my ideas about coaching applications as well as those who gave feedback on individual chapters. These include Alex Linley, Amanda Levy, Reena Govindji, Richard Boyatzis, Sunny Karir, Todd Kashdan, and many others. Thanks to all of you. Finally, I would like to extend my deepest gratitude to my wife and my children, who supported this project in innumerable ways.

PRACTICING POSITIVE
Psychology Coaching

Education to Empowerment: An Introduction to Applying Positive Psychology Coaching

In 2007 an extraordinary thing happened to me: I published my first ever book, *Positive Psychology Coaching*.[1] It was a defining moment, much like getting my doctorate or the birth of my children. Holding the book—the actual book—in my hands represented a huge accomplishment and marked a turning point in my life. We all know about Steven Covey's time matrix: People are likely to continue putting off those tasks that are important but not necessarily urgent. Well, I was lucky enough not to fall into that trap. I was one of those folks who took this lifelong dream—writing a book—off the back burner and made it happen. The book was written with my co-author Ben Dean over the course of a year, and it was the result of countless hours of phone calls, interviews, reviews of the research literature, and even a couple of international trips. Those grueling hours of lonely writing under the emotional pressure of looming deadlines had all paid off. It is difficult to describe the intense mix of relief, accomplishment, pride, and fatigue I felt. I was, at long last, a published author. I had a small book launch in England, received the occasional letter of thanks from strangers in places like India and Australia, and was invited to give talks and coaching demonstrations. My star seemed to be on the rise.

And then a funny thing happened. A few months after the publication of the book, Ben and I received a scathing review on Amazon.com. The author of the review, which ran about 1,200 words—the length of a short magazine article—clearly did not like the book. He referred to Ben and me as "academics with no writing skills" and, at one point, said, "This book was so bad, in so many ways, it's hard to know where to start." The review included stinging phrases like "a shallow rehash" and "I don't know which was more painful: their condescending prose, or the glee with which they seem to think they've said something useful." The reviewer concluded with a list of books people should read instead of *Positive Psychology Coaching*. Again, it is difficult to describe the overwhelming emotions I felt while reading this review. I was crushed. This book had been the major project representing a year of my life. It was the very activity to which I chose to commit myself precisely because I felt it was so worthwhile. I instantly thought of every instance that I told my son "I'm sorry I can't play with you right now, Daddy's working on his book." Would I have been better off to abandon the writing project in favor of more family time?

What other opportunities had I missed while I was—arguably—wasting a year on a useless book? For the first time since I had begun working on the project I began to question the wisdom of my decision and the quality of the product I had produced.

What followed, as you might expect, was a period of depression. I had very definitely been knocked out of my saddle. I quit working on research projects and quit writing magazine articles. I went into each coaching session shaky and uncertain of my own abilities. I wondered if I was really a laughingstock to others and just didn't realize it. And it wasn't just me: The book sales dipped sharply after the review appeared online. Dozens of people on Amazon.com reported that the review was helpful to them and one even took the time to comment: "Saved me reading the book." I wondered what type of person I was that people had to be saved from me and from my best efforts. Even now, more than two years later, I find writing about these events painful.

Fortunately, the depression didn't last. After a couple weeks of floundering I bounced back. I began to see that, between the harsher criticisms and strong opinions about tone and language use, the reviewer was correct on many points. In fact, I should go on record here saying that I really bear the reviewer no personal ill will. It might surprise you to learn this, but he and I have exchanged some very friendly e-mails in the time since his review was published. He apologized for the tone of the review, which he said was written largely for effect and that, upon further consideration, he thought was disrespectful. I accepted his apology and believe he meant it sincerely. Despite all that, I have to acknowledge that the reviewer made some legitimate points and illuminated the differences in expectations I had as a writer from those held by many of my readers. I had thought that, as an expert positive psychology researcher, I would introduce coaches to the fascinating new science of positive psychology. I further expected that readers would simply want to take this information and create their own interventions in their own ways, appropriate to their own coaching practices. These ideas, as I later learned, were somewhat off the mark. In my experience with coaches since that time, I have found that most are eager for ready-made interventions and are principally interested in research results when they are couched in terms of "next steps," "practical skills," or "applications." That is, as an academic I have always been excited by ideas, and I realized, all too late, that coaches are generally excited by action.

What the reviewer wanted—and I think he was right to want this—was practical next steps: clear suggestions for translating the research into workable questions, assessments, and interventions for use with coaching clients. His review expressed, if nothing else, his frustration with what I had done with *Positive Psychology Coaching*. I had discussed many studies but rarely mentioned the relation of these exciting research results to coaching. As an expert, I failed to accept the mantle of leadership and offer clever ways to spin the straw of positive psychology into coaching gold. For my own part, I had assumed that my initial mission of merely educating readers about positive psychology would be enough. The interesting aspect of all this was that it was not the harsh review that changed my thinking—although it certainly presented a red flag that suggested my thinking needed to be changed. What really turned me around was conducting workshops with coaches. I began standing in front of groups of coaches in places like Iceland, Turkey, Canada, and Denmark, and they all wanted the exact same thing as my reviewer: They wanted tools, not concepts or ideas. Over the course of many workshops my attitude evolved from one of wanting to educate people to one of wanting to inspire people to one of wanting to empower people. And here, at last, is the heart of my critic's comments: a plea to be empowered.

I want to be clear, up front, about my goals for this volume. I do not apologize for my earlier book—indeed, I do not believe there is anything to apologize for. I am quite proud of it. Nor do I write this book as a means of compensating for failures related to the first book. Finally, I do not write this book as a defense against my earlier critics. Instead, I wanted to write an additional book that represents my own personal growth. My goal for the first volume was to educate people about the emerging science of positive psychology, and my goal for this book is to present a wide range of useful tools based on that science. As the title of this book implies, I am interested in strategies for assessing and applying positive psychology within the coaching context. To the extent that you, the reader, can walk away from this book with new ideas that you can immediately put into practice in your own coaching, this will have been a successful endeavor.

▶ Why Are You Reading This Book?

It may sound like an unusual question, but I would like you to stop and think about why you are reading this book. Are you hoping to learn something about the science of positive psychology that you didn't know before? Are you hoping to walk away from the experience with actual tools that you can use with your clients? Are you hoping to breathe new life into your existing coaching practice by adopting a new philosophical orientation? Are you hoping that this book will, itself, serve as a sort of coaching education? The answer to the question of why you are reading this book is important because it sets up expectations for the book's contents and its usefulness to you.

It may help you to think about the two coaching books I have written—this volume and the earlier *Positive Psychology Coaching: Putting the science of happiness to work for your clients*—as I do: as a single book divided into two volumes, one intended to present a foundation of science and the second written with the purpose of expanding on this foundation in practical ways. This process, which I call "education to empowerment," reflects the same approach I use in my international workshops. I begin with a seed of knowledge (education), introducing participants to a new idea such as the notion that developing strengths might lead to success more than overcoming weaknesses. From there I move to inspiration, in which I show that this knowledge can be used in exciting ways to improve performance. Using the strengths example, *I demonstrate my ability to accurately spot strengths in strangers using very little information*. In truth, my ability to spot strengths is not some prodigious talent I have, but rather, it is the result of countless hours of practice. Even so, my workshop participants find this inspiring, to watch someone who is masterful at a skill. Psychologists know much about inspiration, which we sometimes call "elevation."[2] Elevation is an emotional reaction related to awe at the performance of another person. This emotional engagement is just what the "education" piece often lacks, and is exactly what my critic was complaining about. Moving people into an elevated state, however, prepares them for action. From here, I try to shift from inspiration to empowerment. There is a subtle but critical difference between seeing that something is possible and realizing that you, yourself, can achieve it. When we watch Olympic athletes perform, for instance, we are amazed at what they are able to do, but we do not for one second think that we could accomplish the same level of mastery. The trick in workshops, coaching, or even book writing is to show people what is possible and then wake them up to the idea that they have the personal resources to enact this change in their own lives. Going back to the strengths example, I show my workshop participants that they, too, have the ability to easily spot strengths in action, even in strangers.

The "Education to Empowerment" Model

Education: Developing strengths might lead to success more than overcoming weaknesses.

Inspiration: Demonstrate my ability to accurately spot strengths in strangers using very little information.

Empowerment: I show my workshop participants that they, too, have the ability to easily spot strengths in action, even in strangers.

Example of the Education-to-Empowerment Continuum

1. **Education** --------------- 2. **Inspiration** --------------- 3. **Empowerment**

"Spotting strengths is a useful skill."   "It is possible to spot strengths."   "You, yourself, can learn to spot strengths."

■ The Two Questions That Inform This Book

In a recent issue of *Choice* magazine, a publication for coaches, I wrote an article about the relationship between coaching and positive psychology.[3] For the uninitiated, positive psychology is a relatively new movement—about a decade old—within the field of psychology. Positive psychology is an emphasis on the scientific study of what is right, rather than what is wrong, with people. It includes research on hope, happiness, strengths, resilience, courage, and other positive aspects of human functioning and flourishing. To be sure, positive psychology owes much to its many intellectual forebears including figures in classical Greek thought, the humanistic movement, and even religious studies. Positive psychologists are not the first to suggest that there is tremendous traction in looking at when people are at their best or discussing how people might achieve their highest potential. Positive psychologists do, however, have the most sophisticated empirical methods of studying these topics. By relying on the virtues of the scientific method, such as representative samples, advanced analytic technique, and controlled laboratory studies, positive psychologists are able to arrive at insights that were previously out of bounds to faith, intuition, reasoning, and logic. It doesn't take much to see that positive psychology and coaching are natural bedfellows. Both professions are principally about helping individuals and groups to perform better and live more satisfying lives.

Positive Psychology in a Nutshell

1. Positive psychology looks at what is right with people, focuses on when people are at their best, and attends to individual and group flourishing.

2. Positive psychology is not the focus of the positive at the expense of the negative. Positive psychologists recognize negative emotions, failure, problems, and other unpleasantries as natural and important aspects of life.

3. Positive psychology is, first and foremost, a science. As such, it is principally concerned with evidence, measurement, and testing. That said, positive psychology is also an applied science, and there is a common understanding that research results will lead to the creation of real-world interventions that will improve school, businesses, governments, and other aspects of individual and social life.

4. Interventions produced by positive psychologists are, by and large, positive interventions. Positive interventions are ways of working with people where the focus is not on alleviating pain or restoring a person to normal functioning from substandard function, but, rather, on promoting superior functioning. Positive psychologists often talk about this in terms of helping clients go from "+3" to "+5."

For many people, coaching is the natural choice for being the applied arm of positive psychology. In fact, many people with an interest and education on positive psychology open coaching practices. Although positive psychology is, itself, an applied science, there is, as yet, no coherent or consistent methodology for delivering positive psychology services. There are people, such as my colleagues at the Centre for Applied Positive Psychology (CAPP), who use strengths science as the centerpiece of their organizational consulting work. There are others who integrate tenets of positive psychology into their psychotherapy practices. And there are many, many others who turn to coaching as a means of putting positive psychology into practice.

▶ What Can Positive Psychology Do for Coaching?

This raises the first, most important, and most obvious question that forms the foundation of this book: What can positive psychology do for coaching? There is an unspoken maxim that holds that, as a science, positive psychology is well poised to inform the coaching profession and help elevate the standards and tools of practice. Indeed, positive psychology has provided a number of empirically validated interventions that might be of interest and use to coaches of all stripes. For instance, researcher Fred Bryant at the University of Chicago has conducted studies of the emotional consequences of using pieces of memorabilia to "positively reminisce" (that is, to savor the past).[4] This has all sorts of practical ramifications for coaching. Just imagine using positive reminiscence with organizational leaders, teams, couples, or individuals seeking more meaning and happiness at home or at work. This is simply a variation on the coaching technique of visioning, but with a retrospective focus instead of a future focus. Positive psychology has produced a number of these types of interventions that, taken together, form the corpus of a scientific toolbox that coaches can add to their existing practices. Positive psychology also has produced new and often counterintuitive insights. Just consider a few of the following: studies show that people are generally poor predictors of how well they will adjust to future situations;[5] that too much satisfaction actually appears to undermine performance;[6] that fantasizing about the future can undermine motivation;[7] and that managing to strengths can produce better performance at work relative to managing to weaknesses (don't worry, I'll talk about all of these later on!).[8] These insights can help coaches approach common client dilemmas with new ideas, appreciation, and ways of working. Positive psychology also provides new assessments of which coaches can avail themselves. There are well-validated surveys of strengths, optimism, life satisfaction, work style, and many other topics that are directly relevant to coaching.

Taken together, the specific set of intervention tools and assessment rooted in the science of positive psychology form the corpus of positive psychology coaching. Interestingly, positive psychology coaching, as an endeavor distinct from other approaches to coaching, is fairly poorly defined. It is unclear who should reasonably call him or herself a positive psychology coach. Should there be some formal certification process by which such coaches can evidence their mastery of both positive psychology and coaching? Should positive psychology coaching be viewed as additional, advanced coach training, in the same way that—say—psychiatric residency is specific training undertaken beyond the basics of medical school? Most readers who are experienced coaches will be familiar with the ways in which these uncertainties mirror the evolution of the field of coaching as a whole. In the early days of coaching, a few brave and visionary pioneers went about the business of motivating others to help them achieve their goals. To transform a loose collection of motivational practices into a coherent profession, however, took time. Professional organizations such as the International Coach Federation have been invaluable in establishing coherent standards for training, practice, and ethical behavior. Researchers such as Anthony Grant and his peers at the Coaching Psychology Unit at University of Sydney have been instrumental in establishing the validity and effectiveness of coaching interventions.[9] Independent coach training schools and university-based programs have been vital in acting as the front lines of creating the profession by balancing market needs with responsible practices.

It is my strong recommendation that positive psychology coaching should be considered with equal gravitas. I am, to be honest, concerned about the number of people who hang up shingles and market themselves as "positive psychology coaches" with limited knowledge of both standard coaching techniques and the science of positive psychology. This is, to some extent, a profession-wide problem, but it is one that concerns me as a practitioner of positive psychology in particular. At the heart of my concern is the fact that positive psychology is a science and, as such, is both technical and dynamic. Although the topics of positive psychology, such as happiness, appear at first glance to be straightforward concerns, the scientific exploration of them is far from simple. A technical understanding of positive psychology, including the ability to critically consume the research literature, effectively use relevant assessments, and create interventions that are within the bounds of the field, is a critical component to being an effective positive psychology coach.

Equally troubling is the fact that, as a science, positive psychology is ever changing. I'll give you an example: In 2002 a collaborator and I published a frequently cited article reviewing the existing research literature connecting income with happiness. Among our reported conclusions was the idea that—at the national level—as income goes up over time happiness stays level.[10] In the United States, for example, household incomes have grown dramatically across the decades, but the average level of happiness appears to have remained flat. This casts doubt on the idea that increasing national wealth, consumption, and infrastructure actually translates to a higher quality of life. This finding, called the "Easterlin Paradox" after the UCLA economist who first reported it, is important.[11] It could, for instance, help policy makers create laws and programs that balance economic concerns with the well-being of citizens. The problem is, it might not be true. In the years since 2002 a number of scientists—economists, sociologists, and psychologists—have published articles (based on data and sophisticated analyses) refuting the Easterlin Paradox.[12,13] It turns out the story of money and happiness might just be a bit more complicated. It could be that the Easterlin Paradox exists in certain countries but not others. If this is the case, then the next logical step would be to identify the factors that lead toward or away from this flattening effect of happiness. An alternative explanation might also be that the Easterlin Paradox depends a little on what type of happiness in which a person is interested. It could be that the Easterlin Paradox holds true for feelings of happiness but not cognitive evaluations of happiness such as life satisfaction judgments.[14] As more research is conducted the story will continue to unfold. Did my collaborator and I misreport? No, we reported conclusions based on the best available data at that time. But as new studies are conducted our conclusions will necessarily be modified. In this spirit of dynamism it is vital that those calling themselves positive psychology coaches have a mechanism for regularly updating their knowledge of the field.

■ Some Suggestions for the Creation of a Formal Positive Psychology Coaching Profession

Following I have listed six core areas that I believe to be crucial for the professionalization of positive psychology coaching as a subdiscipline of both positive psychology and coaching. In addition, I make specific recommendations concerning each of these core areas:

1. Credentialing

   Just as the International Coach Federation has established standards for training and credentialing coaches, I believe that those using the professional label of "positive psychology coach" ought to have formal training in positive psychology. At this time, there is no set standard for the type or duration of this training, and I am not so presumptuous as to think that my opinion can be the sole voice on this topic. While one obvious type of credential is a doctorate degree, there are a variety of other types of training programs as well. Here, I suggest a number of types of programs and Internet information for each (current as of the time of this writing).

   Master's Degree Programs in Positive Psychology: The advantage of these programs—and there are only two in the world that I am aware of—is that they have the backing of established, accredited universities and therefore enjoy a depth and rigor that is a hallmark of university education. The two programs include:

A. University of East London, Master's degree in Applied Positive Psychology http://www.uel.ac.uk/psychology/programmes/postgraduate/positive-msc.htm

B. University of Pennsylvania, Master's degree in Applied Positive Psychology http://www.sas.upenn.edu/lps/graduate/mapp/

Certificate Coaching Programs in Positive Psychology: There are a number of programs for coaches that specifically promise an education in positive psychology research, assessment, and intervention. I have listed three different types of such programs here.

A. San Francisco State University, College of Extended Learning, Core Strengths Coaching http://www.cel.sfsu.edu/coaching/classes.cfm?selection=indprograms&Abbrev=coah&Admin_unit=E

B. MentorCoach, ICF certified training with a positive psychology emphasis http://www.mentorcoach.com

C. Terri Levine Positive Psychology Coaching Program (in the interests of full disclosure, I designed this eight-unit certificate course) http://www.terrilevine.com/positivepsych.htm

2. Keeping Up-to-Date with Positive Psychology

As mentioned previously, positive psychology's knowledge base is continually shifting. It is crucial that those calling themselves positive psychology coaches keep abreast of current developments in the field and that they do so in a rigorous and consistent manner. Reading a book, such as this one, is one means of updating knowledge, but even the research and interventions reported on between these covers will need updating. There are a variety of online listservs and blogs about positive psychology, but I do not consider these adequate sources of current information because they are not primary sources and because they do not necessarily reflect the voices of those most expert in the field. Instead, I highly recommend that people subscribe to the academic journals in which positive psychology research is published, attend skills-based trainings by recognized experts, and join official positive psychology professional groups. I include a brief list of each of these below:

Journals: There are a number of journals, including coaching journals, that publish positive psychology research. However, there are relatively few journals that are wholly devoted to the science of positive psychology.

A. The *Journal of Happiness Studies* http://www.springer.com/social+sciences/quality+of+life+research/journal/10902?detailsPage=description

B. The *Journal of Positive Psychology* http://www.tandf.co.uk/journals/titles/17439760.asp

C. *The British Psychological Society Special Group in Coaching* http://www.bps.org.uk/coachingpsy/journal.cfm

Trainings: There are a number of high-quality trainings in positive psychology application and assessment that are appropriate for coaches. The following examples do not represent a complete list but are intended to act as illustrations of trainings with an emphasis on positive psychology.

A. Realise 2 Practitioner Programme (Centre for Applied Positive Psychology—UK). This two-day program introduces a wide range of practitioners to the science of strengths, to a well-regarded strengths assessment, and to strategies for using a strengths focus as work. http://www.cappeu.com/practitioners .htm

B. Strengths Training (Values in Action Institute—USA). The VIA Institute on character, funded by the Mayerson Foundation, is a leader in character strengths research and offers occasional trainings related to their VIA strengths assessment tool and other positive psychology topics. http://www.viacharacter.org/

C. Resilience trainings (The Happiness Institute—Australia). Under the leadership of Dr. Tim Sharp, the Happiness Institute offers a wide range of courses and trainings in positive psychology. http://www.thehappinessinstitute.com/ events/

3. Remain Vigilant for Signs of Personal Strengths

It may sound obvious to coaches to pay attention to the personal strengths of a client. Indeed, seasoned coaches will already be in the habit of keeping a sharp eye out for potential client resources, including abilities, skills, talents, and other positive personal characteristics. It is the good fit between this pillar of positive psychology and this tried-and-true coaching strategy that leads me to believe it should be a core part of any formal positive psychology coaching. Rather than some vague idea of looking for what the client does well, I endorse a highly specific means of identifying and labeling strengths. Pay attention to the visual and auditory cues from your clients' engagement, such as their posture, inflection, and hand gestures. Just as important, begin to build a strengths vocabulary so that you can label positive qualities when you see them and have a shared language for communicating these virtues to your clients.

4. Use Established Positive Psychology Assessments

One of the best aspects of positive psychology is the fact that it is a science. This means that it is centrally concerned with measurement. Because of this, coaches can benefit from established positive psychology assessments of psychological phenomena such as optimism, self-esteem, motivation, and meaning in life. By relying on measures that are well developed and measure topics of interest to coaches, you can gain additional confidence in the quality of the results as well as contrast your clients' answers to those of comparison groups. Coaches can draw on positive psychologists' sometimes superior knowledge of statistics and test construction to arrive at better surveys.

To illustrate how sophisticated these tests can be, just consider the development of the most widely used life satisfaction measure: the Satisfaction With Life Scale, created by Ed Diener (my father) and his colleagues.[15] In the early 1980s they began with the simple idea that life satisfaction can be reliably measured. The simplest way would be to ask people the single question, "How satisfied are you with your life?" and use a numeric answering system. The problem with single-item scales is that they are sensitive to what researchers broadly call "error." This means that all different people might interpret this item in unique ways or that their answers might be influenced by some momentary circumstance. An improved strategy would be to ask multiple questions that attempt to assess the same concept. So, in this case, instead of simply asking how satisfied you are with your life, I might ask to what extent you feel you have gotten what you want in life, to what extent you feel you are making progress toward your goals, to what extent you harbor regrets, and to what extent you generally feel satisfied. Taken together, these items have the potential to reduce error and produce a more reliable overall satisfaction score. Diener and his colleagues tested hundreds of these items, submitting each to statistical scrutiny, until they arrived at the five items that showed the greatest promise. The researchers examined this elite item pool against other existing measures of happiness, including non-self-report measures.[16] This is a far more stringent approach, sometimes taking years, than the off-the-cuff measures that some coaches create. The good news is, positive psychology is full of free, easy-to-use measures of a wide range of interesting variables.

5. Communicating with Your Client about Your Approach

I recently received a call from a prospective client who was shopping for a good fit with a coach. She had come across my name as being connected to positive psychology, and she was curious about what, exactly, this meant with regard to the way I practiced. She asked a terrific question: "How would your coaching look different from anyone else's?" Her question was important for two reasons: first, it underscores the necessity to distinguish positive psychology coaching from other forms of coaching, and second, it emphasizes the importance of being transparent with clients. One of the things I have long valued about being a coach is the openness and naturalness of the relationship. When I was trained as a therapist—a noble pursuit in my opinion—I was often frustrated with the admonition not to disclose too much personal information or, at times, pull back the curtain and let the client see your inner thinking and process. The caricature of the therapist merely nodding and saying "Mmmmmm-hmmmmm" has become a short-hand joke for the popular view of therapists being unreadable. Coaching works best under a different set of circumstances. It works best when coaches and clients can authentically join together to cocreate the relationship under an umbrella of complete honesty. My clients can tell when I am jazzed about a particular solution and when I feel lukewarm, and we sometimes discuss my emotional reactions as well as theirs.

The other important aspect of my prospective client's question—how does my positive psychology coaching differ from other forms of coaching—is easy. I am explicitly informed in my coaching work by the science and theory of positive psychology. This means I have a tendency to look for solutions rather than explore obstacles, that I use a codified vocabulary for strengths, that I draw upon empirically supported interventions and assessments, and that I attend heavily to the role of positive and negative emotions when I interact with my clients. To be sure, some coaches might do all of these things, and many do some of these things, but there are important points of departure. The most obvious, and perhaps the largest, is that I draw upon a large, first-hand expertise of research.

This means that my coaching style—much as writers talk about their unique voices—vacillates between coaching proper (exploring, supporting, and challenging) and mentorship (giving expert advice and consultation). As I moved from a novice coach to a more advanced coach, I found that my clients not only appreciated my ability to move between these two modalities, but also that they actually sought me out for this skill. In the same way, I think positive psychology coaching, as a niche practice, gives coaches a competitive edge because it promises not only basic coaching acumen but a level of facility with appealing scientific subject matter such as happiness and hope.

Understanding how your knowledge of positive psychology content areas affects your practice is critical to selling your services and establishing your coaching voice. Knowing, for example, that you use an approach based explicitly in appreciative inquiry or solutions focus can help you articulate the nature and process of your work. Telling your clients that you routinely use the Realise 2 strengths assessment with your clients can help them know what to expect when they engage your services.

6. Make a Paradigm Shift

Consider how, when, and why integrating positive psychology in general, and strengths in particular, might benefit your work with each individual client. Those potential benefits may include (a) clients being more predisposed to enjoying positive topics, (b) therapists buffering themselves against burnout, and (c) both clients and therapists experiencing the psychologically tonic effects of using strengths. Positive psychology coaching is, essentially, about a paradigm shift. This might mean a shift for you as a coach, but it will certainly mean a new way of thinking for your client. Even the most upbeat, optimistic clients will sometimes bump into professional, social, or emotional walls. As a coach, you can lend them a fresh perspective by framing questions in a way that assumes solutions are inevitable and that the client is capable of change.

Positive Psychology Coaching Credentialing at a Glance

A certification in positive psychology coaching should rest on the twin laurels of basic coaching competence and a firm grounding in positive psychological science. I believe the latter would ideally cover three core areas:

1. *A positive focus*—At its core, positive psychology is about asking what is right, rather than what is wrong, with people. While this does not mean that we, as coaches, ignore weaknesses or problems, it does mean that we think there is at least as much utility in focusing on the positive. This fundamental philosophical view is a prerequisite for all positive psychology interventions.

2. *The benefits of positive emotion*—Happiness, however defined, is the currency in which we trade. Positive emotions are associated with virtually every desirable goal and outcome ranging from solid friendships to better workplace safety records. Understanding how positive emotions work, and how and when to best promote them, is a core mechanism that makes positive psychology coaching effective.

3. *The science of strengths*—Another pillar of positive psychological science is the study of strengths. The idea that each individual possesses admirable attributes and that these are responsible for success and can be even better developed is essential to a positive psychology coaching practice.

In addition, I think any responsible training would present learners with mechanisms, such as continuing education credits, for keeping up to date with the evolution of positive psychological science. Finally, I would view any responsible training as including a relational component—such as active supervision or peer consultation—between the learner and a credentialed positive psychology coach.

▶ What Can Coaching Do for Positive Psychology?

The second major question that must be considered is just as important but, perhaps, slightly less obvious to coaches: What can coaching do for positive psychology? If positive psychology lends credibility and tools to coaching, then it only makes sense that it is in coaching's best interest for positive psychology to flourish; whatever aid coaches can lend to that process could be considered an investment in their own professional interests. My guess is that most coaches don't feel an explicit professional obligation to positive psychology, any more than they might feel obliged to help sports psychologists or economists. The truth is, however, that there are a number of unique ways coaching can benefit positive psychology and, in turn, its own professional fortunes.

Coaching sessions, themselves, are terrifically fertile ground for ideas and insights about relationships and performance. Who among us hasn't lit up with excitement as we or our clients stumbled upon an intriguing new approach to an age-old problem? Just as clinical therapy sessions have long been a rich source of anecdotal evidence, coaching sessions can be used as instructive case studies, not only for other coaches, but for positive psychologists as well. By sharing the insights and ideas that are borne out of coaching sessions, coaches are well poised to guide new positive psychology research and the creation of useful new assessments. Take the simple idea of brainstorming. There are a number of ways to brainstorm with clients, but experienced coaches likely develop preferences for a particular style based on the results it produces. In their coaching classic, *Co-Active Coaching*, Laura Whitworth and her coauthors describe brainstorming as a skill in which "the coach and client together generate ideas, alternatives, and possible solutions. Some of the proposed ideas may be outrageous and impractical. This is merely a creative exercise to expand the possibilities available to the client. There is no attachment on the part of either coach or client to any of the ideas suggested" (p. 254).[17] I love this definition, and, as a coach, I brainstorm with my clients in this exact way. But as a scientist I also wonder if there are insights we can gain through study that might help us to brainstorm even better. Just consider the following types of research questions:

- Are there certain types of clients for whom rapid-fire brainstorming is more appropriate, and others for whom the rapid-fire style dismantles a more deliberative approach?

- Is there an ideal ratio of outrageous to practical ideas that helps the process be more productive?
- Are there preparatory practices, such as telling jokes, that increase positivity and make brainstorming reliably more productive?
- How does the level of attachment to brainstorming outcomes on the behalf of either the coach or client affect the brainstorming productivity?

Coaches often lack either the tools or the interest to investigate their practices at this micro level. Each of these is a question with empirical merit that could, potentially, be guided by coaches who already have anecdotal evidence and preliminary answers to some of these questions. Imagine a system in which coaches and positive psychology researchers team up together in a dialogue that enhances each of their professional interests. Just as there is a growing number of coach directories listing coaches for prospective clients, there could be a directory through which coaches and researchers could connect and share mutually beneficial ideas. Coaching practices can act as on the ground data collection sites and benefit from the insights related to the research that is produced. Open dialogue between coaches and positive psychologists would also allow the former group to request specific research. It could be, for example, that a coach is particularly interested in a phenomenon local to his or her practice. Here is an example from my own practice: I have had so many occasions that a client has shown up for a session and said, "I wasn't feeling very motivated, but then I thought, 'What will Robert say to me at our session?' The specter of you as my coach really motivated me!" This is interesting to me as a coach, because it suggests a powerful way that the coaching relationship is used by clients through their own imaginations. Now, wouldn't it be exciting to have an even better understanding of when clients are likely to engage in this type of motivating fantasy, or to know which clients are likely to do so? And what about that minority of clients who show up to a session with an extra heap of embarrassment because they were not able to follow through on their commitments? Obviously, personality plays a role in explaining why one person would use a fantasy vision of her coach as motivation and the other would use a fantasy vision of her coach and become embarrassed. But systematic research can open the door wide on this phenomenon, helping us to understand what works, why, and when. Imagine that you had a direct line of access to a research laboratory and could request studies done on specific topics that are relevant to your coaching practice.

The final area where coaching has an obligation to positive psychology is as a market concern. Positive psychology has evolved from a basic science to an applied science. This means that a decade ago researchers were primarily interested in exploring strengths, happiness, and other positive topics. But in recent years there has been an increasing trend toward application of these research results. What this means is that the new wave of people who are being attracted to positive psychologists are just as interested, on average, in application as they are in research. To a large extent they seem themselves as "anti-therapists" providing consultation and intervention services that help promote positive aspects of functioning and boost happiness. The problem is that because positive psychology is such a new discipline there are relatively few established jobs for graduates of programs like the University of Pennsylvania's master's degree in applied positive psychology. Graduates generally choose between research, applying positive psychology to some other established field such as finance or management, or some more applied work. The de facto choice for a third option is coaching. I believe it is in the interest of all working coaches to actively work toward credentialing this new wave of practitioners. By establishing clear criteria, such as those put forward by the ICF in which formal positive psychology programs can work, we will all benefit from a higher quality of responsible practice on the behalf of those with training in positive psychology, but not necessarily in coaching.

The Coaching Obligation to Positive Psychology, at a Glance

1. Insights from coaching sessions and professional trends within coaching suggest areas for research focus.
2. Coaching sessions of all stripes provide an interesting and important testing ground for new positive psychology interventions.
3. Coaching trends related to business and other commercial needs offer a needed guide for the development of solid positive psychology assessments.
4. As positive psychology becomes increasingly applied, and as more students graduate with degrees specific to positive psychology, coaching provides a natural professional landing pad.

▶ How This Book Works—Layout, Types of Coaches, Reader's Responsibility

If you are anything remotely like me, you like books. You buy books—especially professional books—because they are a great way to get inspiration, new ideas, new skills, and to basically grow in your work. If you are like me, you likely purchase books from a wide catalog of topics including management, coaching, psychology, and general nonfiction. Also, if you are anything like me, you do not read these books cover to cover. You probably hop around to the most interesting or relevant chapters or just read the introduction before casting the book aside. My bookshelves are stacked with unapologetically half-read tomes. This is one of the great truths about professional books: Far more are sold than are actually read. And I believe this makes sense. Professional books often present a single sticky idea or list of useful tools, but rarely do they have the kind of narrative arc that best-selling novels have. It is unfair to compare this summer's best beach read to the hot management title you skim while on the plane. This book is no exception. As much as I would like to up the interest level by putting a murder mystery between the chapters on positive diagnosis and positive assessment, it just won't happen. Instead, I expect you, the reader, to jump around the book and use it in a nonlinear fashion as you deem appropriate. I want you to be able to read a chapter as a stand-alone topic, without having to have read the chapters that came before and without being obligated to read what comes after. I want you to be able to mine these pages for exactly the content you can use, without wasting any of your time on the topics that are of less interest to you.

■ What You Will Find in This Book

1. *Strengths:* Everyone—clients and others—are naturally loaded with a wide range of skills at which they naturally excel. Despite the fact that these abilities are second nature, they can also be developed. There is an exciting branch of positive psychological science that focuses exclusively on the study of strengths. This includes ways to assess client strengths, research on the correlates of strengths, and strategies for developing strengths. Strengths scientists also acknowledge the fact that everyone has weaknesses that they may need to overcome en route to achieving their goals. Chapter 2 explores the relationship between strengths and weaknesses and provides what is, essentially, a master class in using a strengths approach with your clients. Strengths is among my favorite areas of research and my training passion. I have attempted to pepper this chapter with some of my favorite insights and activities from years of trainings on the topic.

2. *Happiness:* Feeling good and experiencing a sense of meaning is a concern that touches everyone. Importantly, the science of happiness has shown that feeling upbeat has a wide range of benefits at work, in relationships, and personally. Nowhere is this more pertinent to coaching than in the topic of happiness at work. Research and theory by Richard Boyatzis, Peter Warr, and Sonja Lyubomirsky show a number of ways in which happiness is an entirely appropriate subject for the boardroom. Chapter 3 includes both a brief overview of the science of positivity, especially as it concerns workplaces, and a number of specific applications including the reflected best self, optimal feedback, and visioning. As a researcher, happiness is my primary area of expertise, and I attempted to stretch this chapter well beyond its counterpart in my original book. Rather than covering the fascinating basics of happiness science, as I did in the earlier book, I have tried to present information that is specifically applicable to coaching.

3. *Hope:* Humans are unique in our ability to look into the future. Whether planning a holiday, predicting the weather, or setting strategy for the next business quarter, we can use our ability to think ahead to live a better life. This is especially relevant to coaching clients when it comes to hope. Our belief in our ability to positively influence a future outcome—our hope—is central to coaching success. Many of our most powerful professional tools—championing, acknowledgment, challenging—are employed with the implicit aim of encouraging hope and thereby increasing motivation and self-efficacy. In Chapter 4 I will present the theory and research on hope as it relates to coaching, and offer suggestions for instilling hope in clients.

4. *Positive Diagnosis:* Since the dawn of medicine doctors have been leveraging their diagnostic ability in their fight to beat illness and promote health. By using symptoms to identify syndromes, doctors have been able to target specific treatments. What if there was a positive counterpoint to traditional diagnosis? What if there were such a thing as a "positive diagnosis" in which coaches were able to look at patterns of positive behaviors, feelings, and thoughts to identify performance syndromes and adjust work styles accordingly? Chapter 5 introduces the concept of positive diagnosis and presents suggestions and measures for accomplishing this.

5. *Assessments:* Among the strengths of the coaching profession is a widespread reliance on established measures of personality, interests, strengths, and other personal qualities that influence our performance. As a science, positive psychology similarly relies on well-validated measurements to study individuals and groups. In Chapter 6 I will present some introductory information about measurement in general. But if this sounds suspiciously like a rehash of your undergraduate statistics course, then be rest assured that my goal is to raise interesting questions about measurement and equip you with tools for evaluating competing measures. Once we have dispensed with this brief foray down the psychometric rabbit hole, we will move on to a list of actual assessments on topics such as satisfaction, hope, motivational style, and negative feelings. The assessments will be discussed and reprinted in their entirety for your benefit.

6. *Transitions:* While you might not actively think about it, your day—and, indeed, all your days—is made up of crucial transition points. You transition from bed to breakfast, from home to work, from work to home. You transition from early career to mid-life, from a full house to an empty nest. Both at the micro and macro levels, these transitions can affect how we feel and how we will fare in our next round of activities or next stage of life. I will present an overview of transitions, related research, and case studies from actual coaching sessions. In each case I will emphasize how transition points can be leveraged for better coaching and better client performance.

7. *An overview of PPC sessions:* There are many definitions of coaching, and it is sometimes difficult to tell one form of coaching from another. Sometimes it is even difficult to articulate the subtle differences between coaching and therapy. Nonetheless, these distinctions are real. To the extent that positive psychology coaching can be distinguished from other forms of coaching, I offer a chapter on the mechanics of positive psychology coaching as a unique endeavor. I offer hints and tips from other coaches with whom I have consulted and outline specific issues related to delineating positive psychology coaching from other brands.

8. *A crystal ball:* Although I am not a fortune-teller, I will make an attempt to read the future of positive psychology coaching. I believe this is a discipline that is at the exciting nexus between two young professions—coaching and positive psychology—that seem to generate more excitement and enthusiasm than almost any other field I have come across, and appear to be growing at a rapid rate. I will make specific predictions about coaching trends and positive psychology trends, and offer recommendations for riding the wave of both of these great fields.

▶ An Invitation

I invite you into this book. Read it in order, read only a chapter, check it out from the library, give it as a gift to a colleague. However you choose to use this book, my goal is to present you with at least one novel or challenging idea, one new exercise you can use, one inspiring story or one assessment that improves the quality of your practice. I do not expect you to agree with every point I make or to follow every suggestion. I am relatively unconcerned about convincing you I am right or impressing you with my expertise. I want, instead, for this book to be about you. I want you to walk away from the reading experience with something you can hold onto, something you can use or share with a friend. To that end, I invite you to look at the experience you are about to embark on less as a critical foray into a professional book and more like a treasure hunt. Some points in this book will, undoubtedly, seem dull while others will shine with a crazy luster. I invite you to poke around, hunt all you like until you find, for yourself, where X marks the spot.

CHAPTER TWO

Using Your Best to Make You Better

Take a moment and think back to your childhood. In particular, remember those physical education classes you took in primary school. Perhaps you were made to run around a track or do calisthenics, or maybe you were lucky and were allowed to play dodgeball. Regardless of the particular athletic activity you engaged in, there is a high likelihood that, at some point in your education, you were forced to choose team captains and pick sides. In some ways, this activity is the cruelest part of childhood. Here's how it worked in my school: The PE teacher asked the single most athletic boy (Jude Nolen) and girl (Megan Schott) to be captains. Then, Jude and Megan took turns choosing the most talented, most athletic children. Jeff Miller usually was the first to be drafted. Then Troy Price. Then Susan Sheridan. And so the selection process went until about the halfway point—when all the athletic and semi-athletic kids were chosen. Then, the strategy turned toward limiting the potential damage caused by the athletic dead weight of the awkward and uncoordinated children. I won't be so unkind as to name these kids, but trust me when I say I remember their names even better than I can recall the names of the top picks. It is particularly interesting to note how naturally this selection process is, how intuitive: Strengthen your team by recruiting the most skilled players, until it comes time to limit the deficits by attending to personal weaknesses.

Interestingly, the way children divide up for sports teams is pretty much the same way organizations recruit for talent, sport clubs recruit for superstars, and—to be honest—the way most of us choose a spouse. When shopping for a mate, for example, most people typically focus on the good; the things that are most attractive about the other person. Perhaps it is a sense of humor, trustworthiness, or plain old good looks. You will notice that—when it comes to matters of the heart—a person almost never focuses exclusively on the negative traits. No one says, "I am so excited to be marrying Tom. The thing I like most about him is the fact that I can live with his messiness. I am also really looking forward to a lifetime of not being dragged down by his occasional angry outburst." When it comes to the things we value and the goals we most hope to accomplish, we have a natural tendency to focus on strengths, because we have an intuitive understanding that it is strengths that will help us be at our best, give us the greatest sense of meaning, and enjoy our lives to the fullest.

The concept of strengths, it turns out, is one of the most exciting areas of positive psychology research and application. Strengths, as we will see shortly, are where our greatest successes happen, where we experience enormous growth, and where we enjoy a burst of energy and happiness. So good are strengths, in fact, that there has long been a clamor to focus more heavily on them. In the late 1960s, for example, management guru Peter Drucker[1] said, "To achieve results, one has to use all the available strengths. . . . These strengths are the true opportunities. The unique purpose of organization is to make strength productive." This sentiment was echoed years later by former Gallup CEO Don Clifton: ". . . Gallup has discovered that our talents—defined as our naturally recurring patterns of thought, feeling, or behaviour that can be productively applied—are our greatest opportunities for success."[2] Clifton was instrumental in establishing a scientific basis for claims that strengths are an effective way to engage clients and workers. Today, a number of blue-chip companies are investing heavily in a strengths focus—everything from strengths-based recruitment to strengths-based management and strengths-based outplacement. As a coach or consultant it is in your interest to know that there is increasing interest in the science of strengths.

Activity: Of What Are You Most Proud?

It is easy for me to say that strengths lead directly to success, but is it really true? It makes intuitive sense that our greatest successes are the product of our best qualities and not necessarily of overcoming our weaknesses. Why not put this theory to the test? Take a moment and think about the thing you are most proud of—perhaps it is a business success, or the way you work hard to maintain your health, or maybe it is your 20-year marriage. Try to think, in particular, of a specific moment of tremendous pride related to a way that you yourself behaved. That time you said just the right thing or made a terrific decision. Chances are, as you take stock of these shining moments, the vast majority of them are the direct result of your strengths being at play rather than resulting from you overcoming a weakness. Your proudest moments are almost certainly related to you being at your best.

Before passing too far into the territory of strengths, it makes sense to spend a little time defining this elusive concept. I do not claim to have a monopoly on the definition of strengths, nor do I have a monopoly on strengths coaching or strengths models. What I present here is, in my opinion, a very useful way to look at strengths. I am far more interested in this as an easy-to-understand model than I am in arguing that it is the single truth about strengths. With that caveat aside, let's jump in! At the Centre for Applied Positive Psychology (CAPP) we look at strengths as the product of evolution.[3] This means that certain qualities—those that are useful for individual and group functioning, such as leadership, creativity, and forgiveness—may actually have biological roots as well as be handed down to us through socialization. Each of us has a number of "pre-existing capacities" that can be drawn out by various situations to make us perform at our best. In fact, rather than complicate the idea of strengths with a long discussion of related topics like talents and skills, we try to keep it simple. At CAPP we say

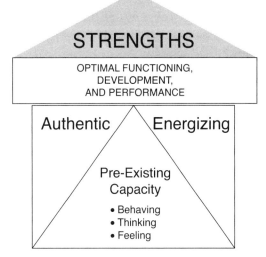

Figure 2.1 Strengths lead to best performance

that strengths are "our pre-existing patterns of thought, feeling, and behavior that are authentic, energizing, and which lead to our best performance" (see Figure 2.1).

It is important to understand what we mean by authentic and energizing. By authentic we mean that the strength is descriptive of the true individual. Here's an example: I am a morning person. This is not a trait I ever wanted, worked for, or asked for. In fact, I find morning people as annoying as you do! And yet, I cannot escape the fact that no matter what time I go to bed I naturally pop awake at 6 in the morning, fully rested and ready to take on the day. The time between the moment I open my eyes and the moment I spring out of bed is less than a second! Despite the fact that I am clearly at my best and most energetic early in the day, every once in a while I get it into my head that I should be a night person. After all, night owls are cool. These are the folks who stay up late, go clubbing, and socialize until the wee hours of the morning. During these misguided periods I promise my wife that I will attend late-night parties and then struggle to stay awake. But it is just not authentic. I find myself nodding off, making excuses to go take a nap in the car, or desperately wishing I were home in my pajamas. Strengths work in much the same way: Each of us is dealt a metaphorical hand in life, and it is this hand we are forced to play. Some of us are creative, others are empathic; some of us are persistent, others are funny. One of the most crucial aspects of working with and developing strengths is making sure you and your clients are working with strengths that are authentic.

Take-Home Lesson:

Strengths are not aspirational! As much as we might want a particular strength, it is far more effective to focus on and work with those strengths that come naturally to us. It is in our best interest to be honest with ourselves and work with those qualities we have, rather than those we wish we had.

When we refer to strengths as energizing we are not necessarily talking about some new-age meaning of the word energy. We simply mean that when strengths are in play they are noticeable for the engagement, energy, and enthusiasm they generate. When people are using their strengths or when they are talking about a situation in which they used their strengths, they tend to come alive, become increasingly animated, more physically communicative, and more alert and excited. Energy is a hallmark feature of strengths and fundamental to identifying them. A person might be good at organization, being persuasive, or comforting others, but unless it is something that gives them an emotional boost or a little burst of energy then it is probably not a strength.

Take-Home Lesson:

Energy is a hallmark feature of strengths. When people use or discuss their strengths they tend to experience a burst of enthusiasm. You can use energy as a marker to recognize when strengths are in play.

The idea of identifying strengths for use and development is not merely an academic concern. Strengths are those personal attributes to which we owe the lion's share of our successes and for which we are most often recognized and admired by others. The ability to spot and label a strength in another person is a crucial skill in recruitment, management, parenting, teaching, mentoring, and—of course—coaching. If strengths are the currency of success, then it is worth building your literacy in this area.

▶ Developing Yourself as a Strengths Coach

At its heart, coaching is about working with clients to help them perform at their absolute best. Whether you are an internal coach or a life coach, the ability to recognize strengths in play and to help your clients develop their strengths is vital to your professional success. In addition to helping them take stock of their financial, social, and professional resources, it makes sense to evaluate their natural personality and psychological resources: their strengths. Unfortunately, many coaches jump right into an "identify and use" model of strengths coaching in which they follow a standard approach: First identify the client's strengths and then brainstorm ways to use these strengths more or more effectively. This is a sensible approach, but in my opinion, it misses some of the complexity, fun, and effectiveness of complete strengths coaching. It is a bit like showing up to Paris, identifying a local, and wanting to start speaking French, without first having any French language instruction. You need to be conversant in the language of strengths before you can throw yourself into using strengths as a focal point in your work with clients. In fact, I recommend that before you work with your clients to identify and develop their strengths, you systematically develop your professional capacity by increasing your own strengths vocabulary.

■ Developing a Strengths Vocabulary

Developing a strengths vocabulary simply means that you take the time to become conversant with a number of strengths, that you have labels for them, and that you can recognize them in others. If you only have the names of 15 or 20 strengths at the ready, then that is all you will ever see in your clients. If, on the other hand, you can readily call to mind the names of 50 or 60 strengths, then you are far more likely to be able to identify nuanced and diverse strengths in your clients. Sometimes strengths coaching can be all about developing new strengths words in tandem with your clients. My own introduction to the idea of building a strengths vocabulary happened in the middle of a coaching session. I had been working with a bright young man who was in his final week of medical school. He was a little panicked because he had a number of important assignments due, including a case presentation, a paper, and an application for a prospective residency. It was Monday when we met, and my client asked if we could meet again on Wednesday to help establish additional accountability. When we spoke on Wednesday, his anxiety had skyrocketed! Not only had he not accomplished his many tasks, he hadn't even started. He confessed that he had spent the week downloading music and podcasts to his iPod—anything but focusing on his responsibilities. Here is how our conversation went:

    Me: How is everything going?

Client: Terrible! I haven't done a thing! I have been procrastinating all week!

    Me: Procrastinating?

Client: You bet! I have been listening to podcasts, building my music collection.... In fact, it seems like I have been doing anything to avoid working on my work.

    Me: I can hear the stress in your voice.

Client: You bet you can! I am pulling out my hair here! I always do this!

Chances are, you have experienced a similar scenario with one of your own clients. Even our most successful, most self-directed clients have a tendency to occasionally avoid obligations or have trouble following through on assignments. What was different in this particular case was my client's fascinating comment: "I always do this!" It caught my attention, in part because it didn't seem consistent with what I knew about him as an extraordinarily bright, hard-working high achiever. So, in the moment, I decided to ask about it.

    Me: You have a pattern of putting off important work?

Client: Yes, I do. I was like this in high school, in college, and all through med school.

    Me: You put off work?

Client: Yeah, always. I save it until the last minute.

    Me: Let me ask you: How often do you hand in papers and assignments on time?

Client: (laughs) All the time, are you kidding?

Me: (mock surprise) Let me get this straight: You put off doing the work until the last minute, but you always get it done?

Client: Always.

This was my first clue that there was more to my client's assertions than first met the eye. I knew my client was successful by almost any definition of the word, and it didn't make sense to me that he achieved all he had by being a procrastinator. Here he was telling me that he put his work off until the last minute, but something about that didn't seem to be classic procrastination to me. In fact, as I listened to him laughing and discussing his work habits, I got the idea that he was actually energized by his unique work style. I decided to probe further.

Me: I guess I have just one question for you, then. . . .

Client: Okay, go ahead.

Me: When you hand in your work at the last minute, how is the quality?

Client: The quality? Ummm . . . superior?

Me: Superior?

Client: Yep, superior.

And there you have it. Here was my client, trying to convince me he was a run-of-the-mill procrastinator. But, procrastination wasn't what I was seeing. I was seeing someone with a gift! I was seeing someone with the talent to know—almost intuitively—exactly how much time he would need to complete his work; a person who didn't waste mental energy motivating himself and let external deadlines do that for him; a person who was able to subconsciously think about a topic over the course of the week while relaxing; a person who moved into action at the 11th hour and, despite the time pressure, was able to rise to the occasion and complete superior quality work! Far from laziness, this seemed like a type of strength to me—one that was just waiting to be labeled.

Me: Do you mind if I challenge you a bit?

Client: Go ahead.

Me: You call yourself a procrastinator, but that isn't what I am seeing.

Client: You're not?

Me: Not at all. If you waited until the last minute and then handed in mediocre work, then maybe it would be procrastination. But I am seeing you rise to the occasion at the last minute and still hand in superior work.

Client: Yeah?

Me: I think you actually have a strength that we are seeing. Let's call it "incubator."

Client: Incubator! I love it. That is exactly me!

Labeling my client's strength was not just a turning point in our session, it was a major step forward in the way he viewed himself, and a major shift in perspective.[4] He went from beating himself up for his supposed procrastination to valuing his natural work style and, better yet, effectively planning for it. It was a defining moment, and the fact that we had a word and definition to describe his strength allowed us to begin a fruitful discussion of how best to develop and use it. It is also worth noting that it was a defining moment for me in my development as a coach. I saw firsthand the power of assigning strengths-based labels, and this has been a mainstay of my coaching practice ever since.

There are innumerable strengths-related phenomena out there in the world right now just waiting for you to label them. In my trainings and workshops I often have participants take the first step toward building a strengths vocabulary by thinking of some personal asset and making up a word for it, whether the word actually exists or not! In the past, I have heard wonderfully creative labels such as "Antennae" (the ability to naturally pay attention to the mood of a group and react accordingly), "Copernicability" (this strength, name after astronomer Copernicus, is the natural ability to take an existing model or thought and see some clever or provocative new side to it), and "Resourcerer" (a kind of wizard at understanding what resources need to be harnessed to achieve a goal, and a master of marshaling these resources effectively). It turns out that labeling strengths works just the opposite of how you might expect: Rather than being confining or boxing clients in, clients tend to respond positively to the labeling process. In part, clients react well to the extent that you, as the coach, have fun with the process. The more clever, outlandish, or fun the label is the more fun it is to play with. In addition, understand that your label will not work for the client 100% of the time. Occasionally, you will come up with a label that doesn't exactly fit for the client. Never fear! Clients are famously forgiving of this type of thing, and they will often suggest a label of their own. In fact, inviting your clients into the dialogue around labels is a terrific way to shift their thinking about strengths. When they modify or accept your label, or when they create one of their own, they begin to take ownership of their own best qualities.

Activity: Create a new strength, right now!

Think about a phenomenon that you are aware of where you, or someone you know, are consistently at peak performance. This may be the way a friend of yours interacts with other people or the way that someone you know from work deals with adversity. Think about what energizes you or the qualities in others that most inspire you. It may help to think about famous people, such as Nelson Mandela or David Bowie. Once you have identified the strengths-related phenomenon, write down several labels for it. Have fun, and don't worry if your labels are particularly clever, just make sure they make sense to you. It can be difficult to do this at first, but stretch yourself beyond this single activity: Set a goal for yourself to keep an eye out for strengths for a week, and each time you see one in action, come up with a label for it, whether that label is as mundane as "creativity" or as playful as "creatasaurus." It is the ongoing practice that will help you master this skill.

■ Identifying Strengths in Your Clients

Even as you build your facility with labeling strengths, you need to expand your capacity to recognize and identify strengths. Strengths vocabulary building and strengths identification are skills that go hand in hand. As a coach, your ability to pick up on and expose your clients' strengths will be directly commensurate with your success. To some extent most seasoned coaches do a form of this naturally. In some cases, coaches bear witness to fluctuations in client energy, noting when clients are enthusiastic and when they fall flat. In some—but not all—cases these fluctuations in energy are directly linked to client strengths being put into play. For other coaches, the idea that it is beneficial to bring strengths to light will not be a revolutionary insight. What might be handy, even for experienced coaches, are practical steps for doing so. In addition to the formal positive psychology assessments discussed later in this book, there are more naturalistic ways of getting at your clients' shiniest qualities.

The easiest way to pick up on strengths is to be on the lookout for boosts in energy. The good news is that this is likely something you are already doing in your coaching practice. Coaching, especially coaching conducted over the telephone, requires constant attention to subtle changes in client energy. But what, specifically, are we seeing when we notice a sharp spike or sudden drop in energy? There are a number of tangible behavioral changes in our clients that are associated with the general concept of energy, and with strengths specifically.[5] First, clients who are discussing areas of high strength tend to speak more quickly and their inflection rises. Their posture straightens, and they become more nonverbally expressive, both in hand gestures and facial expressions. Interestingly, people discussing areas of personal strength are also more likely to use metaphors. People are often so fluent in their best areas that they have a well-developed language—including metaphors—for describing their thoughts and actions. I had a client, for example, who was extremely socially gifted, especially when it came to meeting new people. She was able to instantly click with people of a wide range of backgrounds, even people who were remarkably different from herself. When she spoke about "first contact" situations, she came alive and said things like, "I feel like one of those Lego blocks. You know how every Lego piece can connect with every other piece, regardless of size or color? I am like that!" (Guess what we called this strength: Lego!)

Identifying Strengths. Be on the Lookout for:

1. Rising inflection
2. Rapid speech
3. Better posture
4. Wide eyes, raised eyebrows
5. Smiling and laughing
6. Increased hand gestures
7. Increased use of metaphors
8. More fluent speech

Because energy is a hallmark feature of strengths, you can frame questions to elicit your clients' inner resources. By asking questions that get at enthusiasm and engagement, you open the door to a conversation about strengths. I typically use a past-present-future approach to strengths-eliciting questions. In the "past" question I ask the client about behaviors or activities from the past about which they are particularly proud. It may be a business achievement, a social tie, or an athletic feat. Whatever the case, it is almost assuredly something the client values highly and is likely to reflect a personal strength. Occasionally, because some clients are turned off by the word "proud," I ask about choices they made that they feel good about or compliments they have received from others. The trick here is to get clients out of short-answer mode and into short-story mode. You want the client to tell a little story, to become absorbed in what they are talking about, so that you have the raw material and time to mine their tale for strengths. Sometimes this requires a little narrative nudge, such as a follow-up like "Tell me more about that." In the "present" question I simply ask clients what they currently find exciting. Chances are whatever it is that is revving their engine is also an opportunity for them to be at their best. Finally, for the "future" question I ask clients to think about the near future—the coming weekend, say, or the coming month. I then ask them to tell me what they are looking forward to. Again, this is an instance where clients tend to give brief answers, and usually a short follow-up is required, such as "What is it about X that you are anticipating so eagerly?" You will recognize immediately when your client has shifted into story mode, and it can be amazing how much information you can get! Typically, when I run trainings for coaches and we practice this exercise, we can, as a group, pull about five strengths from about 15 seconds of a person's answer to the question "What are you looking forward to in the future?"

Three Simple but Powerful Questions for Tapping Strengths

1. What are some of the things from your past about which you are most proud?
2. What energizes you in the present?
3. What are you looking forward to in the near future?

One of the things I particularly like about using this method to search for client strengths is how naturalistic it is. Unlike formal assessment measures, which have their own set of advantages, simply asking your clients about their enthusiasm and excitement is informal and can help your relationship. In fact, I find the "future" question the most powerful of the three, and it is a great way to get to know your client. I typically use this question or a close variation in my early sessions. Why don't you try your hand at identifying possible strengths from a real-world example. Remember, everybody has a number of strengths, so there is not one single correct answer. See how many different strengths you can find, and have fun playing with the ways you label them.

What Are You Looking Forward to in the Near Future?

Answer: I wish I could say that what I am looking forward to is something work related, but the truth is I am not all that excited about work right now. Honestly, the thing I am most looking forward to is my vacation in three weeks. I know this sounds kind of weird, but I am going to Mexico for a week with two people that I don't even know! It started when a mutual friend suggested the trip. We all agreed to go, but then the friend had to back out for family reasons. I felt terrible for her, and a little awkward about being stuck on a trip with two strangers. But then, you know, I figured I would just give it a shot. You only live once!

We are going to the Yucatan Peninsula. We are going to hang out at the beach and play in the ocean, which I am really excited about. I have heard the diving is good there. I don't know how to dive, but I am going to learn. I am also looking forward to visiting some of the Mayan ruins. I have always been fascinated by history, and I am excited to learn about the Mayans. I don't know anything about them, really, but I am going to read a book before I go. I actually think this whole experience will be a great way to get to know these new people. Maybe I'll end up with friends for life!

Now, before you read any further, did you read the answer to the question and try to spot some strengths? I realize it is somewhat harder to pick strengths out from the printed page than if this woman were sitting in front of you, but I believe you can still find some possible strengths. If you have given it a shot and are ready to go forward then, by all means, read on! There are a number of activities that this woman expresses obvious enthusiasm for, such as going diving and visiting ruins. It might be that she is curious or playful, and these would be good starting points, but it is difficult to tell for certain. After all, wouldn't most people be interested in these activities? There are a couple of traits that seem unique to this particular woman. First, she is adventuresome. Think about it: She is traveling to a foreign country, engaging in a new activity, and doing it all with people whom she does not know. You might call this strength "adventure," as we do at CAPP (people high in this strength are likely to put themselves at the edge of their own comfort zone because they are excited to see how they will respond).[6] You might label it "courage." You might even label it "optimism," because her mild risk-taking seems to suggest a sense that everything will work out for the best in the end. Another possible strength is her desire to learn new things. You can see that she is excited by the prospect of learning about people, learning about Mayan history, and even learning how to scuba dive. In every case, her passion for learning seems wholly self-directed and energizing. You might label this strength "love of learning," as I do, or perhaps you label it "learner," "Try-er," or "Sponge." If you picked up on either of these two types of strengths—her love of learning or her sense of adventure—you are well on your way to being able to identify personal strengths, even without the use of a formal assessment.

If the benefits of a strengths focus seem obvious to you, think again. Although both research and anecdotal evidence point to our strengths as being incredible resources, a huge number of people overlook them in favor of a weakness focus. In fact, self-help books and seminars are a multi-billion-dollar industry worldwide, an industry that is largely centered on recognizing personal deficits and overcoming weaknesses. I don't fault anyone for focusing on deficits; to a large extent it is natural. We are evolutionarily predisposed to be vigilant for risks and problems. Problems and personal failings simply feel emotionally very pressing to us and tend to demand our immediate attention. Not only that, but there is huge pressure to focus on our weaknesses and avoid our strengths. We are often taught, for instance, that we should be humble and modest, and discussing strengths openly can, therefore, seem offensive. As a coach or consultant, you can expect some of your clients to have a natural aptitude for strengths and others to be slow to warm to the topic.

Reasons We Don't Focus on Strengths

1. We are adapted by evolution to be vigilant for problems.
2. Problems often feel pressing.
3. Social norms dictate that we retain some modesty.
4. We are not always aware of our strengths.
5. We often believe that it is our weaknesses, rather than our strengths, that are our greatest areas for growth.

There are, fortunately, several ways to introduce strengths to your clients without turning them off to the topic. The first is to establish the culture of your coaching session as one of strengths and positivity by introducing this topic early on. Much has been made—in life and in the psychological research literature—about first impressions and how quickly they are set. You may know about the primacy effect in which people's first impressions of you color their view of your later behavior.[7] What better way to start off on the right foot with your clients than by throwing some attention to strengths in with your early discussions of goals and resources? As positive psychology has developed over the years a technique for introducing strengths, as a topic, has become increasingly widely used. Not surprisingly, it is called the strengths introduction. In this simple but powerful exercise, people (your client, in this case) are asked to introduce themselves by briefly telling a story about a time when they were at their best. You can easily accomplish this in your intake or early sessions by asking "what do you like best about yourself?" "Tell me about when you were at your best" or "what are you most proud of?" In the interests of both modeling and establishing the coaching relationship, you might consider having your own strengths story at hand. By using the strengths introduction you create a foundation for a positive focus.

There are two things you should know about the strengths introduction before you ever try it out with an actual client. First, most people are initially reluctant to engage fully with the strengths introduction. Second, it is extraordinarily easy to overcome this reluctance. What happens is this: Your client has a lifetime of socialization telling her to be humble and modest, and being frank about her strengths can feel a little uncomfortable. This is where you have a golden opportunity to establish your coaching culture. You can reassure her by saying, "Here, in our sessions, we do not have to worry about everyday social rules. This can be a place where we can speak honestly, and we don't have to worry about anyone judging us. Trust me when I say that I am actually very interested in your strengths. I want you to talk about them. In fact, when you tell me about your achievements I know you aren't bragging or suggesting that you are, somehow, fundamentally better than other people. I know that you are just being honest with me about the strengths that are unique to you." I have conducted coach trainings all over Europe, Asia, Africa, and North America, and in each location I have found that people require a little reassurance, but then are willing and able to throw themselves into the activity. Interestingly, almost everyone who participates in a strengths introduction feels energized and uplifted by the experience. Most folks also appreciate hearing the strengths of other people (you, for instance), and find listening to strengths inspiring. All that said, I also believe it is important to respect cultural differences and understand that for some people speaking openly about their strengths may feel foreign or awkward.

Leading a strengths introduction is rather straightforward. Here is how I do it in large groups. You can modify this approach in any way you feel is locally appropriate with your particular clients or the organizational culture in which you work.

> Typically, when we are introduced to other people we ask about their line of work. The reason we do this, if you think about it, is that knowing a person's profession or trade gives us a tremendous amount of information about that person's educational background, socioeconomic status, aptitudes, and interests. Asking "What do you do for a living" is a type of conversational shorthand for "Who are you?" Imagine, though, what it would be like if we lived in a world where we introduced ourselves by telling about what we do best. It sounds a little crazy at first, to talk about our greatest strengths so openly and publicly. But, in a moment, that is exactly what I am going to ask you to do; I am going to ask you to tell a very brief story about a time when you were at your best. I want to know about your strengths.

> Now, I know that even as I say this your defenses are on the rise. You have a lifetime of socialization telling you not to talk about your strengths. There is tremendous pressure not to brag, not to put yourself above others, and to retain your composure and modesty. I want you to know that I understand that. But here, in this situation, you and I can put those social conventions on the back burner. You can feel free to honestly talk about what you do well and be rest assured that I am honestly interested in hearing about you at your best. When you tell me your story I know that you are not suggesting you are inherently better than anyone else, and I know that you are not bragging. You are simply sharing with me, at my request, a story about something at which you excel. And everyone in the world has such as story.

> So, please, take a second and think about something you have done, a decision you have made, or a feat that you have accomplished about which you feel some sense of pride or satisfaction. Think about what strengths you possess that helped you be successful in this instance. I'd love to hear that story.

A second crucial strategy for introducing strengths to your clients has to do with its opposite: weaknesses. One of the major stumbling blocks for all people, including clients, is the misperception that a strengths focus necessarily means ignoring weaknesses. If this is the case, most folks reason, then the strengths approach is nothing more than Pollyanna-ish optimism and is, at worst, entirely unrealistic. It is for this reason that I strongly recommend you head off such criticisms before they even take root by confronting them head on. When I open the conversation about strengths with my clients or in academic or organizational trainings, I make sure early on to bring up the idea of weaknesses myself. Usually, after introducing strengths—either by defining them or very briefly outlining a few of the benefits of strengths—I plunge right into weaknesses. The first thing I do, where weaknesses are concerned, is emphasize that I believe it is important to address weaknesses. I reassure my clients, or my training group, that I do not advocate looking at strengths at the exclusion of weaknesses. I emphasize that focusing on both strengths and weaknesses is important, but for entirely different reasons. And then I introduce them to the sailboat metaphor (see Figure 2.2).

Let's pretend you are a sailboat. But, unfortunately, you have a leak. Let's call that leak your weaknesses. Now, if you have the least shred of common sense, you will not ignore that weakness, that leak, because you will sink! I absolutely urge you to attend to that leak. In fact, it is critical that you do. In the real world our leaks—our weaknesses—can make us capsize or sink unless we take care of them. So, yes, put some effort into stopping that leak. Having taken care of the leak you should understand one very important thing: Even if you stop the leak 100%, you will still not be able to get anywhere! It is your sails—your strengths in this case—that actually give you forward momentum. You need to take care of your leak to prevent yourself from sinking, but you need to hoist your sails to catch a favorable wind and move forward. Focusing on only strengths or only on weaknesses is not sufficient.[8]

A third strategy for introducing strengths effectively to your clients is by reinforcing the notion that there is a scientific foundation to a strengths focus. Often, when people hear about major positive psychology topics, such as happiness, hope, or strengths, they interpret them as being abstract, elusive, or theoretical. It is important to bear in mind that positive psychology is, at its heart, a science. In its early days, in fact, positive psychology pioneers expressed justifiable concern that positive psychology would be conflated with the self-help movement and dismissed as a pop

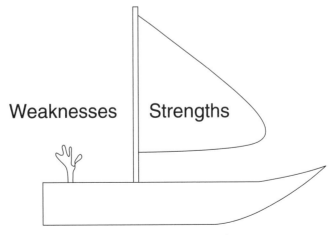

Figure 2.2 Understanding the relationship of strengths to weaknesses

culture phenomenon. In 2002 Martin Seligman, the founder of the modern positive psychology movement, wrote, "science must be descriptive and not prescriptive. It is not the job of Positive Psychology to tell you that you should be optimistic, or spiritual, or kind or good humored; it is rather to describe the consequences of these traits" (p. 129).[9] Although, in the years since 2002, positive psychology has increasingly become an applied science, it is still a science. A strengths approach, then, is not just a catchy idea or a feel-good strategy. There are solid numbers and specific evidence suggesting that it is an approach to work and an approach to life that works.

Strengths Research at a Glance

1. Identifying your strengths is associated with higher happiness and lower rates of depression (Steen, Seligman, Peterson, & Park, 2005).[10]

2. Using your strengths consciously over the course of a week is associated with higher happiness and lower rates of depression (Steen, Seligman, Peterson, & Park, 2005).[11]

3. Manager optimism predicts project performance (Arakawa & Greenberg, 2007).[12]

4. Gratitude is associated with higher levels of social support and lower levels of depression (Wood, Maltby, Gillett, Linley, & Joseph, 2008).[13]

5. Higher levels of strengths such as optimism, forgiveness, and gratitude is associated with lower rates of social anxiety among combat veterans (Kashdan, Julian, Merritt, & Uswatte, 2006).[14]

6. Strengths such as bravery, kindness, and humor, among others, are associated with recovery from illness (Peterson, Park, & Seligman, 2006).[15]

7. Top-performing managers focus on strengths: They are more likely than poor-performing managers to spend time with high producers, to match talents with projects, and to emphasize strengths over seniority (Clifton & Harter, 2003).[16]

8. Therapy that uses an explicit strengths-based focus has been found to outperform "therapy as usual" and "therapy plus anti-depressant medication" comparison groups (Seligman, Rashid, & Parks, 2006).[17]

Finally, it may help you to have a few tips regarding those clients who seem resistant to the strengths approach. I use the word "resistant" here in the kindest possible way. I know, as a coach, you are trained to follow your client's lead and would never want to force your agenda on your client. When I talk about overcoming client resistance, then, I mean working with clients who do not necessarily have a natural language or affinity for strengths, or who are reluctant to take ownership of their authentic strengths. Often, these clients are slow to warm to strengths not because of some difference in worldview or fundamental clash of personal values or coaching agenda, but simply because they do not yet have the language to speak about or understand strengths in a sophisticated way. In addition, they may not have ever received direct or immediate feedback about their strengths. For evidence of this latter notion, one need turn no further than Tom Rath, of the Gallup Organization. In *How Full Is Your Bucket?*[18] Rath writes "Managers take note: praise is rare in most workplaces. One poll found that an astounding 65% of Americans reported receiving no recognition for good work in the past year." Your clients "resistance," then, may be nothing more than the understandable tripping over words in a foreign language. Here are some tips on how to acquaint your clients with their own best sides:

1. *Help your client experience strengths emotionally.* Asking clients to discuss past examples of behavioral strengths, such as leadership or courage, can spark positivity in the client. For more cognitive strengths—those related to thinking processes such as curiosity and creativity—it is possible to engage these qualities within the session, simply by brainstorming or probing with powerful questions, thereby allowing the client an in-the-moment experience of positivity. Be sure to point out and label the strength along with the positive feeling.

2. *Help the client build a strengths vocabulary.* What's good for the goose is good for the gander. Just as you work to fill out your own strengths vocabulary, work to help your clients do the same. Often, the largest hindrance to discussing and accepting strengths is the fact that most people do not have well-developed strengths vocabularies. Offering a definition of strengths, pointing out strengths where you observe them, giving strengths-spotting homework assignments and similar activities can help clients build their strengths vocabularies. As the clients become better at noticing and labeling strengths they often become more at ease with the approach and are better able to develop their own strengths.

3. *Undertake an Individual Strengths Assessment (ISA) or other formal measures.* Formal strengths measures, such as those discussed later in this book, have an added air of authority for some clients. There is often a perceived objectivity and legitimacy that clients are ready to lend to formal assessments. Use the results from the assessment as a springboard to discussion about your client's strengths.

4. *Use the client's language.* This is a particularly important point as matching client language can help fortify the coaching alliance. Reflecting the client's own language back at her can demonstrate that you are paying attention and using terminology with which she is already familiar. More sophisticated aspects of matching client language include using client metaphors as the basis of questions or suggestions.

5. *Engage the client's strengths.* If labeling your client's strengths leads to repeated deflections or disavowal, it is prudent to discontinue that particular strategy. Instead, try leaping forward in the process and simply focus on how the client can best use these internal resources.

Ways to Introduce Strengths to Your Clients

1. Set the culture by introducing strengths early on.
2. Address weaknesses as an important focus.
3. Redirect attention toward successes and away from unnecessary self-criticism.
4. Emphasize scientific basis and benefits of the strengths approach.
5. Use the client's language wherever possible.

▶ Developing Your Client's Strengths

One of the aspects of coaching that I most enjoy is working with clients to use their strengths optimally. Because strengths come naturally to us it might seem a bit counterintuitive that we would need help to better employ them. This is precisely where we see the notion that "it is our strengths rather than our weaknesses that are our greatest areas of growth" in action. We can manage and—even to a certain extent—overcome our weaknesses, but it requires a fair amount of motivation, self-discipline, and perseverance. Developing your strengths, on the other hand, comes easily and is inherently rewarding and motivating. This means that energy invested in strengths will lead to a disproportionately large gain relative to a comparable investment in weaknesses. Of course, this leaves an all-important question: Where, exactly, do we find opportunities to employ and develop our strengths beyond what we ordinarily do? There are various answers to this question.

First, look for strengths that are less developed. Each of us is blessed with a number of different strengths. Some of these we are well aware of, they define us, and we have a long history of receiving direct feedback when we use them. Others, however, are less well developed and lurk below the surface, to be used only occasionally. At CAPP we call these "unrealized strengths," and they are natural areas for growth.[19] To some extent unrealized strengths will be abilities, like "incubator" and "antennae," that are overlooked as strengths. Strangely, people have a tendency to discredit their own strengths precisely because they come so naturally. Working with your clients to identify those strengths that are, as yet, unrealized is the logical first step on the path to strengths development.

Perhaps a personal example will help illustrate this point. A large part of my professional work involves giving presentations. I teach classes at the university, I train coaches and organizational staff, I give keynotes and book readings. My success hinges on my ability to bring my strengths to bear on presenting. Fortunately, I am courageous, funny, and a natural storyteller. As a result I tend to lean heavily upon humor, comfort with the stage, and stories when I give my presentations. Although not every presentation I give is up to my own standards, I recognize that I owe what success I have to my effective use of these natural strengths. But, what happens if I want to be an even better presenter? What happens when I want to grow and develop professionally? I need to look for those strengths that are natural and authentic, but which I am not currently using to the best of my ability. In my case this includes a good intuitive sense of the engagement and interest of my audience. For a long time I overlooked the audience when I gave presentations. I focused, instead, on my content, wanting it to be smooth, rich, and high impact. As soon as I woke up to my ability to consider the audience reaction on a moment-to-moment basis (this was actually pointed out to me by a colleague), the quality of my presentations rose. I was able, for the first time, to shift my focus from my agenda (the content I wanted to convey) to what the audience would find useful. Rather than remaining faithful to my own time frame, I learned to linger on points that resonated with audiences, and this flexible, audience-centered approach resulted in higher ratings of my presentations. Similarly, you can work with your clients first to identify their unrealized strengths and then to see how they can use these to achieve new levels of success.

A second approach to developing strengths lies in not overusing them. If unrealized strengths represent underutilized potentials, then realized strengths—those that we are aware of and use on a regular basis—pose the danger of being overused. Our strengths are often so effective and energizing that we fall into the trap of using them as the hammer with which we strike everything in sight. What many people fail to realize, through no particular fault of their own, is that situations and strengths interact. Remember earlier in this chapter when I compared strengths to the sail on a boat? This metaphor is especially relevant to optimal strengths use because sails need favorable environmental conditions (wind) to propel the boat forward. In the same way you and your clients need to find a match between your strengths and the situations in which you find yourself. Being a funny person can be a tremendous asset, but it might be worthless if you are dealing with a highly emotional crisis. Similarly, being playful and spontaneous can be a boon to a brainstorming session, but it might actually be a liability when it comes to careful strategic planning. Just because a strength leads to success in one instance does not necessarily mean it will automatically be appropriate to a different set of circumstances.

Again, perhaps a specific example will help illustrate this point. I once worked with a client who was tremendously bright. She absorbed knowledge the way a plant absorbs light. In fact, she thirsted for knowledge and felt a rush every time she learned something new. She purchased books by the dozen and subscribed to a dizzying array of professional and general periodicals. And here is where she ran into trouble. My client often had to conduct internal trainings for various departments in her organization. She loved to prepare for these trainings and wanted to include absolutely every possible fact she could. She would spend sleepless nights prepping presentations. The problem was she was spending far too much time on preparation, spending far too much money on background books and journals, and packing her talks full of far too much information. Her basic talent for learning transformed into a kind of knowledge-based hording, and became oppressive when she attempted to transmit her learning to others who lacked her deep reserves for facts. Ironically, to ratchet her strengths development up a notch—to help her get more out of this strength—we worked on dialing it down. We talked specifically about being more selective with the amount and quality of the background materials she chose to read in preparation for her presentations. We discussed limiting both the time she takes to prepare presentations and the number of take-home messages she generally wants to convey. Importantly, we emphasized the difference between love of learning in her own private life and love of learning as it might be optimally used in her professional life.

You should know that with all of my clients and in all of my classes and trainings, the idea of dialing back strengths, of using them less, is one of the ideas with which people most readily connect. The notion that you can underuse a strength is pretty straightforward, and most folks have an "I already knew that" attitude regarding underuse. Overuse, on the other hand, is generally a bit more intriguing to people. It is here that they are likely to need the most support and also feel the most engaged and experience the most rapid growth (see Figure 2.3).

Figure 2.3 Matching strengths to situations

▶ Strengths in Organizations

Up to this point we have discussed strengths as a general topic, with suggestions that might be useful for a broad range of coaching, consulting, and mentoring relationships. There are other, more specific ways in which strengths are particularly appropriate to the organizational setting. First, an organization itself can be a strengths-based organization. This essentially means that the culture of the organization is itself one built around the concept of strengths in general and the strengths of the specific personnel in particular. At CAPP, we pride ourselves on being a strengths-based organization, and we engage in a number of activities that promote a strengths culture. Everyone who works at CAPP, for example, has a "strengths cartoon" drawn of them. These cartoons illustrate a strength or strengths that we can expect to see from our colleagues. My colleague Reena, whose cartoon is shown in Figure 2.4, has a tremendous sense of fairness and is willing to stick up for the underdog. The cartoons are large, framed, and hang on one wall of the CAPP offices. They are a constant and public reminder that every member of the team brings some assets to the organizational table. Other companies offer strengths-based recognition in other ways. If you ever have the opportunity to wander the halls of the Gallup Organization, for instance, you will notice that the placards on office doors contain not only the person's name but also a list of their strengths. Another strategy is conducting face-to-face positive 360s. This does not imply disingenuous praise, but means that team

Figure 2.4 Reena's strength cartoon

members make the effort to give honest, positive feedback about work or decisions that were helpful and appreciated. When it comes time to suggest what might be improved, this praise makes the criticism far easier to swallow. Brainstorming ways to make strengths an institution can lead to more energized, productive workplaces.

Another natural point for creating strengths-based organizations is through strengths-based recruitment. Traditional wisdom dictates that effectively placing people is a matter of matching skills and experience to job openings. For all of the obvious appeal and advantages of this approach, it does not entirely capture the full potential of prospective employees. Knowing that a prospective hire has years of experience at a call-center likely tells you about his competence, reliability, and even ability to get along with others. But it tells you very little about his interests, passions, and engagement. These latter qualities are more than just important; they are vital to productivity and turnover. Recruiters can ask prospective employees about their strengths, which generally leads to different kinds of information and a livelier, more engaged interview process. CAPP recently worked with Norwich Union, the United Kingdom's largest insurer, on developing a strengths-based recruitment project. Instead of targeting specific skills or past experience, such as having worked for X amount of time in a call center, Norwich Union produced advertisements soliciting certain strengths. One of them, called "The Listener," featured a woman named Jo. This is what the ad stated: "As soon as the phone rings Jo comes into her own. Customers love her because she is calm, understanding, and pleasant. She knows the right questions to ask and, more importantly, she knows what to do with the answers. In the world of insurance claims, she's the Listener." Here the emphasis has shifted from skills, which can be acquired, to core strengths and personality traits, which are more natural. How did Norwich Union's campaign fare? Work sites that tested the strengths-based recruitment strategy saw measurable increases in employee engagement, superior performance ratings from on-site managers, and the employee attrition rate was cut in half in the first four months![20]

Why might a strengths approach to recruitment be so successful? One possibility is that today's workplace is changing at a more rapid rate than at any time in history. Centuries ago, a blacksmith's assistant could be certain that his job conditions would be exactly the same from one year to the next. In the modern workplace employees are asked to update computer and other IT skills regularly, and increasing geographic and social mobility means that they are also expected to adapt to new team members, offices, and supervisors on a regular basis. If skills provide insight into what you have done in the past, strengths provide a peek into what you might be capable of in an unforeseeable future. Another possibility is that the strengths recruitment process itself better weeds out people who may not succeed at the job and selects instead people who are unusually well suited to it. Anecdotal evidence from some of the Norwich Union interviews suggests this is the case. One prospective employee, for example, said, "About halfway through the interview I realized the job wasn't for me. I didn't have the right strengths and, strangely, that was okay." Another person said, "The interview was one of the most interesting and enjoyable interviews I have ever had. I was just able to be myself." Finally, a recruiter remarked, "I feel as though I've gotten to know this person better than I've ever known any candidate previously."

Another area where strengths are particularly important in the organizational setting is in strengths-based management. You will remember the Gallup statistics on top managers focusing heavily on strengths.[22] Strengths-based management requires supervisors to be aware of their own strengths and limitations, to value identifying and developing strengths in the people they work with, and the ability to do so. Marcus Buckingham has written extensively on strengths-based management and offers two reasons why it is not a more common tactic.[23] First, it often is at odds with existing organizational culture and protocols. Second, it is just a ton of work! For managers to focus on strengths they must individualize their management strategy and interactions to suit the particular character of each employee. Often, a heavy workload and time pressures discourage managers from adopting individualized attention in favor of a one-size-fits-all approach. Using a formal measure to identify employee strengths, having a public system—like the CAPP cartoons—for remembering these strengths, and spending time with workers to help them match their strengths to projects are all worthwhile strategies. If you are an executive coach you may want to start small with your client, testing the waters with a small change, rather than working toward an immediate overhaul of their management style. Let employee feedback and productivity guide the process.

The final aspect of organizations where strengths are particularly relevant is in outplacement. As I write this chapter the world is experiencing an economic downturn that has resulted in bank failures in places like Iceland and alarming unemployment rates in places like the United States. Unfortunately, a number of large companies across the globe are being forced to lay off personnel. Layoffs, while often necessary for the long-term health of the organization, are tough both on the workers who are made redundant and also on the supervisors who are forced to make those tough decisions and be the bearers of bad news. A strengths approach can be useful to bolster the energy of those people who remain in the workplace, offer a path to resilience for managers, and can be included in outplacement for workers themselves. As a coach in the current work and economics climates you may be forced to deal with the dark specter of outplacement. Fortunately, brainstorming ways that strengths can be used is one possible way to deal effectively with this unpleasantness.

▶ Conclusion

In the end, strengths offer a way to do the smallest thing to make the biggest difference. Strengths are huge natural resources for your clients and potential areas of enormous growth. Working with your clients to label, spot, and develop strengths is a certain way to promote energy, effectiveness, productivity, and a sense of meaning.

▶ Further Reading

Linley, A. (2008). *Average to A+: Realising strengths in yourself and others.* Coventry, UK: CAPP Press.

Rath, T. (2008). *Strengths Finder 2.0.* New York: Gallup Press.

Peterson, C., & Seligman, M. (2004). *Character Strengths and* Virtues. Oxford, UK: Oxford/American Psychological Association.

CHAPTER THREE

Harnessing Positivity

A year ago I traveled to the slums of Kolkata, India, for an unlikely reason: I was interested in conducting strengths interviews with some of the poorest people in the world. I had a hunch that locked away in the squalor of these impoverished neighborhoods were tremendous reserves of human ingenuity, kindness, and inspiration. One morning I visited an illegal slum settlement by the side of a large stagnant pool of water. The homes were made of bamboo and thatch and newspaper. The occupants lived under constant threat of police harassment and forced eviction. In this particular slum I met a charming 10-year-old girl named Putal. Putal told me the horrifying story of the time she went to relieve herself at night, fell into the polluted water, and nearly drowned. She was rushed to the hospital where she recovered, and was much taken with the nurses' smart uniforms. I struggled to understand what day-to-day life was like for Putal. Finally, I made my way to the questions I wanted to ask: Putal, what are you really good at? What do other people compliment you on? What is it you are proud of? She answered me in the way a child would. "I am really fast," she said.

Now, I like to joke around with kids, and I teased her a bit. "Do you think you are faster than I am?" I asked.

"I am definitely faster than you!" She said, her confidence radiating.

"There is no way you are faster than I am," I protested, "I am a grown man and you are just a little girl!"

"Then let's race and see," said Putal.

With that we left the confines of her family's cramped hut and made our way to the street. News of the race spread like a fire across the slum, and soon we were joined by hundreds of people lining the side of the road. Someone blocked traffic and someone else designated a parked, distant taxi cab as our finish line. We shot forward from our starting point, and I thought that I would have to be careful so as not to hurt Putal's self-esteem. The problem was that Putal was exceptionally fast! She blew by me, and I struggled to catch up. Suddenly, it was my own self-esteem I was worried about! I ran as fast as I could, but I had a difficult time staying abreast with Putal. Then, as we drew closer to the taxi, she drew on some unknowable reserves and turned on the speed in earnest, leaving me far behind. The entire slum—her friends, her family members, her neighbors, local vendors, and even my own translator—erupted into cheers. Putal came to shake my hand with an enormous smile beaming from her face. I could hardly catch my breath.

Putal's story tends to put smiles on people's faces. It is a nice story on so many levels. It is pleasing to see a child have success. It is rewarding to see a cocky adult put in his place. It is an inspiring underdog story, in which an underprivileged girl finds equal footing with someone much more advantaged than her. Putal's story also illustrates some important cross-cultural lessons. People, regardless of social, economic, or cultural background, like novelty, they like challenge, they like success; and all of these things tend to put a smile on our collective faces. Happiness, as it turns out, is a vital component to everyday life. People participating in psychological surveys in such diverse places as Turkey, Brazil, and Iran rate happiness as being one of the most worthwhile goals in life. It's even as important as falling in love or getting into heaven! Studies also show that most people are mildly happy most of the time. In Western society, in particular, happiness, like weight loss, has become a self-improvement obsession. In fact, you may even consider happiness as "the line below the bottom line." That is, although people like to make money, win races, and go on vacation, the reason they are doing these things is because—ultimately—they feel good.

Happiness is a crucial but often overlooked aspect of coaching. Client positivity—and I typically refer to it as positivity with clients—translates directly to increased creativity (great for brainstorming solutions), more curiosity and interest in the world (great for visioning), more health (great for everything), better social relationships (great for work and home), and optimism (great for perseverance).[1] To the extent that you can cultivate positivity within a coaching session, you can lay the foundation for your clients to be at their best. What's more, positive coaches matter.

▶ Happiness Is Liquid

When most people think of happiness they think of an emotional pleasantry. Happiness, to most people, is a feel-good outcome. It is a commonsense notion that happiness is the emotional finish line in the race to life. You get the right job, live in the right city, marry the right spouse, find the right parking spot, and you will end up happy. That is, first something happens in life, and then there is the rosy emotional aftermath. Interestingly, recent research from positive psychology shows that the reverse is also true: You get natural bursts of happiness throughout the day, and these moments of energy you can spend on the job, the spouse, and other areas you care about.[2] That's right! Happiness is liquid, in the same way that monetary instruments such as stocks are liquid. Humans are built with emotional systems that include happiness, and that happiness is intended to be spent. It is a type of emotional currency that can be spent, like money, on the outcomes in life you truly value, such as your health, your relationships, and success at work.

The basis for this idea largely comes from studies and theory developed by University of North Carolina–Chapel Hill researcher Barb Fredrickson. Fredrickson noticed a small handful of decades-old studies showing that putting people in a positive mood often leads to interesting consequences. If people spontaneously find money in a phone booth (hidden there by researchers), they are then more likely to help a stranger in need of aid (actually an actor working with the researchers).[3] Similarly, giving a small gift of chocolates to doctors helped them to make better diagnoses![4] Fredrickson realized that positive emotions might actually be useful, as well as feeling good. From this insight she developed her Broaden and Build theory of positive emotion. In short, broaden and build theory suggests that emotions are functional.[5] Negative emotions serve to limit our thoughts and behaviors, helping us to act more decisively during times of stress or danger. Positive emotions, by contrast, serve to expand (to broaden and build) our social, physical, and cognitive resources. That is, when you are in a good mood, you become more curious, more sociable, more creative, and are a bit healthier.[6] Your immune system works better, your cardiovascular system gets a boost,[7] you become a better problem solver, and you persevere longer at tough tasks.

Research evidence for this theory is plentiful. Fredrickson herself has many studies showing the broadening and building effects of positive motion. For instance, in one study working men and women undertook the brief daily practice of meditation, which produced more positive emotions.[8] These emotions, in turn, led to more self-acceptance, receiving more social support from others, feeling more purpose and a greater sense of mastery in life, and fewer symptoms of illness. Similarly, there is preliminary evidence that specific neurochemicals (the intriguingly named "HVA" and "5-HIAA") may be implicated in positive emotion leading to better coping and increased trust in others, and vice versa, creating an "upward spiral" of positivity.[9] Further evidence of the benefits of positive emotions come from a large meta-analysis (a study of studies) by Sonja Lyubomirsky and her colleagues.[10] Across all the studies they examined they found a staggering range of tangible benefits of happiness. What's more, many of these benefits were the direct result of feeling happy, and not the other way around. Take a look at the benefits listed in Box 3.1, and see if these are outcomes in which your clients might be interested.

Box 3.1 Benefits of Positivity (adapted from Lyubomirsky, King, & Diener, 2005)

1. Lower turnover at work
2. Better reports of customer service
3. Better supervisor evaluations
4. Lower emotional exhaustion
5. Higher job satisfaction
6. Better organizational citizenship behavior
7. Fewer work absences
8. Fewer emergency room and hospital visits
9. More social club involvement
10. More volunteerism
11. Others perceive as friendlier, more assertive, and more confident
12. Higher annual salaries
13. Higher longevity
14. Fewer fatal auto accidents
15. Lower incidence of alcohol or other drug abuse

16. Faster recovery from illness or injury

17. More likely to be judged worthy of receiving a pay raise

18. More likely to be judged as creative

19. More likely to resolve conflict through collaboration

20. Increased motivation

21. Better decision-making efficiency

22. Increased creative thinking

23. More inclusive thinking toward others

▶ The Old Positive Psychology Story

If positivity is so terrific—and the data certainly suggest that it is—then the next logical step is to discover how, exactly, to increase your clients' good feelings and how to harness these to gain the types of outcomes clients want at work and in life. Everyday interactions and common sense tell us that there are simple things we can do, like smiling and joking with others, that will boost people's moods. But there isn't much traction in telling people to smile more or make more jokes. And you certainly won't get anywhere if your proposal to organizational leaders never gets more complex than "try to promote humor in the workplace." Discerning clients, managers, and readers of this book will certainly want more sophistication. The good news is that positive psychologists have devoted about a decade's worth of research to identifying interventions that will increase positivity. There is now a solid research basis to back up the effectiveness of certain activities as happiness enhancers. What's more, there are even clever new ways to access and participate in these activities. I recently consulted for a promising new web site that allows subscribers user-friendly access and online reminders to participate in happiness interventions. The bad news is that, despite the progress we have made, these interventions are extraordinarily rudimentary.[11] The same simplicity that makes a catchy iPhone application can also be off-putting to leaders who want to get down to the serious business of business. While effective, current positivity interventions are not often framed in a way that take individual differences or work environments into consideration. The following is an example.

If you are even passingly familiar with positive psychology, you have undoubtedly heard of the "gratitude exercise." People participating in this intervention are asked to keep a daily journal of three things for which they are grateful. They may do so in the morning or in the evening, and they are encouraged to do so every day, and to keep the list to three. Results from multiple studies show that this activity boosts happiness on many measures of happiness.[12] Based on the strength of these studies, this activity has become, effectively, the sledgehammer that we positive psychologists use to smash everyone in sight. Blogs, newspaper articles, coaching web sites and self-help books all allude to this simple powerful activity. What most of them do not discuss are the problems with this activity. Each year in my positive psychology course at Portland State University I assign my students the gratitude exercise. Each year about 80 to 85 out of 100 students say it boosted their mood over the week they participated. Despite this obvious good result, only about 10 to 15 students report that they have kept up with the gratitude habit even a couple weeks later, to say nothing of the end of the term! Something is happening in which this effective exercise is not becoming habitual; it is not emotionally resonant enough or enjoyable enough that people are highly motivated to continue doing it. Researcher Sonja Lyubomirsky wisely cautions her readers that these types of interventions are not one size fits all and need to be adapted for optimal individual use.[13] Which makes a lot of sense if you imagine trying to assign this in a workplace where it will be scrutinized by skeptical leaders with a sharp eye on the bottom line.

In an increasingly competitive world with ever more sophisticated clients, we must do better than the gratitude exercise. One logical step is to modify the gratitude exercise, changing the language and practices to be a better fit with client or organizational values. To some extent, businesses have already done this with appreciation programs such as recognizing the employee of the month or singling out top sales representatives. This is a nice first step to what Tom Rath, of the Gallup Organization, refers to as the "recognition gap" in which 65% of American workers in one poll reported receiving no praise for quality work over the prior year.[14] Rath suggests "shedding light on what's right" as a form of organization-friendly recognition. This can be done through recognizing performance, as in employee-of-the-month programs; or in the form of identifying strengths, as discussed in the previous chapter; or it can come in the form of praise and appreciation. As a coach you can work with your clients to develop new habits in which they become vigilant for and appreciative of what goes well during the workday, the virtues of others, or instances in which they have been supported or helped (see Box 3.2). Perhaps even more important than just being aware of these bright moments is actually extending a word of thanks, whether that means keeping a small stack of thank-you cards in a desk drawer or taking the time to thank a colleague at the water cooler.

Box 3.2 Activity: A New Look at Appreciation

Think about how appreciation links to a positive mood, and how beneficial that can be to clients. Work with your client to make time—even five minutes—to reflect on all that went well during the day. Consider the following questions: Who had a hand in the day's greatest successes? Who rose to the occasion? Who took initiative? Who offered support? How were these people acknowledged? How does it make you feel when you think of these things? What does it make you feel like *doing*?

You might also want to focus on appreciation as it relates to your client. Try asking this: Who acknowledged you today? How did it feel when you were acknowledged? Try visualizing that moment. What else would you like to be acknowledged for?

Although I am personally familiar with the research showing that cultivating and expressing gratitude can boost happiness, these types of activities have never felt like a perfect fit for me. I'll be honest in saying that I do not regularly keep a written gratitude journal, and it is ever so easy for me to fall out of practice with reflecting on the best points of the day. As with every positivity-enhancing exercise, gratitude takes a bit of effort, and I find it difficult to sustain this effort over time. I may just be lazy, but I suspect many of your clients will be in the same boat. This is why I recommend taking the time to make sure the activity matches the client. It is one thing to recommend visioning, savoring, and gratitude exercises with clients for whom a five-minute reflection session at the end of the day will be a natural fit, and quite another for clients who will peter out after a week or two. For this latter group (and this includes me) it is worth noting that there may still be benefits to occasionally visiting these exercises. In fact, this is the hidden side of the research results that not many folks talk about: Psychologists tend not to test gratitude journaling, as an intervention, over the course of months. For expediency's sake they tend to assign the activity over one or two weeks and still show positive results. This means that occasionally practicing gratitude is also beneficial.

▶ The New Positive Psychology Story

As a one-off activity there is an empirically supported positive psychology intervention I like even better than gratitude, and it is the best possible self-exercise. This is a simple activity that asks persons to imagine themselves in the future, to picture achieving most of the things they want in life, to think about making good decisions and to envision the life they want for themselves. It tends to produce a little burst of inspiration in most folks. In part, this activity works because it focuses attention on the good and on the possible. Positive Psychologist Laura King has conducted research on the best possible self-activity and shown that simply writing stream of consciousness thoughts about reaching one's potential is a psychological tonic, producing measurable increases in individual happiness.[15] In part, it works because it sets up goals for immediate work. It is more than just daydreaming or fantasizing in an unrealistic way; it identifies deeply held values and presents an agenda for personal growth. The aspect of this exercise I like the best is that it is widely applicable to clients of all types. Visioning a positive future self is as appropriate in the boardroom as it is in a living room. It is as useful for executive clients as it is for life-coaching clients. Interestingly, a number of people have independently arrived at this particular exercise as being particularly fruitful for increasing positive emotion, affecting personal change, and leading to desirable work outcomes. As a result, a number of models and interventions have emerged, each of them more nuanced and sophisticated than more simplistic (but effective!) activities such as the gratitude exercise.

■ Individual Change Theory

In the late 1980s there was a stereotypical view of business management graduates as being overly analytical, unable to work in groups, and a bit provincial in their thinking. This was, of course, before the heyday of emotional intelligence trainings. At the time many MBA programs were very traditional, with an emphasis on one-way transmission of knowledge through lectures and other conventional teaching methods. Researcher Richard Boyatzis and his colleagues at Case Western University decided to take a second look at their curriculum and teaching methods in an effort to improve the quality of their program and of their graduates.[16] They took a 360-degree approach and evaluated their students on a wide variety of business-related ability and knowledge areas, such as persuasiveness, networking, written communication, and accounting. The faculty obtained student self-evaluations, peer reports, and formal assessments of 38 different topics and used these as the first step in a new course. The course was built around receiving feedback about performance and capabilities, designing individualized learning goals and plans to achieve them, and building positive peer groups. How did the course work out? Students consistently rated the course highly, enrollment increased by 15%, and faculty members were generally supportive and enthusiastic about the changes being made.

What is more important about this shift in thinking in management training is what it led to: Individual Change Theory. This early education project stimulated Boyatzis' thinking about how individuals make change. He began thinking about the feedback element of the course and spent special time considering the evaluation of current ability and performance against the backdrop of dreaming about and visioning a better personal future. Ultimately, he arrived at the idea that the ideal self—a vision of the type of person one aspires to be or the types of things one wishes to accomplish in life—is the fundamental driver of intentional personal change. Affect—and positive affect in particular—is at the heart of Individual Change Theory. Boyatzis argues that spending time taking stock of one's ideal self activates a range of positive emotions that, in turn, serve to motivate people to make and sustain personal changes. In a 2006 article, Boyatzis and Akrivou wrote:

> Positive affect improves the thoroughness, efficiency, and flexibility of complex decision making and influences one's sense of standards to evaluate your progress against a set of standards. Also, it facilitates the quality and quantity of pathways of thought and seems to boost an aspect of executive function, which is the ability to adjust efficiently to new information and undertake new problem solving efforts in congruence with the new information. (p. 625)[17]

The Ideal Self

Each of us carries with us a fantasy of being at our best or achieving our potential. These ideal visions tap our passions, our values, and our past achievements. As silly as it sounds, in my private moments I sometimes pretend to be interviewed on the radio for giving particularly good talks or trainings. This is an emotionally rewarding pastime that serves to reinforce my belief in my ability and motivates me to achieve new heights. In fact, the more articulate this ideal self is—the more I can specify exactly what I want to accomplish and the types of decisions and interactions of which I think I am capable—the better I feel and more motivated I become. You and your clients, similarly, contain conscious and unconscious pictures of the types of people you would like to realistically become over the next one or five or ten years. Helping your client to articulate this vision can give an extraordinarily powerful boost of energy and motivate him or her toward positive personal change.

It is important to note, however, that the ideal self is different from the so-called "ought" self.[18] That is, the ideal self wells up from within an individual and describes her own feelings or values of what she might become. Notions of what a person ought to do are typically external and imposed by others. The problem is, it is often difficult to disentangle the ought from the ideal. To some extent, each of us has internalized family, societal, and organizational values that may not necessarily be our own. We have all experienced the ambivalence that comes from the internal conflict of personal passions and external obligations. As a coach or mentor you will sometimes have to work with people to ease this tension by helping your clients either further integrate the external values or disregard them.

Activity: Creating an ideal self

Imagine yourself in the future. It may be the near future or several years from now. Imagine this is a future in which you have gotten many of the things you want from life and accomplished many of the things to which you aspire. Take a couple of minutes to really picture what you are like and what your life is like. Imagine where you would be living, where you would be working. Imagine what your commute is like, your health is like, your friendships are like. Imagine the skills you have, and the opportunities you have for growth. Picture the types of decisions you have made and the goals you have achieved.

1. Describe where would you be living:

   _____

   _____

2. What is it you value in living arrangements and circumstances that you would like to achieve?

   _____

   _____

3. To what extent is this vision of your future living arrangements internal versus the product of some external factor or someone else's values?

   1 ------------- 2 ------------- 3 ------------- 4 ------------- 5

   Completely   Completely
   My own values and choice   External values and choice

   _____

   _____

4. Describe your work life: your commute, your office, your position, the type of work you would do:

   _____

   _____

5. What is it you value in work that you would like to achieve in this ideal future?

_____

_____

6. To what extent is this vision of your future work the product of internal versus the product of some external factor or someone else's values?

1 -------------- 2 -------------- 3 -------------- 4 -------------- 5

Completely   Completely
My own values and choice   External values and choice

Positive Affect

Simply put, humans are equipped with two motivational systems: one for inhibition and one for activation. One makes us explore and venture forth, and the other makes us recoil and draw away. Boyatzis argues that, similarly, we have two general tendencies, which he calls the positive and negative emotional attractors—the PEA and NEA, respectively.[19] When things are going well for us we tend to be more playful and spontaneous and broaden and build our personal resources. This is where the ideal self comes in, offering an attractive imaginary target for our energies. However, we are often confronted with urgent problems and pressing decisions that sour our moods or force us into immediate action. These are negative emotional attractors. This is where Boyatzis' theory goes from good to elegant, suggesting that both are realistic, beneficial, and operate together as a dynamic system. At times stressful situations call on us to buckle down and perform, while at other times, we have the luxury to dream. Taking stock of your realistic situations—the "real you" contrasted against the "ideal you"—can give crucial feedback for the personal change process. The real/ideal contrast can illuminate areas for growth, possibilities for planning, and expose deep values.

Be aware, however, that when you work with clients this strategy can occasionally backfire. Every once in a while I encounter someone in a training who looks at their current circumstances and where they want to be and comes away feeling dejected instead of inspired. Often this knee-jerk emotional reaction can be easily overcome by redirecting the person's attention to the values, past accomplishments, and goals that form the foundation of the ideal self. You may also want to work with your clients to choose a specific attainable element of the ideal self to begin focusing on by way of boosting positivity.

Although this process sounds straightforward, and although visioning is a common coaching exercise, it is surprising how little advantage we sometimes take of the ideal self and its motivational consequences. It is also noteworthy how little attention we give to the important role that positive emotions play in the change process, helping us to leverage our current feelings for the ability to take risks and try new behaviors. In fact, it is here, as a coach or mentor, that you can be of particular assistance. In a recent article on leadership development, Boyatzis wrote:

> To try new behavior, a person often needs a type of permission to let go of old habits and try new ones. This permission typically comes from interacting with trusted others. Clients or students must spend sufficient time in the PEA to be ready for their time in the NEA and the stress of adaptation. In this way, the consultant, coach, or faculty member is simultaneously a cheerleader (predominately positive), guide (conscious of the person's state and progress), and provocateur (pushing, pulling, cajoling the client or student into the PEA or NEA when appropriate). (p. 307)[20]

Astute readers will notice the similarity between individual change theory and the group-oriented positive psychology intervention of Appreciative Inquiry.[21] David Cooperrider, the originator of Appreciative Inquiry, is Boyatzis' colleague at Case Western University. Appreciative Inquiry, which asks teams to identify individual strengths and then dream and design a more ideal future, is an excellent example of an intervention that harnesses positivity to help people change. In truth, there are a number of possible variations by which you might use visioning, goals, and ideals to muster a burst of positive feeling in your clients and thereby help usher them toward the growth they seek.

Coaching Questions for the Ideal Self

1. How well articulated is the ideal self?
2. How important is it to you to achieve the ideal self?
3. When are you planning to make the changes associated with achieving the ideal self?
4. What resources and opportunities do you have that will help you work toward your ideal self?
5. What hurdles do you anticipate? How can these be part of the growth process?
6. What factors inform your vision of your ideal self?
7. How internal (as opposed to external) are the values that inform your ideal self?
8. What person, living or dead, is similar to your ideal self?
9. Name a single, small behavior you can change as a first step toward your ideal self.
10. How can you chart your progress toward your ideal self?

■ The Reflected Best Self

The reflected best self is a feedback-oriented intervention developed by researchers at the business schools of Harvard and the University of Michigan.[22] In this exercise the participants receive feedback about when they are at their best, rather than when they are at their worst, by way of rewarding effective behavior and motivating positive change. Having your best self reflected back to you by people who know you well and know what you are capable of and when you shine can be a hugely positive experience. The reflective best self exercise focuses especially on the performance trifecta when you employ your best attributes (your strengths), when your behaviors are a positive experience for you, and when you create a constructive experience for others. The specific directions for this exercise can be found online at the University of Michigan's Center for Positive Organizational Scholarship web site (http://www.bus.umich .edu/Positive/POS-Teaching-and-Learning/ReflectedBestSelfExercise.htm). Like the ideal self in Individual Change Theory, the reflected best self harnesses positivity to forward motivation, action, and personal change.

Unlike the ideal self, however, the reflected best self is a measure of you at your realistic best. There is an emphasis on what you might be able to achieve, but rather than looking at a fanciful future, the reflected best self points people toward what they have already achieved. Personal development is, according to this model, more a matter of embodying those top moments more of the time than it is about changing from the person you are into some other person. I find that my clients are like me in this respect: They are attracted to the idea that they are already good people, already quite capable, and already accomplished. The trick is not to take on even shinier attributes but to buckle down and be at your best as often as possible.

Fortunately for coaches there are a number of ways to help your clients do this. Among the recommended exercises I like best from the reflected best self model is creating a personal vision statement. Again, this may not—at first blush—seem to be a startling aha moment. Identifying personal values has long been a mainstay technique of coaching. Occasionally we need to be reminded of these basic techniques because they are deceptively easy to overlook and pass by. When, for example, was the last time you took out an hour and wrote—actually wrote—your own personal vision statement? I go through periods where mission statements fall off my professional radar completely, only to be discovered again some months later. When I work with clients—whether they are managers, students, therapists, or people looking for a new profession—they tend to come out of the mission statement process feeling energized. I have used this in coaching sessions, assigned the activity as homework, and used it with groups in workshop format. The following is exactly how I facilitate the writing of mission statements (you and your clients can access an online audio/ visual version of this at my web site at http://www.intentionalhappiness.com).

■ Quick Guide to Writing Mission Statements

Step 1: I begin the process by introducing my clients or workshop participants to Zappos.com, the largest online shoe seller in the world. You may be familiar with the Zappos story: A young dynamic CEO, Tony Hsieh, uses creativity and positivity to create a work culture that is fun and productive and customer service savvy and, in doing so, catapults his company from $1.6 million in gross sales in the year 2000 to a gross billion dollars in sales only eight years later (in the process, printing up employee T-shirts saying "My company sold 5,000,000 dollars in one day and all I got was this lousy T-shirt"). Zappos is so confident in its ability to deliver top-end customer service and employee engagement that it offers $2,000 to anyone who quits its four-week introductory training program, and it publishes a 500-page book of testimonials from employees, managers, and vendors.[23] I tell my clients and workshop participants about this quirky, energetic, and fun young organization because it is so inspiring and tends to excite positive emotion.

I highly recommend you go to http://www.zappos.com to learn more about the company's history and culture. Click the "about us" link at the bottom of the home page. Here you will find all sorts of links about the brand, including a number of videos, media coverage, testimonials, and the company's core values. This is the other reason I choose to make Zappos the launching point of the mission statement exercise: Their unusual core values are worth looking at. They include positive but more traditional values such as "embrace and drive change" and "pursue growth and learning." And they also include some standout values such as "be humble" and "create fun and a little weirdness." To get an idea of how these values are played out in daily work you need look no further than the "random acts of kindness parade" regularly hosted by the finance department. Or consider Hsieh's famous "pizza story": One night he and friends returned to their hotel to find room service closed. Hsieh jokingly suggested they call Zappos to order food, and they did. Although they are an online shoe seller, the customer service agent taking the call compiled a list of local pizza delivery restaurants in the area. Now that's customer service! Watch the videos and let yourself be inspired by this company's success. Note: You may have a company or charity that inspires you more than Zappos, and it is fine to use that, so long as it directly boosts positivity and sets the stage for talking about core values.

I use the Zappos core values as a fun way of introducing people to the idea of listing their own fundamental guiding principles. I have folks start by writing their own core values, not worrying too much if they are perfect, if they overlap, or if they are an exhaustive list. I recommend two to five values.

Step 2: I have people reflect on their strengths. Usually I begin by showing them the VIA list of 24 strengths and have them choose a few that are personally descriptive, but I also talk with them about additional strengths. When time and circumstances allow I have them take the Realise 2 strengths measure. When I work in small groups I help them identify strengths by asking them what they are looking forward to in the near future, an activity I discussed in the previous chapter. I encourage them to write down two to five strengths they commonly use.

Step 3: I have them take another look at their values. There are a number of ways in which to do this, but I typically ask them questions like "What do you feel most proud of accomplishing?" "What would you want your legacy to the world to be?" and "When are you at your best?" Although these questions address, broadly, areas we have already covered, I want to usher them from reflective mode into action mode. To accomplish this I have them do free-form writing for a couple of minutes, always reminding them there are no right or wrong answers.

Step 4: Now, what you have gathered to this point is your clients' values + their strengths + their values in action. This will be the basis for their mission statement. Have them look for thematic similarities, things that keep popping up again and again. For many people the theme of "helping others" emerges, but it is often fascinating to see how this common value manifests differently in different individuals. Some folks say, for instance, that they want to be supportive and helpful to family members, others want to brighten the lives of friends, and still others are committed to helping strangers in faraway lands. When my clients feel ready to actually tackle the mission statement I encourage them to follow a two-paragraph format. The first paragraph should be personally descriptive, describing personal values. The second paragraph should be about how, specifically, these values would be put into play.

So, by way of example, my own statement might read:

> Paragraph 1 (descriptive of core value): I value growth. I am interested in my own lifelong learning and in fostering similar development of others, of any age or background. I believe that extending help to others will make the world a better place because it will lead directly to more evolved people and better relationships.
>
> Paragraph 2 (more specific about how I want to deliver the values in paragraph 1): Positivity is crucial for personal growth. I will use humor and storytelling to create a supportive, nonthreatening, broadening environment in which people can grow. I will look to use my roles as teacher, mentor, coach, researcher, and writer to provide platforms for others to grow. I also know that I grow most when I help others reach their potential.

It's just that easy. Most people walk away from the experience feeling centered, energized, focused, and hopeful. Now the troubleshooting part: It is common for people to freeze up before they start the actual writing process. This usually happens because they want their statement to be perfect or all encompassing. As a coach you may need to hold their hand through this phase. Support them by telling them that this is similar to a last will and testament or a national constitution in that it is a living document, one that should be revisited and changed on an occasional basis (I recommend the day after their birthday). So don't worry about small errors or it not being a perfect bulls eye; there can always be revision.

■ The Best Possible Self, or the Better Possible Self?

Finally, I would like to mention a third exercise related to taking stock of one's self that uses positive emotions as a core element. In the previous two models—the ideal self and the reflected best self—the emphasis was on boosting positive emotional energy and harnessing it to motivate people toward growth and change. It is interesting to take a step back and ask whether these types of exercises are better described as relating to the best possible self or to a better possible self. On the one hand they are about being better than one currently is, and on the other hand they often contain the hidden assumption that there is an endpoint to personal development. Although I am certain that, if pressed, everyone would agree that growth is a dynamic process and that personal excellence is a moving target, I also believe that it is common for people to fall into the trap of thinking about growth targets as fixed. This can be easily seen in widely used satisfaction measures.

Many coaches give their clients some type of satisfaction measure by way of assessing areas for potential work and areas of potential strength. Sometimes these measures are presented as wheels, as in the "wheel of life," and sometimes as traditional written scales with numerical response choices. They sometimes address general life matters, such as satisfaction with relationships or health, and sometimes they focus on work concerns such as sales performance or team communication.

Regardless of the particular format, these measures generally work by having clients assign a low number, such as a 0 or 1, to indicate dissatisfaction or very low satisfaction and higher numbers, such as a 9 or 10, to indicate extreme satisfaction. Contained within these measures is an assumption about the ideal self. The real self is the current satisfaction score, and the ideal self is a "10." The coaching process is a discussion about how to push upward from the current score toward the ideal 10. Many coaches facilitate this process by asking questions such as "What would it take you to raise from a 5 to a 5.5 or 6 in satisfaction?" This is a time-tested coaching intervention and tends to be effective because it reduces the investment in change to baby steps that clients feel hopeful can be accomplished quickly.

New research on satisfaction suggests an intriguing new spin on this traditional intervention. One of the most interesting findings from positive psychology in recent years is the idea of optimal happiness.[24] That is, although happiness is widely beneficial, data are now suggesting that having too much of it can be a bad thing. This only holds true, however, for achievement-oriented domains; those that are benchmarks of performance such as making money or getting good grades. For social domains, such as your satisfaction with your marriage, it appears that you can—and hopefully do—have all the happiness in the world without any deleterious effects. In one study, people from 33 different countries who scored an 8 out of a possible 10 on life satisfaction made significantly more money than their more satisfied counterparts who scored a 9 or 10! Similarly, university students in another study who scored an 8 out of 10 on life satisfaction had better grade point averages, were more conscientious about work, and attended class more. In general, people who are pretty satisfied, but not perfectly satisfied, strive a little more and work a little harder resulting in more rewards. Although happy with their lives, they retain a little bit of hunger that drives them to excel. People who are perfectly satisfied, by contrast, are less likely to want to exert extra effort to make changes in their circumstances. Again, this only holds true of life domains related to achievement and not those related to social relationships. For those achievement areas, this research presents a new way of using the satisfaction scales to harness positivity.

Here's the new scaling intervention: Ask your clients to complete a satisfaction questionnaire in the same manner you would normally. Undoubtedly, they will have a range of scores, some higher and some lower. Pay particular attention to the scores of achievement-related domains, such as the ones in Figure 3.1. When it comes time to discuss their various scores, take a moment and educate them about the new research findings. You need not be a personal expert in the science of happiness to report on the results from these studies. In fact, most clients get the basic relationship of satisfaction to striving right away. It makes sense to them that perfect satisfaction can result in complacency while a hint of hunger results in drive. You can also reassure them that there is nothing wrong with a score of a 9 or 10. It likely reflects favorable circumstances at work or a recent string of successes. People naturally rise and fall within a range, over time, as their life circumstances change. The take-home message, where your clients are concerned, is that a satisfaction score of 8 is the optimal target. When this idea hits home you can sense a huge wave of relief off your clients. Instead of motivating them to work toward a 10, you have just brought the finish line two points closer to them, and they haven't even begun working yet! The reason this intervention works—it is well received among my

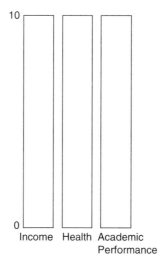

Figure 3.1   Satisfaction with achievement-oriented domains of life

clients and in my workshops—and the reason this intervention is not just a gimmick or a trick of numbers, is that it cautions people against the type of perfectionism that so easily crops up in our most highly motivated, high-achieving clients. I have found that shifting the focus from being the best to simply being better offers my clients permission to strive without the burden of emotional self-flagellation. What's more, the relief they often feel comes across as an emotional boost that you can then use to begin your work together.

▶ How to Increase Positivity in the Workplace

Although we have talked, to this point, largely about working with individuals and promoting and harnessing individual happiness, it also makes sense to discuss creating a culture of positivity at work. This emphasis on group happiness rather than individual happiness will be a familiar topic for readers working with organizational clients. How many times have you heard complaints about some psychologically defeating aspect of corporate culture? Coaching sessions can be a litany of talk about bad bosses, unclear expectations, heavy workloads and tight deadlines, the stress associated with organizational change, poor quality training, and a lack of opportunity for creativity. These are the same types of complaints most of us hear from our friends and spouses as well. Work makes up so much of what we do during the day that it is to be expected that when jobs are stifling or stressful these negative feelings get carried home with us. Interestingly, it isn't just that office politics, the demands of the job, and other work-related stressors get us down; positive psychology research shows that harnessing positivity—at the group level—can translate to more worker productivity and a greater sense of satisfaction for individuals.

Psychologist Peter Warr has carried out studies on job satisfaction and well-being at work for decades. He has identified 10 aspects in which workplaces differ from one another and which directly contribute to employee well-being.[25] They are:

1. Opportunities for personal control
2. Opportunities to use skills

3. Externally generated goals

4. Task variety

5. Clarity (clear expectations and feedback)

6. Adequate pay

7. Workplace safety

8. Supportive supervision

9. Opportunities for interpersonal contact

10. Social rank or position

The best offices have all of these qualities. Really good offices have many of them. Warr thinks about work in terms of its emotional content and consequences. Warr describes emotion in a common two-by-two format, where feelings modulate according to how pleasant (or unpleasant) they are as well as how arousing they are (see Figure 3.2). He suggests that when these 10 elements are in place, workers will experience more pleasant than unpleasant emotions. Further, some of these aspects of work, such as externally generated goals and task variety, can lead to more arousal, while others, such as safety, can lead to lower arousal of positive emotions. You may have taken particular note of item 3, externally generated goals. Although there is a wealth of information suggesting intrinsic motivation—that which wells up from within—trumps extrinsic motivation, Warr suggests there is a helpful amount of externally generated goals. He defines these, in part, as workload, attentional demand, demands relative to resources, and role responsibility. Some amount of these things can be stimulating, but too much can lead, according to Warr, to high anxiety and low comfort. Interestingly, having too few opportunities for personal control tends to lead to greater depression and lower enthusiasm as opposed to higher anxiety. Thus, it is not just that these 10 elements are the markers of good workplaces, it is that each affects worker well-being in a different way.

Warr's model presents some interesting inroads for the coaching conversation. You can work with your clients to assess how satisfied they are with each of these 10 features of workplaces and target areas for future work. The idea is to create as many pleasurable emotions as possible, and to ensure that a good portion of those are also high arousal. Warr's model is bottom-up, focusing on constituent parts, such as having supportive supervision and adequate pay, of a larger whole, well-being.

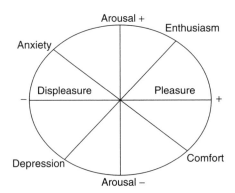

Figure 3.2   Emotional arousal and pleasure at work

Others have focused on top-down approaches in which an emphasis is placed on the positive emotion, and that is used as a mechanism to change the constituent parts. This can also be used as a coaching device: asking your clients about the times and amounts they feel anxious, enthusiastic, dejected, or comfortable at work and discussing ways to boost the positive emotions.

In their book, *The Levity Effect*, authors Adrian Gostick and Scott Christopher take this latter approach, arguing that levity—humor, laughter, and a light sense of camaraderie—translates directly to desirable work outcomes including more productivity and less turnover.[26] They cite survey research by the Great Place to Work® Institute used to create *Fortune's* "100 best companies to work for" list. It turns out that 81% of all employees who work in organizations rated as "great" report that they work in a fun environment, such as the one at Zappos. Only 62% of people working at organizations that received the designation of "good," by contrast, reported having much fun on the job. Not only is this "fun gap" deserving of attention, according to Gostick and Christopher, it is also one of the widest gaps in the entire survey, making it one of the most distinguishing differences between good and great places to work.

How do these great companies do it? How do businesses like Zappos take something as traditionally nuts and bolts as a finance department and turn them into a costume-wearing, parading bunch of fun-loving weirdos who love their jobs? There are several ways (in fact, Gostick and Christopher list more than 140 of them in their book!). First, your clients can hire fun people. Introducing play and fun can begin with the recruitment interview and can be one of the elements upon which candidates are evaluated. Second, new hires can learn on the first day that the office is fun as opposed to oppressive. They receive these signals from open-minded managers, such as Dr. Vic at Zappos, who keeps a throne in his office and photographs employees and guests sitting in it while wearing crowns. Most importantly, however, Gostick and Christopher caution that levity in the workplace is predicated on trust. Before your clients force their employees to play swivel chair soccer they must earn their trust by treating these workers with respect. A survey of 100,000 workers at the Boeing Corporation revealed that top managers at one site were able to get better work-related results, in part, because they asked their supervisees about their families, their weekends, and their health. They showed concern and appreciation. In the same way, you can work with your clients to start small and create a foundation of trust with a spoonful of fun by creating a public bulletin board for compliments or hosting an appreciation party during work hours. Work with your clients to take the emotional pulse of their workforce and make changes accordingly.

Giving Feedback That Leaves People Feeling Motivated and Positive[27]

1. *The power of expectation*—The person receiving the feedback owns their own emotional reaction, and this is largely dependent on their expectations not only of the feedback itself, but also of the feedback process in general. If you know you are going to give someone feedback, it is helpful to establish at the outset what the feedback is intended to accomplish, what form it will take, and that further work is expected.

2. *The power of accuracy*—It almost goes without saying that the closer to the target the feedback is the more helpful it will be. This puts the onus of responsibility on the person giving the feedback, and suggests thought should be given to parts of the feedback that might be superfluous or might be seen as a criticism of character rather than performance.

3. *Feedback is directed at the future, not the present*—There is an important difference between focusing on what is right and wrong with current work and discussing what needs to happen to make that work great in later iterations. The latter case depends on the ability of the person giving the feedback to focus on that terrific future work, painting a picture of it for the other person, and then providing steps for getting there.

4. *Believing in the project*—You might think that investing in the feedback process is tantamount to investing in the improvement process. You'd be wrong. I once had an editor who took weeks to get back to me about an article I had submitted for publication. His only comment on the manuscript, which took me a full week to write, was "it just doesn't sing." Not only was that not very specific (see next item), but it also indicated a real lack of personal investment. Worthwhile feedback has to indicate that the project can truly be great and that the person giving the feedback believes in the project and in its potential for success.

5. *Specificity*—This one is pretty straightforward. The more specific the feedback is the more understandable it is and therefore can be better actioned.

6. *The power of relationship*—The feedback is, fundamentally, a relationship. Just consider how you would give feedback on a short story to your best friend, a total stranger, or your parish priest. Even if it were the exact same story, you would tailor your feedback to the relationship. Looked at another way, you can harness your relationship and what you know about the person (and his or her strengths) to give better feedback and to hold them more accountable for change.

▶ Coaching and Positivity

To a large extent, the coaching endeavor itself is built around inspiring and harnessing client positivity. As such, the results of positive psychology studies should be welcome news to coaches as it provides a scientific rationale and new intervention ideas for creating change. That said, it is worth stepping back and asking a reflective question for coaches: What should the coach's role be regarding positivity? Take a few minutes and think about this issue. What obligation do coaches have to put clients in a positive mood? What tools do we have for creating and maintaining positivity? When might it be inappropriate to facilitate positivity? How do you honor the client's agenda but still avoid the trap of chronic problem talk and negativity? Feel free to write answers to the following questions to help you reflect on your own practice:

1. What is the emotional tenor of my coaching sessions? What influences this?

2. How do I boost positivity? Am I a supporter? A comedian? A self-effacer? What tools do I have at my disposal for increasing my clients' happiness in session?

3. How do I typically deal with negative emotions in session?

4. What is my own attitude about the function and appropriateness of emotion? Where did I acquire these views?

▶ Conclusion

In recent years happiness has begun to overcome the bad reputation it once had. Although there are still some stodgy naysayers who believe happiness is selfish or silly, many people are waking up to the fact that workers want to be happy, and that positivity leads to success in just about every walk of life. Research evidence now presents a compelling argument that positivity directly leads to better functioning at work and at home. Working with your clients to create more positive emotion, maintain these highs appropriately, and harness their power will give you an additional route to facilitating personal change and success.

▶ Further Reading

Gostick, A., & Christopher, S. (2008). *The Levity Effect*. Hoboken, NJ: John Wiley & Sons.

Rath, T., & Clifton, D. (2004). *How full is your bucket? Positive strategies for work and life*. New York: Gallup Press.

Diener, E., & Biswas-Diener, R. (2008). *Happiness: Unlocking the mysteries of psychological wealth*. Oxford, UK: Blackwell.

Fredrickson, B. (2009). *Positivity: Groundbreaking research reveals how to embrace the hidden strength of positive emotions, overcome negativity, and thrive*. New York: Crown Publishers.

CHAPTER FOUR

Making Molehills out of Mountains: Coaching Goals and Hope for the Future

At 13,000 feet our porter began coughing up blood. It was the summer of 1997, and I was climbing Tanzania's Mt. Kilimanjaro with my brother-in-law, Robindra. Along with Mt. Fuji and Portland's Mt. Hood, Kilimanjaro is one of the most recognized and frequently climbed peaks in the world. Although some routes on this—the tallest mountain in Africa—are technically demanding, many are simply physically strenuous hikes requiring little specialized equipment or skill. Because of this reputation as a "walk up," Kilimanjaro lures thousands of nonclimbers to its flanks annually. But standing at over 19,000 feet, the mountain catches many of these adventurous tourists unprepared for conditions of extreme cold and altitude. About 10 people die each year on Kilimanjaro. I was afraid our porter would be one of them.

We were four days into our climb and preparing for the final summit push—a grueling marathon of elevation gain—the following morning when our head expedition guide, Wilson, brought us the bad news about the porter. Robindra and I were spending the afternoon reading in our tent when Wilson stooped down and peered inside the open flap. "Robs," he called in softly; he always called us "the Robs." We came out of the tent and saw the worried look on his face. At 51 years old, Wilson had climbed Kilimanjaro well over a hundred times. I imagine he has seen every emergency of weather, sickness, and route finding imaginable. If Wilson was worried it must be important. "One of the porters is spitting up blood," he informed us. Robindra, Wilson, and I sat together outside our tent pitched high on a rocky escarpment of the Karanga Valley on Kili's south side. We discussed the porter's condition. Apparently the porter had begun our climb with a mild cold, which he concealed, perhaps fearing that his livelihood would be endangered if it were known that he was ill. Over the days he developed a cough, which steadily worsened. By the time we arrived at the Karanga Valley he was lagging behind and producing blood when he coughed. It was a clear symptom of pulmonary edema.

Pulmonary edema, also called "dry land drowning," is a potentially fatal form of altitude sickness. Edema occurs high in the mountains when fluid is produced in the lungs faster than the body's ability to reabsorb it. As the lungs slowly fill with fluid less oxygen gets to the blood stream, and the resulting symptoms include headache, dizziness, shortness of breath, nausea, and finally coma and death. Essentially, the victim drowns in his or her own fluids. The easiest form of treatment for expeditions without specialized medical equipment is a rapid descent. Because the illness is caused by altitude, a descent of only a few thousand feet can begin clearing up the symptoms.

However, as the three of us sat discussing a plan, we had a difficult time agreeing on a simple course of action. In retrospect I see that there were factors at work beyond those of which I was aware high on the mountain. As for myself, I was willing to defer to Wilson's judgment. After all, he was the head guide and, having climbed Kilimanjaro more than 100 times, he was far more experienced than either Robindra or myself. But Wilson was reluctant to take charge, asking instead what we thought ought to happen. It could be that because we were paying clients he felt a certain professional obligation to give us an opportunity to try for the summit. Or it could be that he, in turn, wanted to defer to Robindra. My bother-in-law is a climber with technical and high-altitude experience on major peaks in both North America and in the Andes. It is possible that Wilson erroneously saw Robindra as the more experienced climber. We went round and round playing hot potato with the responsibility for making a decision.

The practicalities of our situation also made the decision before us difficult. We were in a valley at 13,000 feet, and there was no easy descent to be had. A trip forward or backward along the trail would take us up and over 14,500 feet before we could descend in earnest. In addition, it was rapidly getting dark, and a nighttime hike would have been difficult, although by no means impossible. Last—and I'm not sure how much this factor weighed in our decision making—a descent would cancel any hope of summiting the mountain, the whole reason we were in Africa. In the end, we took a wait-and-see approach; we agreed to stay put in our camp and to reevaluate the situation at sunrise.

That night I lay awake a long time. At that altitude our blue tent was encrusted on the inside with a layer of frost. Every time Robindra shifted in his sleeping bag it caused a mini-blizzard in our tent that stung my face and crept into the neckline of my long underwear. I thought of our porter, asleep on the ground outside near the fire. I thought for a moment about modern adventure stories like Jon Krakauer's bestselling *Into Thin Air*. There are dozens of published accounts of heroic men and women who survived tough odds in the mountains. Somewhat selfishly, I imagined emerging from my tent and single-handedly assisting the porter down the mountain. But the reality was, lying in my sleeping bag, uncomfortable, unwashed, constipated, tired, and cold, I did not feel at all like a hero.

I awoke in the early morning to the panicked jiggling of our nylon rain-fly. It was Wilson, telling us to wake up quickly. I was ahead of Robindra as I grabbed my fleece jacket and boots. I unzipped the tent and headed out into the frozen morning. Wilson was there telling me the porter was dead. I ran to the place where the fire had died out in the night, hoping Wilson was wrong. I tried to tell myself the porter might just appear dead; had anyone taken his pulse? I ran to where the porter was, but when I approached him I saw that his mouth was wet and there was a yellow fluid overflowing down his cheeks. He was clearly dead. I was stunned. I stopped and turned away, backing up and sitting on a nearby rock.

The rest of the morning was a surreal blur. The Tanzanians held an impromptu funeral in Swahili, and Robindra and I stood on the outside of the circle of men with heads bowed. They wrapped the dead man in a bright yellow nylon tarp and fastened it with duct tape. We sent Wilson's younger brother running to the next camp over, a day's hike away. Then we all sat silently as the sun crept across the sheer cliff above us, waiting for a national park official to arrive. Unbelievably, during our wait Wilson asked us if we wanted to prepare for a summit push or if we would rather abandon our attempt for the summit. He informed us that if we chose to climb to the top he could try to arrange to acquire some alternate porters culled from other expeditions. I was shocked by his question. It seemed only right that this man's life was more important than our vacation. I told Wilson we would help evacuate the body off the mountain. Wilson shared this news in Swahili, and he told us that the group very much approved of our decision.

The park official, who arrived at noon, was dressed in army fatigues and wore a beret and carried a radio. After making a perfunctory report to him we loaded the porter's body onto a wooden litter and began the long hike off the mountain. We passed over 14,000 feet in the hot afternoon sun and came to the barren moorlands, where Robindra and I ran out of water. It was difficult hiking over loose gravel and large rocks and the litter bearers had to stop often to rest. Our large party pressed on into the approaching darkness and by six o'clock we were close to a campsite. Wilson suggested that Robindra and I stay the night at the camp while he and his men pushed on. We declined his offer and our group, which had swelled to 30 in number, began the long nighttime descent with only three flashlights between us. By midnight we had come down out of the barren moonscape and made our way through the mud tracks of the rainforest. We had hiked 23 miles at altitude, without water for the last eight hours and much of it in the dark. I was beginning to sag and stumble often. If I would have been alone, I am certain I would have collapsed. Only the seemingly indefatigable Africans kept me moving forward.

At some point, I'm not sure when, we came upon an ambulance, merely a Range Rover painted white with a red cross on the rear doors. Nine of us crowded into the vehicle. We laid the body, wrapped in yellow on the bench in back and then, having nowhere else to set our backpacks, stacked them on top. For the next hour the rover slid and lilted in the deep mud, sometimes leaning impossibly far over. I was smashed between two porters and constantly jerked by the erratic driving. At long last, deep in the middle of the Tanzanian night, we delivered the body to the police station, and then Robindra and I were dropped at our hotel. I don't even remember making it to my bed before I succumbed to a black sleep.

Contained within this ill-fated story of my trip to Kilimanjaro are some of the most important lessons I have learned about goals, motivation, and optimism. For me, the trip was an intense, firsthand experience of how commitment to a major goal can both help and hinder a person psychologically. While investing heavily in an outcome, such as reaching a summit—metaphorical or literal—can provide the extra dash of drive needed to succeed, it also means that there will be an extra sting if you are met with failure. Contained within this story, also, are important lessons about how outside forces act on our goals, no matter how worthy or how well planned they are. Finally, embedded in this tale is an important lesson about hope. Hope was the force that pulled me toward Africa, allowing me to fantasize that I might stand at the top of the continent's highest peak. Hope was the power that tugged me onward on the flank of the mountain even when I was exhausted. Hope was also the force that distracted me from taking immediate life-saving action when our porter fell ill. Goals, motivation, and hope—all three presented both their best and worst sides to me that day.

In this chapter, I discuss all three of these important concepts: goals, hope, and motivation. As you, no doubt, are already aware, these powerful psychological processes are not just relevant to your coaching work, but are vital to it. Since the very beginning, coaching has been largely about setting goals and increasing motivation to better achieve success. Seasoned coaches will recognize the many ways they can leverage positivity, hope, fantasy, and visualization to stretch their clients. Although I will briefly cover some of the lesser-known research in this topic, I will largely confine my discussion to interesting new ways this area of positive psychological science can be used in hands-on practical ways.

The Power of Storytelling

As a natural storyteller, I often use real-world narratives to inspire, challenge, or instruct my coaching and mentoring clients. They quickly grow accustomed to hearing me ask, "Do you mind if I tell you a quick 30-second story related to that point?" More importantly, my clients report that these stories are among the most powerful parts of the coaching session, offering examples and insights that further their agendas. I intentionally told the story of my ill-fated climb on Kilimanjaro in a detailed and thorough manner. I could have reduced the tale to a couple of paragraphs to get my main message across. Hopefully, by adding additional detail I laid the foundation for increased emotional resonance and set the stage for a more nuanced lesson. This story could, potentially, provide the launching pad for a number of interesting and useful discussion points. For instance, when I tell this story to my undergraduate students at Portland State University it leads to fascinating conversations about personal responsibility: Who was at fault for the porter's death? How did each person in the story contribute? This story also contains interesting lessons about redefining goals as circumstances shift: In the beginning I wanted nothing more than to climb Kilimanjaro; at the end I wanted nothing more than to respect the death of this man by *not* climbing Kilimanjaro. Other people I have talked with, however, think that a successful summit would have been the best way to honor his memory. In the same way stories can be used to create and communicate a vision for the future or to help people wrestle with sticky issues at work, especially true-life stories taken from real organizational occurrences.

Just as my Kilimanjaro story highlights the issues of personal responsibility and goal setting, stories from organizational culture and history can lay the foundation for talking about interesting or difficult issues. Storytelling consultant Peter Christie suggests that there are (at least) four primary types of stories: anecdotal, historical, allegorical, and biographical.[1] In organizations there are a number of natural storytelling opportunities, and it can be helpful to be aware of these. Managers can use stories to articulate a vision and motivate staff. Marketing staff can use stories to strengthen brand identity. Staff at all levels set the culture of the organization with their spontaneous water-cooler stories. Facilitators can enhance learning through the use of stories. Consider the ways in which your clients use stories: What language do they use? Who are the recurring characters, and what are the recurring themes? How might you use the concepts of authorship and revision to change their stories in positive ways?

I recently attended the First World Congress of the International Positive Psychology Association in Philadelphia. At this meeting Martin Seligman, the founder of modern positive psychology, proposed an interesting idea: "We are not pushed by the past," he said, "so much as we are pulled by the future." He meant that our visions and aspirations are what motivate and drive us, far more than our histories support us. Our direction in life—both as individuals and as a collective—is largely about obstacles and opportunities in the road ahead rather than what has happened in the past. Whether this is completely true in some provable way is less important than the fact that it is an intriguing notion. It speaks directly to the idea that humans, by nature of our highly evolved frontal lobes, are built to look ahead. We predict weather, plan vacations and retirement, prepare for meetings, lock our cars, save money, and many other activities that hint at our tremendous capacity to think about the future.

Goals are future-oriented benchmarks that help us organize our behavior. By establishing goals, both large and small, we establish a gauge for success, a guide for making decisions, and a target to move toward. Pursuing goals isn't just second nature, it is vital to our functioning. In the absence of goals we tend to flounder. Perhaps this is the reason that establishing a client agenda (an attainable short-term goal) and working with clients to achieve their visions (a tapestry of longer-term goals) is such a foundational part of coaching. Much has been written about SMART goals and other approaches to designing goals that are achievable and measurable, and I do not wish to retrace that same ground here. Instead, I will introduce you to some areas of goal-related research with which you are likely *not* already familiar. Also, I want to emphasize application and suggest ways you might translate this research into usable coaching interventions.

Let's begin by talking about the future, and our ability to think about it. Although squirrels hoard nuts for the winter and bears find caves in which to hibernate, these are instinctual behaviors. You never hear about a squirrel putting away two years worth of nuts so he can rest easy over the summer or a bear choosing not to hibernate. Indeed, it is humans who have the unique skill of making volitional decisions about the future: planning, anticipating problems, marshaling resources in anticipation, and modifying plans as circumstances dictate. It makes sense, then, that we are naturally predisposed toward setting and pursuing goals. In recent years, researchers have found that goals are directly related to increased happiness and a deeper sense of meaning and connection.[2]

Unfortunately, that is where the good news ends. A new line of research on affective forecasting shows that although we are terrific about planning for the future we are far from perfect at predicting how we will feel in the future.[3] This is a fascinating and counterintuitive way of looking at things: We make decisions all the time because—implicitly or explicitly—we believe they will make us happy. We take on projects, agree to dates, move, take vacations, and make purchases all because we think we will feel an emotional boost or experience a jump in quality of life. This is especially important for your coaching work because it means your clients are making decisions and setting goals every single day based, in part, on erroneous information. The projects and targets they lay out for themselves might be achievable, and might even be rewarding, but often not in the way your clients will predict. Familiarizing yourself with this research can provide a whole new avenue for helping your clients make choices that will return psychological dividends.

What researchers Tim Wilson and Dan Gilbert have found suggests that we make consistent and predictable errors in forecasting our future state of mind.[4] We often mispredict both the intensity and duration of these feelings. Take the example of a young university professor up for tenure. If you were to ask her how she would feel if she did or did not receive tenure, as these researchers have done, she would likely say that she would be elated to win tenure and crushed not to. When the researchers followed up with actual professors who did and did not receive tenure they discovered an interesting thing: The young lecturers who did not receive tenure felt the emotional sting, but it was neither as severe as they predicted nor did it last as long. They recovered relatively quickly. Similarly, those lucky young professionals who received tenure experienced an emotional high, but it was not the euphoria they expected, and it passed pretty quickly. These findings have been replicated across situations, including the emotional impact of an election, dating, and athletic competitions.

In addition to duration and impact errors we have a tendency to mess up, cognitively speaking, when it comes to situations that we have never before experienced.[5] Although we are pretty accurate in terms of valence—knowing that achievement will feel good and failure will feel bad, for instance—we are not perfect. When we are in novel situations, such as riding on a roller coaster, we sometimes find that we are surprised that what we thought would be scary was fun and exhilarating, or what we thought would be a rush was jarring and terrifying instead. In the case of novel situations we often do not have adequate information to make an accurate guess about our future feelings. One way to avoid this problem is to talk to someone who has experienced the activity and use their advance knowledge to make a better decision. Although this might sound like commonsense advice, it is surprising how often we charge ahead without doing exactly this.

Duration Neglect = the propensity to under- or overestimate the emotional impact of the duration of an event. For example, a wonderful seven-day trip to Hawaii might produce exactly the same amount of remembered happiness as a ten-day trip to Hawaii of exactly the same quality.

Impact Bias = the propensity to under- or overestimate the emotional intensity of an event. For example, a win by our favored football club—Real Madrid—might boost our mood, but only to a moderate rather than extreme degree.

Valence Prediction = we are generally good a predicting valence but less accurate when it is a new or novel situation. For example, going on a date might be widely predicted to be fun, but the actual experience could turn out either fun or disappointing.

To give you an example of how this information might be used in a coaching context consider a client of mine who was deciding whether to accept an attractive job offer in San Francisco. My client approached this decision in much the same way as many of us do: After feeling an initial burst of euphoria over the job offer she sunk into a deep funk, paralyzed by uncertainty and indecision. I have seen it many times: People fret over large life decisions such as the choice to take a new job, move to a new city, have a child, or go to graduate school. These decisions can seem so important that they take on a life of their own, dominating a person's attention, emotions, and relationships. It is surprisingly easy to get hung up on making exactly the right choice. Some folks spin their metaphorical wheels trying to decide on the absolute best course of action. Ironically, putting too much emphasis on an outcome can lead to inaction. My client quickly plunged into a kind of permanent ambivalence. Interestingly, when looked at through the lens of affective forecasting, we can see that my client's indecision was related to her predictions of her future emotional states: If she made the right decision, she would end up happy, but if she made the wrong decision, she would be miserable. When I spoke to her it was clear that she suffered, particularly, from duration neglect related to moving to the new city where she would begin her new career. Consider some of her comments:

Client: I am really worried about the move.

Me: What, specifically, are you worried about?

Client (sighing): There is so much! I have spent so long building a social network here, and I don't know anyone in San Francisco. I don't know the city; I don't have friends; I don't have a car; I don't know the job. It just seems like I will be bewildered. Bewildered and lonely.

Me: No doubt, moving can be really stressful.

Client: I know! And you know me; I don't handle change all that well. I am pretty slow to adapt.

It is interesting to notice a couple of facts in this brief dialogue. First, my client focused heavily on the short term. She focused on the days and weeks immediately following the move. This is a natural tendency for all of us because it is much easier to paint a mental picture of this shorter-term time frame. It is harder, by contrast, to imagine what life will look like five years down the road. However, it is a longer-term focus that helped move my client forward, as illustrated by the rest of the dialogue:

Me: That's one of the things we both know about you. You are good at planting roots. And trying to disrupt those roots can be tough.

Client: Yeah.

Me: There is one thing I am curious about, if you don't mind my asking . . .

Client: Go ahead.

Me: I'd like you to try to imagine life in San Francisco six months after your move.

Client: Okay, It's kind of hard.

Me: Do you think you'll have any friends?

Client: Well, sure.

Me: Do you think you'll know your way around the city?

Client: Of course.

Me: What about work? How much will you feel like "the new guy"?

Client: I might still be learning the ropes, but I won't be brand new. I'll know some things.

With each successive question I asked my client, the mood became lighter and lighter. As my client began to visualize herself and her life in the post-transition period she gained new awareness that, essentially, things would turn out fine. Her biggest stresses, such as not knowing her way around the city and not having any social contacts, would certainly be overcome. There is no question the transition period would be stressful, but also no question that my client was capable of weathering it and creating a fulfilling life for herself. Once we had arrived at this new perspective we were able to shift the coaching conversation from "Should I move to San Francisco?" to "If I move to San Francisco what are some of the things I would like to create for myself in my new life there." This new question felt better to my client and opened the door for visioning and brainstorming. Ultimately, she did make the move, and I am happy to report that she enjoys an active social life and is happy in her new life.

The Dark Side of Goals

We have all experienced a time when heavily investing in an important goal has led to crushing anxiety rather than hope and inspiration. Research by Eva Pomerantz suggests that the difference between these two emotional reactions lies in where a person focuses.[6] When someone looks at what Pomerantz calls "failure impact predictions"—what will go wrong in the event of failure—stress skyrockets! If a person focuses, instead, on how much progress has been made toward the goal, he or she is more likely to feel energized and happy. As a coach, you can use emotion diagnostically: When your clients complain about anxiety, this is a red flag that they are focusing on the effects of possible failure. Try reviewing progress, resources, and short-term milestones to put them back on a positive emotional track. Consider the following questions. Although all of them will look like the type of standard, open-ended coaching questions you already use, each is crafted to point client attention toward gains and away from potential failure, thereby increasing positivity and decreasing worry:

1. What progress *have* you made?
2. When have you been successful at similar goals in the past?
3. What resources are at your disposal to help with this goal?
4. What do you like best about this goal?
5. What have you tried so far?
6. Who could help you with this goal?
7. What keeps you working at this goal?
8. What kind of energy reserves do you have left around this goal?
9. *How* can you make this goal work?

■ Markers of Motivational Behavior

There are few areas in all the world of coaching as well reported on as goals and motivation. Because so much of our professional work centers around establishing, working toward, and achieving client goals, it is no wonder that coaches seem to have an insatiable appetite for research and insights on goals and motivation. Much has been written, for example, about the architecture of good goals, such as the characteristics embodied in the SMART acronym. And much has been written about types of motivation, such as intrinsic and introjected motivation, just as the framing of goals as "approach" or "avoidant" is well-trod territory.[7] I have as little interest in covering this discovered country as you do in reading about it (see suggested further reading at the end of this chapter if you want to dive more deeply into these waters).

One area of motivation-related research and theory that has been, I believe, underreported in the annals of coaching is that of the specific markers of motivated behavior. Broadly speaking, behavior can be motivated or passive.[8] Your client can be highly engaged with a goal or completely disengaged in effort. This is easy to understand in the case of a large and important goal, such as marketing a new product. An active marketer would take the reins and initiate a strategic campaign targeted toward a presumed customer base. A passive marketer would be more likely, by contrast, to hope that word of mouth or other viral marketing strategies did their work for them. The distinction between motivated and passive behavior is far less clear, however, in other instances. Take, for example, the case of stereotyping. Everyone stereotypes to some degree; we all place people in mental categories because it offers a sort of social shortcut. We raise our guard, for instance, when we pass a man, rather than a woman, on a dark street at night, because we understand that, on the basis of group averages alone, a man poses a greater potential threat to us than does a woman. When we tense up as we pass the stranger, is this passive or motivated action? Was the stereotyping itself automatic or motivated? It turns out that there are specific markers that help us tell the difference between automatic and motivated behavior. These can be useful benchmarks for coaches for exploring and understanding client motivation and behavior:

1. *Persistence-Until:* As the name implies, "persistence-until" is the tendency for a person to continue pursuing a goal until such time as that goal is attained. Highly motivated behavior, whether it is setting the dinner table or writing a report at work, is worked on until it is accomplished. One of the factors that researchers have uncovered that is directly related to the persistence-until marker of motivated behavior is accessibility. High commitment to a goal leads individuals to be more vigilant for information, resources, and other factors that are relevant to their goal. The more readily accessible mental information related to a goal is the more likely the chances of success. As a coach it can be worth exploring client persistence as well as taking note of how accessible goal-relevant information seems to be to your clients.

2. *Equifinality:* This simply means that when it comes to motivated behavior there is a greater tendency to focus on the final outcome than on the process by which it is achieved. You eat until you are full. You drive until you arrive at work, even if you have to take an alternate route. You pass a test even if you have to cheat

to do so. And here, in this final example, is the rub. Coaches and clients alike should be aware of the "by any means" mentality. Especially because researchers have uncovered what has come to be known as the self-affirmation hypothesis. This means that when people engage in behavior that is inconsistent with their attitudes, they often change their attitudes to bring them in line with their behavior rather than changing the behavior itself! As a coach it might be particularly helpful to be watchful for instances in which clients are externally pressured (motivated) by others at home or at work to engage in behaviors that are not congruent with their values.

3. *Docility:* Imagine a coach with the goal of becoming a skilled public speaker. Initially, she does not possess enough expertise to determine what elements of her talk were successful on their own merits and which were due to random or environmental factors. After repeated speaking engagements, however, she begins to learn that certain techniques—telling jokes or opening with a story—lead to success while others—letting one audience member dominate the discussion or presenting complicated diagrams—turn audiences off. This process of dropping failed behaviors is docility, and it acts in a dynamic way with the process of picking up or retaining successful behaviors. Interestingly, further expertise in public speaking can lead the coach in our example right back to docility by making her behavior so overlearned, so automatic, that she can "do it in her sleep." Motivated behavior requires updating, and it is here that you, as coach, can bring your powers to bear. By checking in with clients about how they continue to sharpen their skills and learn and grow you can keep them in the highly engaged state of motivation and avoid docility.

4. *Affect:* Positive emotions are a terrific indicator of motivated behavior. When people make progress toward a goal they generally feel good, and when they feel good they generally have the energy and enthusiasm and creativity to make progress on goals. Understanding your client's emotional state as it relates to his or her progress on a goal can be subdivided into three categories:

   A. *Discrepancy*—Your clients tend to make mental contrasts of their current performance or progress relative to the end goal. In general terms, the smaller the discrepancy the better they feel. This is why authors feel better when they reach the halfway point of their book than they do after they complete the eleventh page of writing.

   B. *Direction*—Your clients also are interested in whether they are moving toward or away from a goal. If your client has a goal of hiring a new assistant, they may initially feel good about advertising the job listing and interviewing a candidate, but then worse about the fact that none of the top candidates accepted the job offer.

   C. *Rate*—Again, generally speaking, your clients like to make quicker, rather than slower progress on a goal. As a coach, if you are looking to raise motivation, positivity, or both in your clients, pay attention to all three of these areas. Each may be used uniquely to ratchet up the emotional experience.

Using Discrepancy, Direction, and Rate to Motivate Clients

Consider the following questions, each of which explores one of these three aspects of client affect and motivation:

1. How far are you from achieving your goal?
2. How do you know? What standard do you use to assess goal progress?
3. How far have you come since embarking on this goal?
4. Are you moving toward or away from this goal?
5. Would your answer to the question of movement (question #3) be the same each day? Across a week? Each month?
6. When do you expect to reach your goal?
7. How fast is your progress these days, compared to when you began this process?
8. How satisfied are you with the speed of your progress?
9. All things considered, how quickly should you be able to reach your goal?

5. *Effort:* The final reliable marker of motivated behavior is, of course, effort. The more invested a client is in her goal the more effort she is likely to invest. Whether this is mental or physical energy, the effort seems to increase in the face of obstacles for highly motivated individuals. As a coach, you can help your client track her effort both as a sign of progress and as a finite resource. In the former case it can be reassuring to clients to keep in mind that they have given it their all or made their best attempt. But effort can be costly as well. From the external vantage point of coach, you can help your client keep track of and regulate effort to avoid burnout.

■ Optimism

Another one of the goal-relevant areas I find the most fascinating personally, and which my clients find the most useful, is optimism. It makes sense that having an optimistic outlook might help people take appropriate risks to pursue goals in the first place, and to persevere with their goals, because they believe a favorable outcome is possible. Let me give you an example: My sister, Mary Beth, and I were once hiking in the Olympic Mountains of northwest Washington state. It was late in the day, and we were descending from one of the lesser peaks. It was cold and misty out, and we lost our way. As we veered off course we accidentally descended into a dangerous ravine that served as a runoff chute for rock fall and which terminated in a steep cliff. We were, understandably, a little nervous. We were scared that we might be hit with random rocks and worried that we would have to try and find another route after the sun had set and the temperature dropped. But not for one second were we hopeless that we would find our way back to the car. In fact, we were optimistic. We thought that finding the car was not only possible, but certain. It was this certainty that we would reach our destination sooner or later—perhaps taking a few wrong turns before we arrived—that helped spur us on. In exactly the same way the idea that your dreams will come true with a bit of planning, effort, and luck likely puts you on the course to chase them.

■ Is Optimism Realistic?

There can be little question that the degree of hope we have, the amount of planning and future mindedness we engage in, and the extent to which we are naturally optimistic all affect our motivation. Every mountain climber starts at the base believing there is a good chance of reaching the summit. Every planned pregnancy assumes that good parenting is possible. Every entrepreneur, similarly, can envision business success. It is our hope—our expectation of a positive future outcome and our belief in being able to personally influence that outcome—that allows us to take risks and persevere. And here we arrive at one of the stickiest areas related to thinking in future terms: How do we know that our optimism is realistic? What makes us so certain that the risks are worth taking? Might we become blind to very real costs of hope and goal pursuit? The answer to these questions can be found in the scores of bodies of climbers who died trying to reach the summit; in the many examples of terrible parenting; and in the ashes of failed businesses. It makes sense when thinking about optimism to try to determine the difference between fantasy and reality. As coaches, one of our best services can be to help clients gain exactly this type of perspective.

When a client expresses excitement about a new goal, it is enjoyable to be excited right along with her. In fact, one of our charges as coaches is to share enthusiasm in an effort to support our clients' successes. But there are many instances in which exploring the realism base for optimism is a prudent and important service. Consider the following methods for arriving at a realistic versus unrealistic hope for the future:

1. *Client disconnect:* As a coach you can be vigilant for signs that the client harbors reservations about a goal or about the future. Tentative speech, slouching posture, distraction, and a drop in emotional energy can all signal the possibility that the client has doubts. Take these signs as invitations to open a conversation about personal resources, timelines, and other factors that will impact the ultimate success of the goal.

2. *Coach disconnect:* As much as you might admire your client, there are times when you have red flags of your own raised. These could come in the form of nagging doubts, seeming contradictions, or emotional uneasiness. Not only should you pay attention to these misgivings, but you should ask permission to raise and explore them.

3. *Resource-Goal match:* Even when there is no cause to suspect anything other than success, it can be helpful to take stock of client resources. To the extent that these resources are well aligned with the client's goal, you have every reason to be optimistic. Even on those occasions when you discover that the resources are a poor fit, it can be a blessing: This gives you and the client an opportunity to modify goals and timelines to raise the possibility of success.

4. *Establishing success criteria:* Hope for success in the future rests on each person's individual definition of what success means. Exploring your client's definition can go a long way toward establishing the reality basis for optimism. By having

clients clearly articulate what would constitute a success, and consider how open-minded they are to alternative definitions, can help both parties understand whether goals are worth the risks and efforts.

Interestingly, there is another way in which unrealistic goals can undermine your clients' performance. Gloria Oettingen, a researcher at New York University, has conducted studies on the way people think about the future.[9] Broadly speaking, people focus on future outcomes in two basic ways: expectations and fantasies. Expectations are simple judgments that a given outcome is likely, as in "I expect my children to come home after school." And fantasies, by contrast, are, well, fantasies. We all fantasize from time to time. Perhaps, in your private moments on your morning commute you practice your Oscar award acceptance speech or you play with the idea of sipping champagne on your private jet. Sometimes our fantasies can even be brief and mundane: How many times have you looked at a beautiful photo in a calendar and thought, "I'd like to visit Tuscany!" The interesting thing about such fantasies is that they tend to heavily weight the enjoyable aspects of the vision while overlooking effort and hardship. Oettingen describes positive fantasies:

> Positive fantasy can pertain to mentally enjoying future outcomes, and to mentally enjoying a future smooth and effortless progress toward that outcome. In other words, the positive versus negative tone of one's fantasies about the future can be based on mentally experiencing having attained the outcome, moving smoothly toward it, or both. (p. 1199)

It turns out that indulging such fantasies can actually undermine motivation. In several studies Oettingen and her colleague found that mentally dwelling on a positive future led people to invest less effort in that very outcome. This makes sense: Visualizing the positive aspects of achieving a goal—essentially reaping the emotional rewards without having to suffer any of the hard work or setbacks—pays out immediately, psychologically speaking. If this is true, where does it leave us, as coaches? Aren't we supposed to use visualization as a powerful tool with clients? Fortunately, Oettingen offers some helpful advice: Positive fantasies are particularly helpful in exactly the types of ways that coaches use visualization: for personal exploration. In circumstances where clients have the opportunity to mentally experience different potential futures or "try on" various identities, positive fantasy can be just the type of emotional experience she needs to think creatively and increase hope. Beware, however, once these initial insights are gleaned, dwelling in the positive fantasy too long might start to work against your clients.

Positive Fantasy Take-Home:

Positively visualizing the future is recommended in instances where clients want to focus on growth and change, but may be contraindicated when clients want to focus explicitly on personal achievement.

Curiosity and Goals

For most people the link between curiosity and goals is pretty straightforward. Curiosity can act like a psychological spotlight, casting light on possible goals that might be interesting or worthwhile. Curiosity can also activate us, tugging at our hearts and minds and pushing us to expend energy, commitment, and responsibility in the pursuit of goals. What's more, curiosity, as a mental state of openness to experience, can enhance our performance. Harvard researcher Ellen Langer was, herself, curious to see how openness and curiosity might affect performance anxiety.[10] Participants in her research were asked to engage in that old workhorse of anxiety: public speaking. Langer assigned study participants to one of three conditions: a high-performance condition in which participants were told that "mistakes are bad," a forgiveness condition in which participants were reassured about the inevitability of mistakes, and a curiosity condition in which participants were instructed to make a mistake and to incorporate any accidental mistakes into their presentation. Members of this third group reported the most comfort and least anxiety and audience members rated their speeches the highest of the three groups.

When working with your clients, especially high-achieving clients with a perfectionist streak, try assigning mistakes and activating curiosity. When clients shift their focus from performance ("I must do well at this") to personal growth ("I wonder what I will learn from this") they can reduce anxiety without sacrificing quality. What's more, people often appreciate an imperfect performance, feeling the small squeaks, minor errors, and tiny stumbles lend character and authenticity to a person. Curiosity researcher Todd Kashdan makes this point by arguing, "This is why people are willing to pay exorbitant prices to hear their favorite bands perform live. We can buy ten CDs of our favorite band or pay for one live performance. Why would we want to see them live on stage? After all, those CDs are edited to be absolutely perfect so you get to hear the best possible performance. We pay to see bands perform live for the spontaneity, the possibility that anything can happen" (p. 175).[11] Try to find ways to remind your clients that, oftentimes, the most magical moments in trainings, presentations, brainstorming, and social interactions of all types are those that are spontaneous and imperfect.

■ Future Me

One area of future mindedness that is sometimes overlooked is the sense of self. We often take an outward view when we imagine the future: What will the weather be like tomorrow? What will my new office look like after I decorate? What financial surprises will next year hold? Of all these questions the one we are least likely to ask is: Who will I be tomorrow? Who will I be next week? or Who will I be next year? The reason for this is simple: Most folks, especially those who hail from Western cultures, tend to think of their identities and personalities as relatively fixed. It doesn't make sense that I am a cool, level-headed guy this week and an emotional hot button next week. And yet, many of us do tend to fluctuate between what culture researcher Hazel Markus calls "possible selves."[12] Because situations exert an influence on how we think and behave, it is only natural to expect that we might be a somewhat different person tomorrow at the board meeting compared with this weekend on holiday with the family. Hard-headed assertiveness, for instance, might mellow into a laid-back attitude.

This more flexible view of the self bears directly on your client's performance. Stanford researcher Carol Dweck has pioneered an area of study she calls "mindset."[13] Simply put, people tend to have either "fixed" or "growth" mindsets. Fixed mindsets are familiar to all of us. These include personality traits and natural abilities. You can hear a fixed mindset in comments such as "He is so musically gifted" or "Jennifer is so smart." These statements assume the personal characteristic is relatively unchangeable. The problem is Dweck has found that folks with a fixed mindset tend to underperform. In a series of studies with children, for example, she found that those with a fixed mindset concerning their intelligence or ability tended to underperform. The reason is that they sabotaged their own test taking by withholding effort. They were stuck in a no-win situation: If they performed well it would reinforce their fixed positive view of themselves, but if they failed it would threaten their very sense of self. What kind of choice is that? On the one hand you might win further proof about something you already believe to be true, and on the other hand you might have your own psychological foundation pulled out from under you. A fixed mindset about positive traits, such as talents, can be a drawback socially as well. In many instances, people who believe themselves to be naturally gifted also tend to view themselves as entitled or superior, and this attitude can be a social turnoff. Dweck and her colleagues also found that fixed-mindset individuals tended to be more likely to be depressed.

The alternative to the fixed mindset is the "growth mindset." In this way of thinking personal attributes, even positive ones like artistic ability or intelligence, are growth endeavors. That is, they are changeable, manageable, and can be learned. Here Dweck makes a terrific point about people who are "natural artists." Just because one person can do something well without much training, she says, doesn't mean another person can't do it well with training. This is even true of those qualities we consider the most basic and unchangeable, such as athletic ability. This can be evidenced, for example, by people whose portrait skills improve when they take a figure drawing class. Or in the case of athletes who get better and better with practice and experience. In fact, the assistant coach of the Chicago Bulls basketball team said about Michael Jordan—arguably the greatest player in the history of the game—"he is a genius who consistently wants to upgrade his genius."

This is where you come in as a coach. You can consider yourself a type of upgrade software for your clients. When you catch them falling into a fixed mindset, even if it is in regard to high self-esteem or a positive personal attribute, you can help them move to a more psychologically healthy growth mindset. But don't just ask, "How can you take this great quality and use it even better?" That kind of question, without proper context, can leave people feeling just as inadequate as a failure can. Instead, why not try sounding out your clients about growth experiences that will leave them feeling energized and self-assured. Consider the following types of questions:

1. Tell me about a time you performed in a way in which you didn't think you were capable.
2. What have you gotten better at over the years?
3. Tell me about an important lesson you have learned from your mistakes.

4. How have you developed professionally in the last year?

5. When were the exceptions to the "rules" of your personality? For example, if you consider yourself a shy person, tell me about a time when you didn't act shy?

6. When you have to perform X specific task, what do you hope to learn from it?

The Importance of Failure

A lot of future mindedness is wrapped up in a positive view of the future. It includes hopes for a better future and optimism that success is possible. Occasionally, it also includes fear of failure or anxiety about the unknown. To the extent that we all want to foster a degree of positivity in our clients, it makes sense to remember that failure is an important part of the learning and growth process. Clients without failure are clients who are stagnating. Trying new things and taking risks come not just with the possibility of failure but with the assurance of failure. While failure almost always leaves a bad taste in one's mouth, it can provide new insights about strategies that work and those that don't. This is more than a Pollyanna-ish reframing: Failure is feedback and even though it can sting it should be valued as a useful source of information about performance.

I love being a time traveler! Every day I am thankful for the ability to mentally project myself back to the past or into the future. I love reliving my former achievements and even my most harrowing experiences. Similarly, I love thinking about what tomorrow holds in store for me and making lists of goals and dreams. It turns out our future orientation is a rich and rewarding part of how we set and pursue goals, how we come to know about ourselves, and the sense we make of failure. As a coach, you can harness your knowledge of affective forecasting errors, the motivational consequences of optimism, and the idea of a growth mindset to help your clients reach their potential and continue reaching it.

▶ Further Reading

Dweck, C. (2006). *Mindset: The new psychology of success.* New York: Ballantine Books.

Gilbert, D. (2006). *Stumbling on happiness.* New York: Knopf.

Kashdan, T. (2008). *Curious? Discover the missing ingredients to a fulfilling life.* New York: William Morrow.

Moskowitz, G. B., & Grant, H. (2008). *The psychology of goals.* New York: Guilford Press.

Positive Diagnosis

Early in my coaching career I made lots of mistakes. I sometimes sat back and let clients talk on and on without jumping in. I occasionally got distracted, caught up in my own thoughts and plans for what I could say next. Sometimes I would ask the wrong questions and derail a client. In particular, I had the habit of being a slave to the client's agenda. I was taught—as are all trained coaches—that the client owns the coaching session and it is our job as coaches to confine our comments and discussion to the client's explicitly stated agenda. This makes sense, since it protects clients against unwanted advice and maximizes the prospects of actually getting what they want. The down side, as I learned over time, is that it can also serve to limit clients. I had clients, for example, walking in the door wanting to talk about a recent interaction with a colleague that left them fuming. Even as I respected their right to address whatever topics they wanted, I harbored reservations that this was the best use of our time together. As I became a more skilled coach I began voicing these concerns and often found it very helpful in working with the client to establish an agenda that met their primary goals for entering the coaching relationship in the first place.

Client agendas are often influenced by recent problems, salient interactions, and limited self-knowledge. Not that any of these, in isolation, is a problem or that current life circumstances shouldn't be addressed in coaching sessions. It's just that clients will establish agendas based on the tools and perceptions they have available to them in the current moment and will naturally be unduly weighted toward in-the-moment difficulties. To the extent that problems loom larger than all that goes well, it makes sense that one of the greatest uses of coaching is to access the coach's external, relatively unobstructed view of the client. As coaches, if we pass up the opportunity to help clients expand their view of themselves and their own potential, then we may be missing a critical chance to make an importance difference. Experienced coaches know that while it makes sense to stick with the client's agenda for the session, it can also be useful to touch on recurring themes, past agendas, client resources, or ongoing client concerns. To put it bluntly: Client agendas serve as a guide for the session, but do not necessarily prevent us from helping the client grow in a more general way. Just because a client wants accountability in meeting a deadline or wants to brainstorm ideas for next week's presentation doesn't mean that more thematic growth cannot occur.

Much of the foundational work of coaching happens long before we get to the motivation, support, and accountability aspects of the change process. In fact, one of the most important parts of coaching is identifying areas for growth. By taking the time, up front, to identify goals, patterns of behavior, strengths, and weaknesses we can help our clients establish plans for personal development that are maximally effective. Many coaches already do this, not only through interviews and powerful questions, but also by administering formal assessments such as the Myers-Briggs Type Indicator (MBTI), a personality-based questionnaire, or the Strong Interest Inventory, a measure of career interest. These types of formal assessments provide a structure for identifying current problems and current potential, and lay the groundwork for learning and development both by reporting feedback and by suggesting directions for coaching work. Although many of these assessments are useful, they are not specifically part of the positive psychology repertoire, as they do not highlight specifically positive traits or behaviors. For example, although the MBTI distinguishes between various personal facets such as introversion or extroversion, there is no understanding of either of these as being superior to or more desirable than the other. In this chapter, I would love to introduce you to a formal strategy for assessing the positive, and in the next chapter I will introduce you to a wide range of commonly used positive psychology assessments.

▶ Positive Psychology and Positive Diagnosis

For as long as people have been interested in cause and effect they have used the concept of diagnosis. For millennia, doctors have used diagnostic systems in which they look at symptoms and health indicators—whether imbalance in bodily humors as in the case of ancient Greece physicians or sperm counts and heart rhythms as we do in modern times—to identify medical maladies and prescribe treatment. While we often use the word "diagnosis" specifically for clinical use, it is true that people in many professions use symptoms to identify problems or plan strategy and solutions. Auto mechanics and computer technicians, for example, follow structured protocols that help them assess problems and performance related to cars and computers, respectively. Similarly, marketing consultants track purchasing statistics of their target demographic to help plan their commercial campaigns. In many companies, indicators of productivity, tardiness, absence, safety, and other variables are used to diagnose problems with individual workers as well as organization-wide difficulties.

In contemporary mental health care the preeminent system of diagnosis is embodied in a taxonomic manual published by the American Psychiatric Association. *The Diagnostic and Statistical Manual of Mental Disorders* (*DSM*; APA, 1994) presents a sophisticated guide for clinicians to recognize client problems, arrive at differential diagnoses, and to develop effective treatment plans.[1] In essence, the *DSM* uses a series of symptom checklists by which counselors can explore the most common complaints of patients and use these to understand what might and might not be ailing their clients.

Understanding *DSM* Diagnosis

Psychiatrists, psychologists, and other counselors use structured interviews or their own expert knowledge of the diagnostic criteria to ask their clients about recent symptoms that might point to one disorder or another. Here is an example from the *DSM-IV* criterion for panic attack, a critical feature of panic disorder.

Criteria for Panic Attack

A discrete period of intense fear and discomfort, in which four (or more) of the following symptoms developed abruptly and reached a peak within 10 minutes:

1. Palpitations, pounding heart, or accelerated heart rate
2. Sweating
3. Trembling or shaking
4. Sensations of shortness of breath or smothering
5. Feeling of choking
6. Chest pain or discomfort
7. Nausea or abdominal distress
8. Feeling dizzy, unsteady, lightheaded, or faint
9. Derealization (feelings of uncertainty) or depersonalization (being detached from one's self)
10. Fear of losing control or going crazy
11. Fear of dying
12. Paresthesias (numbness or tingling)
13. Chills or hot flashes

What is so nice about this symptom checklist is that it provides practitioners a shared vocabulary for discussing syndromes with one another as well as with clients. In addition, this long list covers all of the common symptoms that people report being associated with panic attacks, making diagnosis fairly straightforward. Clients who present with an episode of panic, in which they feel dizzy, chilled, and as if they are dying, point counselors toward a diagnosis of panic disorder and away from other disorders such as bipolar disorder or schizophrenia. This helps counselors narrow in on approaches for working most effectively with their clients, whether that is prescribing the correct type of medication or using the indicated counseling approaches.

Interestingly, although the word diagnosis has a clinical ring and appears to be related specifically to problems, it can also be used in a positive way. Symptoms can be used to identify potential and peak performance as well as problems. Consider a mechanic can look at a well-maintained engine in an old car and can point to those components that are in good shape and unlikely to fail. In fact, when someone goes about the business of purchasing a used vehicle they often take it to a mechanic for inspection. In most cases they are as concerned with what is right with the car—those components that will hold up over time—as they are with any glaring problems. A doctor, similarly, can look at a person's excellent genetic markers, good diet, and frequent exercise to draw conclusions about health and longevity. The idea of positive diagnosis wells out of the fact that, for most of us, it is easy to overlook our ability to classify and use information relating to success and peak performance in favor of a focus on weaknesses and problems. If the word diagnosis still sounds overly clinical and problem-oriented to you, feel free to replace it with phrases such as "positive assessment" or "measure of potential" that will resonate better with your clients.

I freely admit that I am not the originator of the idea of positive diagnosis. Many noteworthy thinkers before me have proposed this idea in one form or another. For instance, Abraham Maslow—the psychologist known for his hierarchy of needs theory—was eager to codify behaviors that were related to his concept of self-actualization.[2] Maslow arrived at self-actualization by observing two of his mentors who, he believed, were exceptional people. According to Maslow, they stood out from the run-of-the-mill crowd in that they were so wholly given over to a sense of mission and performed at such a high level that they appeared at a different stage of personal development than most people. They were, in essence, the human development equivalent of Olympic athletes. Maslow set about the business of identifying more such people until he had amassed a couple dozen examples of self-actualizers. From these he attempted to identify behaviors that were commonly or consistently associated with self-actualization. He arrived at the following nine criterion behaviors. Although they are less discrete than the symptom checklist for panic disorder, you can still see that they provide a preliminary diagnostic checklist.

▶ Self-Actualization Behaviors

1. Experiences of flow states that represent total absorption and selflessness.
2. Make daily choices that move one toward growth and away from defensiveness.
3. Have knowledge of and the ability to listen to one's true self.
4. Honesty.
5. A deep sense of understanding of one's mission, destiny, and primary relationships.
6. An ongoing dedication to personal growth even if this means difficult practices and choices.
7. Setting up peak experiences, in part by understanding what to avoid in one's weaknesses and lack of potential.
8. Engaging in self-reflection to better understand one's preferences, identity, behavioral leanings, bad habits, and other aspects of the self.
9. "Resacralization." That is, breathing a sense of wonder, sacredness, and true understanding into one's perception of the world, into one's relationships, and into one's actions.

Imagine using this approach or a very similar one with your clients. Picture the types of questions you might ask your clients to better understand their self-actualizing tendencies. You might ask, "How much time do you reserve in a typical week for self-reflection?" or "What would happen if, when you made choices, you asked yourself 'How will this choice lead to my own personal growth'?" or "When do you have the hardest time being honest with others? With yourself?" While these questions will not in and of themselves elevate your clients into self-actualization, they will provide stepping-stones for important personal growth and higher functioning. These questions, and the target behaviors they represent, offer an early glimpse into a positive diagnostic system.

Another area of potential for those interested in the concept of positive diagnosis, especially coaches, is motivation. Most coaches will be familiar with the concepts of intrinsic (the activity is inherently rewarding) and extrinsic (external rewards motivate you to engage in an unpleasant activity) motivation. Further, within this theory of motivation there are also finer shades of motivation including introjected motivation (when you, yourself, act as an external motivator, as in "I *ought* to do this" or "I *should* do this") and identified motivation (when you have fully internalized the motivation and want to engage in an activity, even if it isn't enjoyable).[3] Together, these forms of motivation form a kind of continuum that ranges from the most externally to the most internally rewarding forms of motivation, as illustrated in Figure 5.1.

Unlike the MBTI or other more neutral assessments, there is a value judgment inherent in these different levels of motivation. Most folks assume that it is generally better to be intrinsically than extrinsically motivated. In fact, the assumption is that every step from left to right in Figure 5.1 is a desirable step. This creates a nice basic example of a framework for positive diagnosis. Coaches can use this chart to place their clients along a developmental continuum and appreciate their progress as well as their struggles. Imagine, for example, having a client come into session and report that they rose to the occasion and completed an unpleasant task because they imagined what you, as her coach, would have said. Here you are able to see a client on the cusp of an exciting changeover from extrinsic to introjected motivation. Instead of being forced into action by a boss, spouse, or other influential person, your client is beginning to be able to motivate herself, even if it is by using external pressures such as an impending coaching session. Being able to distinguish between different forms of motivation allows you to place your client in a specific place on the motivational continuum and offers insights into how best to spur them to action.

This is similar to my own theory and research on incubators. Incubators are those people—often highly intelligent or creative—who have a history of procrastination.[4] They put off work until the last possible moment. Unlike procrastinators, however,

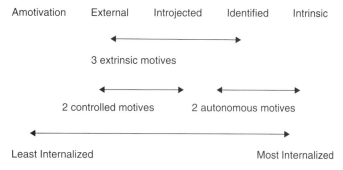

Figure 5.1   The motivation continuum

incubators become energized in the 11th hour, thrive under pressure, and produce consistently high-quality work. This distinction is more than academic; it is of profound importance to people because their identities are caught up in such labels. Incubators, for example, are almost always labeled as procrastinators or underachievers and have a habit of being hard on themselves. Most of the incubators I have worked with beat themselves up for their tendency to wait until the last possible moment before kicking into action. Once saddled with the label of incubator and understanding their natural work style, however, they tend to feel a huge sweep of relief and let themselves off the hook for putting off projects. You can easily diagnose your clients' work style by using two simple questions: First, ask about how far in advance of deadline they begin working. Are they generally an advance planner who works well ahead of schedule? Or do they tend to put work off? Next, ask about the general quality of their work. Do they generally produce high-quality work? Or mediocre or substandard work? In a pilot study with university students these two questions, alone, were able to distinguish between motivational work styles. Table 5.1 can help you understand how responses to these two simple questions can provide clients with insight about their natural work habits, areas of potential pride, and areas that might require personal development.

Maslow and other motivation researchers were not alone in their push for a more holistic understanding of high performance. From the very inception of the modern positive psychology movement, its founder, Martin Seligman, argued that traditional psychology—with its emphasis on mental illness—was only "half a psychology." Early on he argued for a research agenda that included strengths and suggested that therapists were more effective when they were amplifying client strengths as well as addressing weaknesses.[5] Seligman was eager to find a formal way to help psychologists identify what is right with their clients as well as what might be wrong with them. He and his colleague, Chris Peterson, created the VIA assessment of strengths, which listed 24 personal virtues such as courage, forgiveness, and creativity that exist across cultures and have endured across history.[6] Peterson and Seligman champion their work as an intellectual counterpoint to the *DSM*—an un-*DSM*, if you will. Today, many coaches, especially those branding themselves positive psychology coaches, use the VIA in their work with their clients.

Although the VIA strengths assessment represents a huge step forward in our understanding of strengths, and presents a nice preliminary step toward positive diagnosis, it falls short in some important ways. Consider the *DSM*: Among the most noteworthy features of the *DSM* system is its multiaxial nature. *DSM* diagnosis involves information from different domains—such as physical health,

Table 5.1   Work styles based on deadline and quality

	The Quality of My Work Is Consistently Superior	The Quality of My Work Is Often Mediocre
It takes a looming deadline to motivate me	INCUBATOR	PROCRASTINATOR
I like to get to work early on a project	PLANNER	TRIFLER

symptoms of mental disorders, and social stressors—to develop a more complete picture of client difficulties. According to the American Psychiatric Association (the publishers of the *DSM*), multiaxial diagnosis provides "a convenient format for. . . . [c]apturing the complexity of clinical situations and for describing the heterogeneity of individuals presenting with the same diagnosis" (p. 25).[7] This multidimensional approach is precisely what the VIA lacks, and where positive diagnosis needs to head. Assessing an individual's strengths is unquestionably a worthwhile pursuit, but undertaken in isolation it does not give a very comprehensive view of the client as a whole person.

▶ A Suggestion for a Positive Diagnostic System

With input from other experts, I have developed a preliminary positive diagnosis and assessment system that provides a comprehensive answer to the question "What is going right (rather than wrong) with this individual?" This system builds on the foundation of the ideas of Maslow, Seligman, and other researchers. Once again, my use of the word "diagnosis" is intended to connote the most general definition, identifying the cause of a phenomenon, rather than being problem or deficit specific. Like the *DSM*, my system aims at gathering multiple streams of information representing different aspects of positive human functioning. Each axis was included in this diagnostic system if it fulfilled the following three criteria:

1. It represents a well-researched area of positive functioning.

2. It represents an area substantively different from those of the other axes, even if these areas interact.

3. It provides useful information for making desirable changes or living a subjectively better life.

This system is primarily intended for use by coaches, therapists, educators, and other change agents to enable them to better work with their clients. Taken together, the five positive functioning axes contained within this system offer a broad view of multiple areas of functioning and present a global picture of client potential. This diagnostic need not replace other assessments, such as the MBTI, but can act as an adjunct to these commonly used coaching methods. Further, this positive diagnostic system is, by my own admonition, a preliminary step. I believe that a blue ribbon panel should be convened to improve on these ideas and set a professional standard for a comprehensive system for use by coaches. Although the system I propose here will likely see minor modifications over the years, it is useful for coaches, even in its current form.

Amanda Levy, an executive coach and co-founder of the Positive Workplace Alliance (http://www.positiveworkplace.com) was kind enough to pilot test this diagnostic system with six people in her Polaris year-long coaching program for emerging leaders and managers.[8] In each case, these clients were excited about the prospect of taking the assessment, which Amanda introduced all at once under the name "Taking Stock of Your Positives (Asset-Based Thinking Focus)." She lists the following as benefits of using this approach with coaching clients:

What I Learned from the Positive Diagnosis Results

- Works particularly well when relationship is already established with client.

- Clients appreciate an assessment of "what is right with me."

- All assessments at one time provides big picture.

- Very useful to have such an asset-based perspective, especially in tough times.

- There are business/organizational conversations to be derived from the assessment.

- The individuals were more self-aware and open than when we first began working together, which allows us to do more and better work together, an opportunity for broader ranging, and deeper conversations.

What Clients Learned from Positive Diagnosis

- "It's nice to get the other side of the story."

- More about their strengths/perspectives (than they usually ever have an opportunity to review).

- How good it is to see the good/feel good.

- Our focus tends always to be on the negative/opportunities for improvement ("sometimes difficult to feel OK about so much positive self-focus").

- More about the assets/resources available to them.

- Probable/possible impact of perspectives on self/life/others (especially around the less-than-optimal results).

- Areas where changes might be made.

- How much positive they overlook/don't consider/take for granted/for which they do not take time to acknowledge/savor/show gratitude.

- The shades/subtleties/varieties of positive experience.

- Ways to describe the positive without using the word positive and simply sounding soft.

- What if someone does not have the kind of results I have? How might they be feeling? Are they coping okay with life's challenges?

A Suggested Positive Diagnostic System, at a Glance:

Axis 1: Capacities

Axis 2: Well-being

Axis 3: Future orientation

Axis 4: Situational benefactors

Axis 5: Sense of mission

Capacities are your client's potentials. They consist of three related areas: strengths, interests, and resources.

■ Strengths

Ironically, capacities is likely the aspect of positive diagnosis and assessment with which you are already the most familiar, and also the area where you are currently missing big opportunities. The capacities refers to the client's innate potential, and is largely made up of strengths and personal resources, broadly defined. Although most coaches ask clients about their personal resources and current opportunities, they sometimes miss innate strengths. To capture a complete view of client capacities I recommend using both a strengths measure and a resource checklist. For the strengths measure I encourage you to use the Realise 2 strengths assessment tool (http://www.realise2.com) to identify client strengths and begin a discussion about what the client does well. I am a particular fan of the Realise 2 because of its ability to distinguish between strengths, weaknesses, and learned behaviors, lending it a more sophisticated approach to strengths assessment.[9] Similarly, other strengths measures such as the Clifton StrengthsFinder[10] or the VIA[11] (http://www.viastrengths.org) can be used to identify client strengths.

A Brief Guide to Using Strengths Assessments:

1. The most basic, and most common way to use the Realise 2, VIA, or other strengths assessment is to use this measure to identify your client's top signature strengths and open a discussion about these. Typical questions include the following: Which of these strengths are you surprised by? How might you use this strength more? Which of these do you consider natural to you? Which might not, in your opinion, even be a strength?

2. A more sophisticated way to use this information is by discussing optimal use of strengths. Questions here might include those that are counterintuitive or less obvious: When might you want to tone down this strength? Which situations bring out this strength in you? Which situations block you from using this strength? What could you change that would give you an opportunity to use this strength more? How might you use two or more of these strengths in conjunction with one another? Name instances in which two strengths together produced a superior result than either alone might have.

3. To take the strengths aspect of capacities a step further, try working with clients to recognize, develop, and use a wide range of strengths. Work with them to begin building a strengths vocabulary so that they can readily identify and label strengths in their own lives. There is no need to put restrictions as to what qualifies—hospitality, rising to the occasion at the last minute, having a calming effect on others—all are fair game. Note: The better you can do this yourself the easier it will be to work with this material. In my experience this is where the biggest gains are made in coaching.

■ Interests

In addition to strengths, the capacities axis is comprised of interests. You may be familiar with interests from the work of John Holland, who created a classification of interests that could be used to assess career fit. Holland's interest categories (shown in Figure 5.2) include realistic, investigative, artistic, social, enterprising, and conventional.[12] According to Holland, the interest categories that are close to one another on the diagram are more likely to be related than those opposite one another on the diagram. A person who is called by the siren song of Investigative activities, for example, is generally more likely to be interested in the nonconforming thinking associated with Artistic interests than she is with those associated with the competitive environment of Enterprising interests. Interests are guideposts to career and activity fit. You and your clients can take the Self-Directed Search, an interest inventory based on Holland's work that does not require certification (find out more at http://www.self-directed-search.com/). Similarly, you and your clients can take the Strong Interest Inventory (SII), which measures career-specific interests by visiting https://www.cpp.com/. Certification is required to administer and interpret SII results.

Gauging your client's interest can be vital to better understanding their strengths, because individual preferences and interests dictate—in part—how people choose to develop their strengths. That's right, most people think of strengths as being natural capacities that either exist or do not within a person. Someone might be artistic, for example, or they might not be. Interestingly, it turns out that strengths interact with interests to dictate how people make important life decisions and choose to develop their own excellence. Consider a series of studies by Vanderbilt researcher David Lubinski and his colleagues:[13] In one study, the Lubinski team examined the work preferences of intellectually talented graduate students and then did so again years later when the research participants were about 35 years old. The researchers found dramatic shifts in work preferences over the years. For example, the young men in the study were principally concerned with their education and "finding a niche," but at follow-up they were more concerned with "making their mark." At work, a leaning toward friendships, satisfaction, and enjoyment was gradually replaced with an emphasis on leadership opportunities and merit-based pay. There were interesting differences with the talented women as well. Although they were just as likely as men, on follow-up, to have tenure track research positions at universities they were also 9 times more likely to be homemakers. Moreover, while all

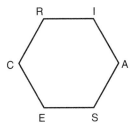

Figure 5.2   Common interests according to Holland

the young people in the study thought a flexible work schedule and fewer hours were important, the 35-year-old women who were mothers thought these facets of work were even more important than their peers at follow-up. In a second study, the Lubinski team looked at the work performance among hundreds of profoundly gifted people; these people, by the age of 13, were identified as being in the top 1 percent on standardized tests of intellectual ability. At follow-up 20 years later the researchers found that it was not basic intellectual ability that predicted specific achievements later in life but, rather, it was "intellectual tilt." When the researchers subtracted verbal scores from mathematical scores, effectively pinpointing whether the 13-year-olds leaned more toward humanities or quantitative reasoning, they found this tilt could predict not *whether* the individual was successful but the *type* of success he or she had:

Verbal tilt	Science, technology, engineering tilt
More likely to publish novels	More likely to file patents
More likely to get PhD in humanities	More likely to get MD

To put it another way, the natural interests of precocious children, as assessed in a single three-hour test administered at age 13, reliably predicted the specific types of work success they enjoyed later in life. Taken together, these studies provide evidence that people's natural leanings and interests interact with their basic strengths to project them forward in one direction and away from others. It doesn't matter if these leanings are the product of genetics, socialization, or individual preferences; they strongly influence how a person chooses to manifest her talents. Thus, strengths should not be viewed in isolation but should be paired with interests to get a better understanding of the best, most optimal way they will likely be employed by each individual client.

A Brief Guide to Coaching Interests as an Aspect of Capacities:

1. Use a formal measurement tool or structured interview to assess your clients' interests. Your clients' interests will be grounded in their basic values and provide a strong sense of motivation for them. Keep these interests in mind, as a theme, and touch on them in your sessions as appropriate. Consider questions such as "When are you most engaged at work?" "Which of your colleagues shares your interests?" "What choices have you made in the past that allow you to pursue your interests more fully?" "What could you change to make your work more interesting to you?"

2. Work with your clients to understand how their strengths and interests interact with one another. For example, you might consider asking questions such as "When you use a certain strength, how engaged are you in that activity? What does this say about your interest level?" "How might you use a strength in a way that would sap your interest?" "Where are your strengths and interests most aligned? What are those activities that bring these two areas together? How often do you get to engage in these activities?"

3. Consider a "strengths × interest" timeline activity. Here is an example: Have your client turn a piece of paper sideways (landscape) and draw a line across the middle. Then, at various points along that line, have your client indicate major life shifts. These will likely include graduating from university, getting married, changing careers or other important transitions. At each juncture have your client report on what choices they had to make and how their strengths and interests helped guide these decisions. As coach, listen for overarching themes that combine all of these major life events and feed these themes back to the client for discussion.

4. Work with the concept of "strength tilt." How do your client's specific strengths manifest in unique ways based on her own interests, values, and preferences? How might one person high in courage, for instance, use this strength differently than another brave person? It is easy to imagine a courageous person who places a premium on helping others becoming a trauma doctor and another courageous person who values justice becoming a whistleblower. Ask your clients "How does this strength interact with your interests and values?" "How are you different from other people who have this same strength?" "What choices have you made around using this strength, and what prompted you to make those specific decisions?"

■ Resources

The final aspect of capacities is resources. Resources include money, time, health, social support, expertise, and other factors a client can bring to bear on his or her pursuit of excellence. The Resources Checklist assessment included here can be a useful instrument to identify potential solutions to problems that your clients may be overlooking. Using a structured assessment allows you to quickly ask about a wide range of potential resources without fear that you will overlook any. Studies from both motivation and happiness psychology show that personal resources such as intelligence and family support are predictive of perseverance, success, and well-being.[14] The critical factor is not so much whether one has resources or not (we all do) but whether those resources are relevant to the goal. Wherever you see high relevance scores you have an entrée for a coaching discussion about how to increase that particular resource or use it more optimally. It can also be instructive in helping to identify areas for work and areas where your client might be self-critical.

Resource Relevance Checklist

Following is a list of common personal resources. Please use a 1–10 scale to report how satisfied you are with each of these resources in your own life. Write your score on the "satisfaction" line provided. Next, use a 1–10 scale to rate how relevant each of these resources is to the problem or challenge you are currently facing, with 10 indicating the greatest degree of relevance. Write your score on the "relevance" line provided.

```
1-----------------------------------5--------------------------------------10
```
Least amount   Greatest amount
of satisfaction   of satisfaction

		Satisfaction	Relevance
1.	Family support	____	____
2.	Energy/passion	____	____
3.	Confidence	____	____
4.	Social skills	____	____
5.	Available mentor	____	____
6.	Position of authority	____	____
7.	Health	____	____
8.	Money	____	____
9.	Assertiveness	____	____
10.	Intelligence	____	____
11.	Self-discipline for work	____	____
12.	Public speaking skills	____	____
13.	Expert knowledge	____	____
14.	Influential or expert connections	____	____
15.	Emotional self-control	____	____
16.	Past experience	____	____

In the end, you may want to put strengths, interests, and resources together in a single package that represents your client's overall capacities. To do this have your client list two or three of their most commonly used strengths, examine how these strengths are influenced by their unique interests, and what resources they have at their disposal that are relevant to the goal or issue they are currently addressing.

CAPACITIES = STRENGTHS + INTERESTS + RELEVANT RESOURCES

▶ Axis 2 of 5: Well-Being—Life Satisfaction and Psychological Well-Being

Although it might seem obvious upon reflection, good coaching rests upon a foundation of knowing how your client is faring, both in the moment and in life in general. When we open a session we often begin with the standard check-in question: "How are you doing?" This provides a kind of social shorthand to understand our client's current emotional state and pressing concerns. When clients are overly emotional we use "clearing" to offer them the space to vent a bit before buckling down to the work of coaching. The truth is, using some form of "How are you doing" is a terrific way to establish the coaching agenda, earmark topics for ongoing discussion, and track progress. Fortunately, positive psychologists have spent literally decades developing widely used, reliable, and valid measures of well-being. You can use these measures, many of which come with normative samples for comparison, to establish a benchmark for your clients' well-being and track its evolution over time. I offer the following two short and easy-to-use assessments.

The Satisfaction With Life Scale[15]

Next are four statements that you may agree or disagree with. Using the 1–7 scale shown, indicate your agreement with each item by placing the appropriate number on the line preceding that item. Please be open and honest in your responding.

7 — Strongly agree

6 — Agree

5 — Slightly agree

4 — Neither agree nor disagree

3 — Slightly disagree

2 — Disagree

1 — Strongly disagree

1. _____ In most ways my life is close to the ideal.

2. _____ The conditions of my life are excellent.

3. _____ I am satisfied with my life.

4. _____ So far, I have gotten the things I want in life.

5. _____ If I could live my life over I would change almost nothing.

To score the SWLS simply add up the numbers to arrive at a score ranging from 5 to 35, with 20 representing the neutral point. Scores above 20 are increasingly satisfied. "Normal" scores on the SWLS range from 21 to 25, indicating that most people are mildly satisfied with their lives.

Satisfaction measures, such as the SWLS, are widely used in many walks of life. Hotels and restaurants give out customer satisfaction surveys and organizations sometimes keep track of worker job satisfaction. Satisfaction is a mental judgment of quality, using a variety of different information. The SWLS has been empirically validated (see suggestions for further reading at the end of this chapter) and is the most widely used measure of satisfaction in the world. Because it asks such sweeping questions, the SWLS shows good stability over time. You can use this assessment easily by asking questions such as "What would you do to increase your score by half a point?" or "What would have to be different for your score to increase by 1?" You can also use the SWLS by looking at answers to specific items. For example, most adults have a few things we regret in life, and it is, therefore, not unusual to see slightly lower scores on item 5. For coaching purposes, you may consider follow-up questions to each individual item (shown in the next box).

Following-up the SWLS: Items and follow-up questions

1. In most ways my life is close to the ideal.
   "Tell me about your 'ideals'"
   "Where in your life are you the closest to your ideals?"
   "How have your ideals changed?"
   "What could you do to make your life more ideal?"

2. The conditions of my life are excellent.
   "Which areas of your life are going well?"
   "Which areas are going less well?"
   "Describe what a balanced life would look like"
   "What are the factors that have helped you achieve this excellence?"

3. I am satisfied with my life.
   "Which areas of your life are you most satisfied with?"
   "In which areas of your life would you like to experience growth?"
   "What would others say about your life?"
   "How much do you want to savor your current circumstances versus try to change things for the better?"

4. So far, I have gotten the things I want in life.
   "What are the things you have gotten that you most value?"
   "What is there you still want to achieve?"
   "Who all is responsible for you having gotten the things you want in life?"
   "Why do you think you want these particular things?"

5. If I could live my life over, I would change almost nothing.
   "What could you change now that would ease some of your regrets?"
   "What important lessons have you learned from the mistakes you have made?"
   "How do your regrets influence your current decision-making process?"
   "What do you think the link is between your regrets and your willingness to take risks?"

Another common concept in the study of happiness is called "psychological well-being." Rather than examining positive feelings or life satisfaction, researchers interested in PWB assume that a person is flourishing to the extent that he or she is achieving basic psychological needs. The best known of these were articulated by University of Wisconsin researcher Carol Ryff and her colleagues.[16] These needs include self-acceptance, growth, purpose in life, autonomy, connectedness, and mastery. My colleagues and I have developed a useful short measure of psychological well-being and have found it to have good convergent validity with longer measures of this same concept (see the suggestions for further reading at the end of this chapter for a more in-depth look at the psychometric properties of this scale).[17] The Psychological Well-Being Scale is presented here (see page 90).

Psychological Well-Being Scale

Next are eight statements with which you may agree or disagree. Using the 1–7 scale shown, indicate your agreement with each item by placing your response for each statement in the blank provided.

1	2	3	4	5	6	7
strongly disagree	disagree somewhat	disagree slightly	neutral	agree slightly	agree somewhat	strongly agree

1. _____ I lead a purposeful and meaningful life.
2. _____ My social relationships are supportive and rewarding.
3. _____ I am engaged and interested in my daily activities.
4. _____ I actively contribute to the happiness and well-being of others.
5. _____ I am competent and capable in the activities that are important to me.
6. _____ I am a good person and live a good life.
7. _____ I am optimistic about my future.
8. _____ People respect me.

To score the PWBS simply add up the numbers for items one through eight. You will arrive at a score ranging from 8 to 56, with higher scores representing higher overall well-being.

The PWBS can be used with your coaching clients in much the same way as the SWLS. Not only does it provide a reliable thumbnail sketch of your client's overall well-being, but the specific items on the PWBS can be used as an entrée to a more in-depth conversation related to the concepts of mastery, purpose, relationships, self-acceptance, autonomy, and growth.

▶ Axis 3 of 5: Future Orientation

The professional coaching literature is full of examples of experts offering definitions of coaching. Oftentimes, discussions of what exactly coaching is includes contrasting coaching from psychotherapy and other professional helping relationships. Among these distinctions is a common emphasis on the time orientation of coaching. Time orientation is the amount a person (or a coach and client) focuses on the past, the present, and the future, respectively. As individuals we all spend some time remembering the past, experiencing the present, and planning for the future. According to psychologists Phil Zimbardo and Ilona Boniwell, it is healthy to have a fairly balanced time orientation.[18] Looking to the past offers traditions and identity, experiencing the present keeps us mindful and aware, and planning for the future helps set up fun and success. As a professional conversation, coaching tends to focus toward the future when contrasted with psychotherapy, which has a slight leaning toward the past. While this is not, of course, the only difference between the two endeavors, and is a simplistic distinction in itself, it is true that much of coaching plans for upcoming performance and assumes progress toward future goals. As such, it is important that you understand how your clients feel about the future. Knowing the extent to which they harbor doubts or hopes for future success can be useful and a predictor of coaching success. Axis 3 of positive diagnosis is future orientation, which includes hope for a better future.

Hope theory, pioneered by the late psychologist Rick Snyder, suggests that optimism is primarily a way of thinking about the future and that hopeful individuals are high in two types of thinking: in particular, agency thinking and pathways thinking.[19] *Agency thinking* means that an individual believes themselves to be capable and in control—at least partially—of future outcomes. This makes sense because people who think they are capable of influencing positive future outcomes are far more likely to be hopeful, take risks, persevere, and ultimately achieve success. *Pathways thinking* means that an individual can think of alternative solutions if they are blocked or experience a setback. Essentially, people high in pathways thinking are creative and are wedded more to their ultimate goal than to one specific process for achieving it.

The Adult Hope Scale[20]

Directions: Read each item carefully. Using the scale shown, please select the number that best describes YOU and put that number in the blank provided.

1 = Definitely false
2 = Mostly false
3 = Somewhat false
4 = Slightly false
5 = Slightly true
6 = Somewhat true
7 = Mostly true
8 = Definitely true

_____ 1. I can think of many ways to get out of a jam.

_____ 2. I energetically pursue my goals.

_____ 3. I feel tired most of the time.

_____ 4. There are lots of ways around any problem.

_____ 5. I am easily downed in an argument.

_____ 6. I can think of many ways to get the things in life that are important to me.

_____ 7. I worry about my health.

_____ 8. Even when others get discouraged, I know I can find a way to solve the problem.

_____ 9. My past experiences have prepared me well for my future.

_____ 10. I've been pretty successful in life.

_____ 11. I usually find myself worrying about something.

_____ 12. I meet the goals that I set for myself.

Notes: When administering the scale, it is called "The Future Scale." The Agency subscale score is derived by summing items 2, 9, 10, and 12; the Pathway subscale score is derived by adding items 1, 4, 6, and 8. The total Hope Scale score is derived by summing the four Agency and the four Pathway items.

There are a variety of ways to use hope theory with your clients. First, you can use it diagnostically. When you hear a distinct lack of hope in your clients try to listen for which type of thinking it represents. Comments such as "I'll never be able to do it," for example, hint at troubles with agency thinking, while statements such as "I just can't see how to do this" appear to suggest issues with pathways thinking. Try using techniques that promote a positive view of the self to raise agency thinking. Using acknowledgement or finding a skills mentor may help clients feel more competent and, therefore, more hopeful. Where pathways thinking is a problem, try using brainstorming to help your clients shift into a more creative way of attaching obstacles.

▶ Axis 4 of 5: Situational Benefactors

Although it has been said that a large part of success is just showing up, I would like to amend this saying. I think the phrase should read "a large part of success is showing up at the right place and at the right time." For many people the problem with "just showing up" doesn't have anything to do with a lack of courage or motivation. Instead, these difficulties can hinge on a lack of self-knowledge or an uncertainty about where one's talents are best employed or which opportunities are the most worthwhile. Knowing your own best work habits and the types of situations that will support your success is a crucial step in understanding your potential. Axis 4 of positive diagnosis is "situational benefactors." These are the situations—whether time of day, physical workspace, or social support—that help a person succeed.

I have coached no fewer than 10 clients who all had the same basic problem: They knew they wanted one kind of work but were engaged in another because it paid better or there were better opportunities for employment. I worked with one woman whom I'll call Candace, for example, who knew she wanted to open her own consultancy. Candace was an intelligent, resourceful, and highly motivated person. Even so, she wasn't sure exactly where to start in the process of opening her own business. We identified a mentor and relevant books, and she began the learning process. All the while, however, Candace was distracted by the lure of full-time employment for others. Employment was less risky, and the stability it offered appealed to her. On the other hand, she had a strong independent streak and felt stifled by working for others. In the end, Candace and I examined the types of situations that generally brought out the best in her. We talked about her most productive work habits, her most fervent supporters, and the professional opportunities in her life. Ultimately, she understood that while she did not want to work "under" someone else she also did not want to work alone. In the end, understanding her situational benefactors helped Candace get a clear picture that taking on a partner and collaborating on a consulting business would provide her both the stability and independence she craved.

Situational Benefactors Scale

Please think of the times when you are most successful. Use the 1 to 7 scale to indicate the degree to which you agree with each statement about when you are at your best, work most efficiently, or are the most successful.

1. I know when I am at my best.

1	2	3	4	5	6	7
strongly disagree	disagree somewhat	disagree slightly	neutral	agree slightly	agree somewhat	strongly agree

2. I thrive on collaboration.

1	2	3	4	5	6	7
strongly disagree	disagree somewhat	disagree slightly	neutral	agree slightly	agree somewhat	strongly agree

3. I generally like to work independently.

1	2	3	4	5	6	7
strongly disagree	disagree somewhat	disagree slightly	neutral	agree slightly	agree somewhat	strongly agree

4. I work better when I have time for careful planning.

1	2	3	4	5	6	7
strongly disagree	disagree somewhat	disagree slightly	neutral	agree slightly	agree somewhat	strongly agree

5. I can keep calm under pressure or in an emergency.

1	2	3	4	5	6	7
strongly disagree	disagree somewhat	disagree slightly	neutral	agree slightly	agree somewhat	strongly agree

6. I know the physical environment that is most conducive to my working effectively.

1	2	3	4	5	6	7
strongly disagree	disagree somewhat	disagree slightly	neutral	agree slightly	agree somewhat	strongly agree

7. I know when during the day I tend to be at my most productive.

1	2	3	4	5	6	7
strongly disagree	disagree somewhat	disagree slightly	neutral	agree slightly	agree somewhat	strongly agree

8. The support I receive from my spouse/partner is an important part of my success.

1	2	3	4	5	6	7
strongly disagree	disagree somewhat	disagree slightly	neutral	agree slightly	agree somewhat	strongly agree

9. The support I receive from my friends is an important part of my success.

1	2	3	4	5	6	7
strongly disagree	disagree somewhat	disagree slightly	neutral	agree slightly	agree somewhat	strongly agree

10. The support I receive from my supervisor is an important part of my success.

1	2	3	4	5	6	7
strongly disagree	disagree somewhat	disagree slightly	neutral	agree slightly	agree somewhat	strongly agree

11. I can easily name opportunities available to me at this time.

1	2	3	4	5	6	7
strongly disagree	disagree somewhat	disagree slightly	neutral	agree slightly	agree somewhat	strongly agree

To score the Situational Benefactors Scale, simply tally the numbers for items 1 and 6–11 to derive a score between 7 and 49. The higher the score the greater the client's knowledge of her own most productive work style, opportunities, and supporters. Items 2 through 5 will help clients identify specific work preferences.

This measure of situational benefactors serves two purposes. First, it is a gauge of your client's self-knowledge. Some clients may be less aware of their own most productive work habits or of the many ways in which support helps them succeed. This scale can act like a spotlight, shining a beam onto areas of support and opportunity that clients were previously unaware of. Second, this assessment can open the door to a more in-depth conversation about when, where, and with whom clients should be working to be at their best. To use the idea of situational benefactors as part of your coaching conversation, consider asking some of the following questions:

1. Who are the people who are most supportive of you?

(What do they see in you? How do they show their support? What might you be able to count on from them in the future?)

2. When are you at your best?

(Are you a morning person or evening person? How do you feel about deadlines? Meetings? Working on weekends? When do you get most of your good ideas?)

3. Where are you at your best?

(When you have been the most successful, where—physically—were you working? What was the room like? Lighting? Decor? Organization? How public a space was it? How long did you spend there?)

4. What types of situations bring out the best in you?

(Do you flourish in groups or prefer to work alone? How do you feel about receptive versus experiential learning? How much time do you take to process information? How physical a person are you, how physical a work environment do you need? What is your relationship to humor?)

The final axis of positive diagnosis is values. Values are, of course, those personal beliefs and ideals that a person believes are important and uses as a guide for making decisions and evaluating the behavior of others. Our values are the product of our genetics, our family upbringing, the culture in which we were raised, and our unique experiences as we go through life. While we might not all agree on the same set of values everyone has a set. As a coach it is important for you to understand your own values as well as those of your clients. A knowledge of your client's values can aid you both in making decisions and plotting a trajectory for personal and professional growth. The cross-cultural psychologist Shalom Schwartz undertook research with tens of thousands of respondents from dozens of countries to identify culturally universal values themes.[21] He identified 10 such themes. He believed that these themes were not only prevalent around the globe but also "orthogonal," meaning that a person high in one would be more likely to also endorse a neighboring value than one from directly opposite on the circumplex.

Personal Values Survey

Following are 10 short descriptions. Please use the scale to describe how similar each description is to yourself.

  5—Exactly like me

  4—Somewhat like me

  3—Neither like me nor unlike me

  2—Somewhat unlike me

  1—Does not describe me at all

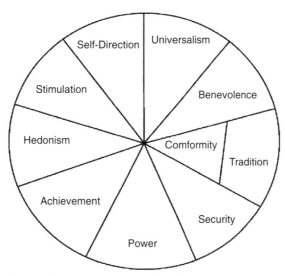

Source: Schwartz and Boehnke (2004).

Figure 5.3   Personal values

1. I love to try new and exciting things._____ (Stimulation)
2. Helping others is the most important thing. ____ (Benevolence)
3. I believe in fighting for equality. ____ (Universalism)
4. It is important to be successful. ____ (Achievement)
5. I think it is important to follow the rules. ____ (Conformity)
6. I value my creativity and individuality. ____ (Self-Direction)
7. If it feels good, do it. ____ (Hedonism)
8. Tradition is my foundation. ____ (Tradition)
9. I aspire to power. ____ (Power)
10. I like routine and dislike the unexpected. ____ (Security)
11. I usually do what others tell me. ____ (Conformity)
12. I like to stick up for the "underdog." ____ (Universalism)
13. I seek out pleasure in life. ____ (Hedonism)
14. I like to tell others what to do. ____ (Power)
15. Caring for others is one of the most important things in life. ____ (Benevolence)
16. I crave novelty. ____ (Stimulation)
17. I hold to my core values no matter what. ____ (Self-Direction)
18. Rituals are important to me. ____ (Tradition)
19. Achieving my goals is one of the greatest joys in life. _____ (Achievement)
20. I crave a predictable life. ____ (Security)
21. I like to feel a rush. ____ (Stimulation)
22. I enjoy being in charge of a situation. ____ (Power)
23. It helps me to know what to expect. _____ (Security)
24. The highest goal is in serving humanity. _____ (Benevolence)
25. Doing things as they have always been done is more important than trying to change things. _____ (Tradition)
26. It is important for me to feel authentic to who I really am. _____ (Self-Direction)
27. It makes sense to seek out pleasure and avoid pain. ____ (Hedonism)
28. All people are fundamentally equal. ____ (Universalism)
29. Things go more smoothly when people follow established rules. ____ (Conformity)
30. Getting what I want in life is among my most important values. ____ (Achievement)

When presenting the Personal Values Survey to clients, remove the values listed in parentheses after each item. These are for your scoring purposes and should be removed in advance of administration so as not to influence the responses of your clients. To score the Personal Values Survey add up the numbers for each of the 10 values themes individually. Each theme is addressed by three items so you should have three scores for each theme ranging from 5 to 15. Pay particular attention to scores that are 12 to 15.

The Personal Values Survey can be used to increase client self-awareness and to open conversations with clients about how they go about the business of fulfilling these values or how they use these values to guide their decisions. Consider asking questions such as "How have your values shifted or stayed the same across your adult life?" "How accurate a reflection do you think this survey is of your values?" "How do these values manifest in your daily life?" "Where do you have reminders of these values in your daily life? Are they posted in the form of a mission statement or do you keep symbols of them in your office?" The Personal Values Survey can also be used to identify potential sources of values conflict, either within your clients or between your clients and those with whom they interact.

An Overview of Positive Diagnosis

Axis 1: Capacities—Strengths, Interests, and Resources

A. Strengths measure such as the *Realise 2*

B. Interest inventory such as the *Self-Directed Search*

C. Resource Relevance Checklist

Axis 2: Well-Being—Life Satisfaction and Psychological Well-Being

A. The Satisfaction With Life Scale

B. The Psychological Well-Being Scale

Axis 3: Future Orientation

A. The Adult Hope Scale

Axis 4: Situational Benefactors

A. The Situational Benefactors Scale

Axis 5: Values

A. The Personal Values Survey

In the end, positive diagnosis is one of the greatest areas of development for positive psychology and a potentially tremendous boon to the field of coaching. Positive diagnosis, while still a method in its infancy, offers a chance to normalize success, measure potential, and create a shared vocabulary for discussing basic human capacities. The system presented here represents an important first step toward creating a truly holistic science of mental health rather than mental illness. It is, however, preliminary. Amanda Levy, the coach who piloted positive diagnosis, reports that there were several difficulties with this system in her trial run. For example, it can be a bit cumbersome to score all of the measures listed here. If you intend to use this system on a wide-scale basis, it may be in your interests to create scoring templates or programs to make this work easier. I would welcome stories of how you have used this system or improved its administration (http://www.intentionalhappiness.com). Despite the fact that positive diagnosis is in its early stages it can be inspiring, refreshing, and useful for your client.

► **Further Reading**

Maslow, A. (1971). *The farther reaches of human nature*. New York: Penguin Compass.

American Psychiatric Association (1994). *Diagnostic and Statistical Manual of Mental Disorders* (4th ed). Washington, DC: Author.

Diener, E. (2009). *Assessing well-being* (The collected works of Ed Diener), Social Indicators Research Series (Vol. 39). Dordrecht, Netherlands: Springer.

Peterson, C., & Seligman, M. (2004). *Character strengths and virtues*. Oxford, UK: American Psychological Association.

Zimbardo, P., & Boyd, J. (2008). *The time paradox: The new psychology of time that will change your life*. New York: Free Press.

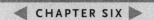

Positive Assessment

While I was in graduate school I took an entire course on a single psychological test—the Minnesota Multiphasic Personality Inventory-II (MMPI 2).[1] The MMPI, a test of psychological disorders that was first published in the 1950s, is a monster of an assessment. It contains 567 true-false questions such as "My father was a good man," "My hands and feet are usually warm enough," "I am sure I get a raw deal from life," and my favorite, "I often feel as if there is a tight band around my head." The MMPI was developed using a clever method called "empirical keying," which means the creators of this test were interested in how people with established clinical disorders answered each of these items. A statement such as "I like mechanics magazines" might seem innocent enough, but it can measure traditional masculinity. Similarly, those items that ask about bodily sensations are far more likely to be endorsed by hypochondriacs. The beauty of this method is that the items are not necessarily "face valid." The MMPI contains 10 scales of major psychological disorders, such as paranoia and anxiety, a variety of subscales, and even scales measuring whether test users are lying or trying to fake their answers.

For three hours every week my fellow students and I would gather in the classroom and listen to lectures of the psychometric properties of the test. We would practice interpreting test reports and had to memorize hundreds of profiles. It was, like the test itself, a bit daunting. At one point I raised my hand and asked, "Isn't this all just a little much? The test is hundreds of items long, it takes so long to complete, and the reports are so detailed. Isn't it just too much?" My instructor smiled and shook his head. "When else," he asked me, "are you going to have an opportunity to ask a client more than 500 questions in a single hour?"

I realized immediately that my teacher was right; although assessments can sometimes seem artificial, time consuming, or difficult to answer they are extraordinarily efficient ways to get information. If a typical one-hour coaching call includes 30 powerful questions, it would take 20 hours to ask as many questions as the MMPI contains. Since grad school I have seen this truth born out time and again. Take, for instance, measures of personal strengths. The VIA contains 240 questions, and the Realise 2 contains 180 items.[2,3] People often lodge the mild complaint that they seem long and that taking such a long test can be kind of a drag. But consider the vast amount of information these tests produce. The Realise 2, for instance, evaluates 60 different candidate qualities and places them into one of four categories: learned behaviors, weaknesses, unrealized and realized strengths. You simply cannot do that in only a handful of questions. Plus, the test only takes people about a half hour to complete and yields extraordinarily helpful information. And herein lies the beauty of assessments: If your client can struggle through a half hour of sluggish test-taking, you both can gain powerful insights that might not be readily available through regular coaching conversations.

Assessments Work Because They:

- Are "official," thereby encouraging people to answer questions they may otherwise be reluctant to,
- Are comprehensive, thereby covering a topic in more depth than an interviewer might,
- Provide a common language, thereby giving everyone the same vocabulary for discussing topics, and
- Are empirical, allowing us to quantify and compare data easily.

Imagine, for a moment, sitting beside someone in the waiting room at your doctor's office. Picture yourself wanting to find out more about them. Consider three simple ways you could learn about them: observation, dialogue, and assessment. In observation you would carefully watch them. You would take note of their clothing, grooming, age, mannerisms, and facial expressions. You could probably make some reasonable guesses about their socioeconomic status and emotional state. Now, imagine that you began chatting with them. You could ask questions about where they live, what they do for a living, how many children they have, and about their interests. This method would, of course, provide more detailed information. You would know much about the person's life, interests, education, and work, even after a short conversation. But what about using a formal assessment? What if you handed them a survey about health history, political attitudes, shopping habits, or sex life? You would be far more likely to elicit this kind of personal information in a questionnaire, and would be far more likely to get a comprehensive view of these by using a survey.

▶ Measuring the Immeasurable

As a happiness researcher, I am often criticized by people I meet. Whether they are a seatmate on the plane or a student in one of my positive psychology courses at the university, many people just have a difficult time accepting that happiness can be measured. Just last week, for example, I had a total stranger send me an e-mail saying that I would "never find any answers to happiness." And this criticism isn't limited to happiness, it is common across many areas of psychology. There are many folks out there who simply believe that the abstract concepts of perception, emotion, and attitude are immeasurable. To the extent that this criticism holds water—and I think it is a criticism worth considering—it makes sense to take a step back and consider how, when, and if we should be using formal assessments of psychological constructs in coaching.

Assessment: A Self-Assessment

Take a moment and consider your own views on the limits and potentials of using formal assessments. Do you believe that we can measure abstract concepts reliably? Can we use surveys, for example, to measure spirituality, intelligence, and depression? Are there things we cannot measure? How comfortable are you with assigning numbers and using labels and formal questionnaires? How do your beliefs influence the way you use assessments in your coaching practice?

The truth is, the world around us is full of examples of measures of a huge range of abstract concepts. Take rock-climbing ability, for example. When you think about it, the ability to climb cliff faces should be very difficult to quantify. Just consider this: There are no two cliffs that are the same. Each is made of a different kind of rock and has different features. Each day the weather is different and each individual person brings with him or her a different level of fear, skill, and equipment. And yet, formal measures such as the Yosemite Rating System are commonly used and accepted by climbers around the world. This system works by rating the most difficult move, or crux, of each climb. A climber only has to say to another climber "That is a 5.11 route," and the second person will automatically know how difficult the climbing is and whether they are up to the task. It is a type of categorical shorthand that allows climbers to estimate which routes are the most appropriate for their own skill level. It is easy to find similar examples of measures of all sorts of personal qualities, including intellectual pursuits such as chess ability, physical pursuits such as tennis ability, preferences such as spending behaviors, and even interpersonal pursuits such as kindness and forgiveness. Measures extend beyond just behavioral assessments as well. They include commonly used assessments of more abstract concepts such as depression, worker engagement, leadership, and scientific impact of research publications. Fortunately for us coaches, positive psychologists have also developed a number of assessments that are appropriate for use with high-functioning clients, such as measures of meaning in life.

In fact, psychologists have built an entire science around defining and measuring abstract personal concepts. Although there are some controversies, as there are in every field, we have made enormous gains in the measurement of intelligence, behavior, emotions, and attitudes. Similarly, many coaches are interested in psychological variables such as motivation, satisfaction, engagement, and success. In this chapter I present 10 assessments from positive psychology. Each measure was chosen because it met all or almost all of the following criteria:

- The test has been empirically validated.
- The test is widely used.
- The test focuses on a topic related to positive human functioning.
- The test is appropriate to coaching.
- The test is free of charge and easy to use and interpret.

What Scientists Mean When They Say "Empirically Validated"

I frequently receive letters and e-mails from people interested in "empirically validated" positive psychology interventions. They are curious about whether keeping a gratitude journal will really make them happier, or whether it is possible to tamper with an intervention and still claim that it is "valid." The difficulty with understanding the answers to these questions is that, in everyday English, we use "valid" in a different way than is meant scientifically. When you and I hang out at the bus stop, and you ask me whether writing about your "best possible self" is a valid route to happiness, you mean "Will it work?" Valid, in lay terms, is generally equivalent to "effective." Scientists take a much more complex view of validity. In fact, scientists don't even recognize validity as a single entity. Around the laboratory we talk about "face validity," "construct validity," and "criterion validity" to name a few types. Construct validity refers to assessments and is basically the idea that a particular test actually measures what it claims to measure. Do intelligence tests really measure intelligence, for instance, or might that measure familiarity with test-taking procedures (the answer is a little of both)? Criterion validity means that a test or a personal attribute can predict later performance. A job recruiter might be interested, for example, in how a person's educational status predicts later work performance. Educational status, in this instance, might be a valid predictor of productivity.

So what do these fancy terms have to do with "empirically validated" positive psychology interventions? Everything. Much has been made recently about the fact that we now have such interventions. What is really being said is that we now have data (evidence) that are suggestive of the effectiveness of these interventions. In simple terms, there are early reports that activities such as keeping a gratitude journal actually work. An interesting question, however, is "What, exactly, do these interventions do?" When we say gratitude, altruism, and other positive interventions "work," we mean that they work to make most people a bit happier. That is, these interventions are valid for a specific purpose. They may not be valid for making people better artists or more self-reflective, but they are valid for boosting mood.

Important Lesson #1: Validity Often Means Valid for a Specific Purpose

Having said that, I want to let you in on a little secret: Validity is not incontrovertible proof. Take the commonly used gratitude exercise: Studies show that there is benefit in writing down three things for which you are grateful each day.[4] In my classes of 100 students at the university, however, only about 20% of the people continue doing this activity, even though about 85% report that it makes them feel happier! What is going on? First, it is important to notice that although the evidence is strong for this intervention it is not perfect. The gratitude exercise will not work for 100% of people. Second, the exercise is effortful, requiring people to develop new habits and many people simply drop the activity before it ever becomes part of their daily routine. Even empirically validated interventions will not work for everyone.

Important Lesson #2: Empirical Support Does Not Mean Irrefutable Proof

Finally, let's look the sticky issue of modifying interventions. Some people I speak with want to play a bit with the standard instructions but are understandably worried that, in doing so, they will undermine the empirical support. Again, let's look at the gratitude exercise. What would happen if we deviated from the standard protocol and required people to write down seven instead of three things for which they are grateful? What would happen, for that matter, if we asked them to journal every other day instead of every day? Would these modifications "invalidate" the intervention? The basic answer to these questions lies in what makes the gratitude exercise work in the first place. The data are suggestive that writing down only a few things, rather than a huge list, and that doing this pretty regularly helps boost happiness. So, if you wanted to toy with four items instead of three, or switch to every other day, the data from past studies suggest that this might also work, especially if there is a good rationale for doing it (e.g., it fits better with your particular schedule or values system). If you changed the intervention in a more radical way—say, writing down 100 things for which you are grateful only one time a year—it is reasonable to think that this strays sufficiently far from the original that it might no longer be effective.

Important Lesson #3: Small Changes to Empirically Supported Interventions Are Entirely Appropriate; Large Changes May Not Be.

In the end, it is smart to look for empirical support, trusting in the scientific seal of approval. It is also artful to realize that support is different from proof. At times there are good reasons to make small changes to tried-and-true interventions so that they fit better and are more effective.

▶ The Dark Side of Positive Labels: A Cautionary Note

A necessary part of measuring how people function, what they are interested in, or how they are feeling is the use of labels. We, by necessity, have to use specific vocabulary to describe the human condition. We have to use terms such as depression, successful, unmotivated, and intelligent. Of course, some people are naturally reluctant to use such labels as they feel these words unfairly suggest that some people are superior or inferior to others. Another common complaint is that labels place people into conceptual "boxes" that restrict creativity or a more multifaceted sense of self. The truth is, we should listen to these cautions and be judicious in our use of labels. Research from positive psychology has shown that even positive labels, such as "genius," can be counterproductive. Carol Dweck, a researcher at Stanford University, has found in a number of studies that children who are labeled as intelligent, even those who are accurately labeled as gifted, can underperform.[5] This isn't because the kids aren't smart, of course, but because they sometimes don't expend effort. Think about it: Success on a task will only reinforce how they already view themselves—as intelligent—and failure offers a distinct threat to this sense of identify. Labels should be carefully handled by coaches. Making sure to reinforce the notion that even natural strengths can be areas for further development can be a recipe for acknowledging what is best about your clients while also encouraging them to grow.

The Assessments in This Chapter: At a Glance

1. *Domain Satisfaction Scales*: measures satisfaction with various areas of life.
2. *SPANE*: measures positive and negative emotions.
3. *Subjective Happiness Scale*: A measure of general happiness.
4. *Meaning in Life Questionnaire*: measures a sense of meaning in life.
5. *Work-Life Questionnaire*: identifies whether one is in a job, career, or calling.
6. *Purposeful Work Scale*: a measure of the meaning derived from work.
7. *Curiosity and Exploration Inventory*: A measure of novelty seeking.
8. *Savoring Beliefs Inventory*: A measure of anticipation, reminiscing, and savoring.
9. *Work-Style Scale*: A measure of motivational approaches to work.
10. *Authenticity Scale*: A measure of authentic living and susceptibility to outside influence.
11. *Strengths Use Scale*: A measure of general strengths use.

In the last chapter I presented two measures with which you can assess client well-being. Here, I would like to offer three additional surveys: one of positive and negative emotions, one of life satisfaction, and one of general happiness. Each of these is a well-validated instrument and can be useful in assessing various aspects of your clients' well-being. Consider the many ways in which your clients' current emotional state, emotional leanings, areas of greatest satisfaction, and overall view of their lives could be useful starting points for coaching conversations.

One way of avoiding the label trap is by thinking about personal attributes as being "dimensional" rather than "categorical." So, it isn't that someone is a genius or that they are stupid, or that they are an introvert or an extrovert, or that they are motivated or unmotivated. Rather, it is that they exist somewhere along a continuum, which might place them apart from some others, similar to some others, or in a different position relative to their own past performance. As a matter of necessity, we use cut-off scores to determine whether someone qualifies as an introvert or extrovert, but these are limits we force onto dimensional variables. In truth, we could change those cut-off values and thereby change who was included and excluded from the group. While using labels such as smart, forgiving, and brave is a handy way to communicate, it also runs the risk of marginalizing people who don't quite make the cut. When I work with clients I use assessments to get a general sense of "where" the client is at, but then talk about their traits or qualities in dimensional terms, exploring how and when they might slide up or down on the scale.

▶ Assessment #1: Domain Satisfaction Scales

Like the Satisfaction With Life Scale (SWLS)[6] described in the previous chapter, you can also measure your client's satisfaction with specific areas of her life. For example, you can ask about satisfaction with her supervisor, commute, pay, workload, and relationship with colleagues. Getting a gauge of these areas can be a helpful way to set a coaching agenda and identify areas of strength and areas for development. Using a so-called "domain satisfaction measure" is at the core of Dr. Michael Frisch's Quality of Life Therapy (QOLT).[7] This empirically validated approach to therapy begins by assessing a client's satisfaction with all different aspects—or domains—of life. Dr. Frisch recommends using domain satisfaction scores to open conversations about the sources of dissatisfaction, current opportunities, perceived progress, and good choices. You can modify the following assessment to include work specific, relationship specific, parenting specific, or other life domains that are relevant to your coaching practice. Note that there is no copyright holder for this assessment.

Domain Satisfaction

Please use the following scale to rate your satisfaction with each area of life listed below:

7 = Totally satisfied
6 = Satisfied
5 = Slightly satisfied
4 = Neutral, neither satisfied nor dissatisfied
3 = Slightly dissatisfied
2 = Dissatisfied
1 = Totally dissatisfied

1. _____ Income
2. _____ Friendships
3. _____ Health
4. _____ Commute
5. _____ Housing
6. _____ Marriage/Partnership
7. _____ Colleagues
8. _____ Recreation
9. _____ Work
10. _____ Family

I have used domain satisfaction measures in many different ways. One simple way is to present your client with some blank domains and ask her to include those domains she cares about most. This way you can ensure that the domains you measure are relevant and important to your client. Taking this quick "psychological snapshot" of your client's satisfaction can help you both identify areas for potential work as well as areas that are consistent sources of success and, as such, models for savoring. Another easy way to use this type of measure is by discussing the optimal amount of satisfaction your client thinks she *should* experience in each domain. If you used a 1 to 10 scale in which 10 was perfectly satisfied, most clients automatically assume that a 10 represents the target for success. Often, if a person scores a 7

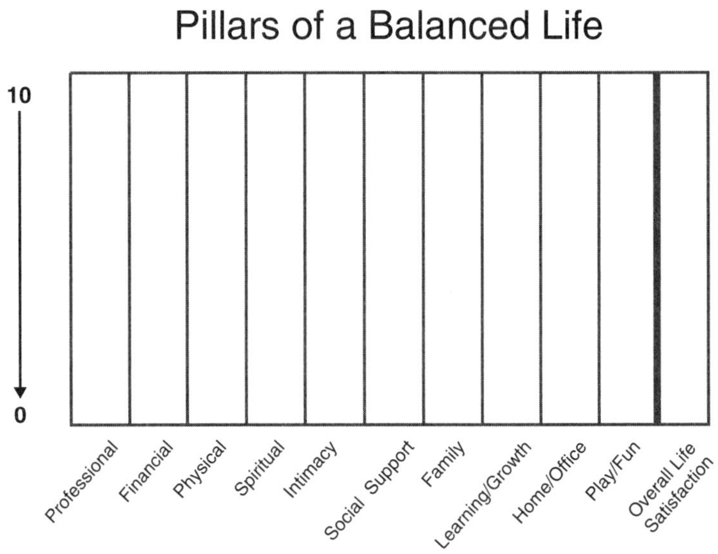

Pillars of a Balanced Life

Figure 6.1   Pillars of a balanced life
Source: Copyright © 2010 Ben Degan

on, say, their leisure time, it is assumed that they are 3 away from a "perfect" score of 10. The truth is few of us want to be perfectly satisfied with every area of our lives. Some small hunger for improvement can be extraordinarily helpful, especially in achievement-oriented domains. This notion is supported by research as well. Ed Diener (my father) and his colleagues examined outcomes related to people who scored an 8 out of 10 on life satisfaction versus those who scored a 9 or 10 out of 10. It turns out that the "8s" were higher achievers.[8] They made more money (in the case of workers) and got better grades (in the case of students). Those who were perfectly satisfied were just slightly less conscientious in their approach to work. It should be noted, however, that these findings were isolated to achievement-related domains such as scholastic performance and did not hold true for social domains. Being a 10 out of 10 on satisfaction with friendships may be better than an 8 out of 10. This "optimal level of happiness" finding translated directly to important conversations with clients. I sometimes share these findings with my clients and ask about how comfortable they feel "shooting for an 8" rather than assuming they should "go for a 10." In nearly every case they report a huge pressure lifting from their shoulders, and this "lightness" often turns into energy and enthusiasm to take on new challenges.

Figure 6.1 shows an alternative, more visually appealing domain satisfaction measure.

▶ Assessment #2: Scale of Positive and Negative Experience (SPANE)

A very basic way to assess how your client is "doing" is to get a measure of her emotional state. This can be done a single time, as a gauge of current feelings, or it can be done over time, to identify emotional leanings. My colleagues and I have created a simple scale of positive and negative emotional experience. Although we own the copyright for this assessment you can reproduce it and use it with your clients so long as you do not charge money for it. This scale shows good psychometric properties including reliability scores and "temporal stability scores."

Scale of Positive and Negative Experience (SPANE)[9]

Copyright © January 2009 by Ed Diener and Robert Biswas-Diener

Please think about what you have been doing and experiencing during the past four weeks. Then report how much you experienced each of the following feelings, using the scale below. For each item, select a number from 1 to 5, and indicate that number on your response sheet. It also shows good convergence with other widely used measures of emotion.

1 = Very rarely or never
2 = Rarely
3 = Sometimes
4 = Often
5 = Very often or always

_____ Positive

_____ Negative

_____ Good

_____ Bad

_____ Pleasant

_____ Unpleasant

_____ Happy

_____ Sad

_____ Afraid

_____ Joyful

_____ Angry

_____ Contented

Scoring:

The measure can be used to derive an overall affect balance score, but it can also be divided into positive and negative feelings scales.

Positive Feelings (SPANE-P): Add the scores, varying from 1 to 5, for the six items: positive, good, pleasant, happy, joyful, and contented. The score can vary from 6 (lowest possible) to 30 (highest positive feelings score).

Negative Feelings (SPANE-N): Add the scores, varying from 1 to 5, for the six items: negative, bad, unpleasant, sad, afraid, and angry. The score can vary from 6 (lowest possible) to 30 (highest negative feelings score).

Affect Balance (SPANE-B): The negative feelings score is subtracted from the positive feelings score, and the resultant difference score can vary from –24 (unhappiest possible) to 24 (highest affect balance possible). A respondent with a very high score of 24 reports that she or he rarely or never experiences any of the negative feelings, and very often or always has all of the positive feelings.

The third assessment I wanted to include is an alternative to the Satisfaction With Life Scale that was presented in the previous chapter. Researcher Sonja Lyubomirsky created this short, easy-to-use survey of general happiness to assess personal happiness, defined broadly.[10] The beauty of this measure is that it harnesses the fact that the word "happiness" can be so widely interpreted. Rather than forcing people into thinking of this concept as a "sense of inner peace" or "the experience of joy," Lyubomirsky wisely leaves the interpretation up to the individual. This measure is a short, simple way to gauge your client's overall well-being and to track overall progress over months of work.

Subjective Happiness Scale (SHS)

Copyright © by Sonja Lyubomirsky, PhD

For each of the following statements and/or questions, please circle the point on the scale that you feel is most appropriate in describing you.

1. In general, I consider myself:

   | 1 | 2 | 3 | 4 | 5 | 6 | 7 |

   not a very   a very
   happy person   happy person

2. Compared to most of my peers, I consider myself:

   | 1 | 2 | 3 | 4 | 5 | 6 | 7 |

   less happy   more happy

3. Some people are generally very happy. They enjoy life regardless of what is going on, getting the most out of everything. To what extent does this characterization describe you?

   | 1 | 2 | 3 | 4 | 5 | 6 | 7 |

   not at all   a great
                                                     deal

4. Some people are generally not very happy. Although they are not depressed, they never seem as happy as they might be. To what extent does this characterization describe you?

   | 1 | 2 | 3 | 4 | 5 | 6 | 7 |

   not at all   a great
                                                     deal

Note: Item #4 is reverse coded.

▶ Assessment #4: Meaning in Life Questionnaire

Meaning in life is one of those areas that has long been squarely in the domain of philosophers and which has, only recently, come under scientific scrutiny by psychologists. I particularly like meaning in life because it is a fundamental need of all people and is germane to the coaching endeavor. The Meaning in Life Questionnaire (MLQ) was created by researcher Michael Steger and his colleagues.[11] This group of scientists was interested in improving on older measures of meaning in life that often overlapped with distress in life. Across three studies they reduced the scale from 44 candidate items to 10 theoretically important and statistically discriminating items and found that the MLQ exhibits good psychometric properties such as discriminate validity and a stable factor structure. One of the aspects I like best about this particular measure is the fact that it can be used to create two distinct subscales, one on the presence of meaning in a person's life and the other on the search for meaning in a person's life. By further breaking down this broad topic into the smaller areas of "presence" and "search" it is possible to open productive conversations with clients about the gains they have made in their natural process of making meaning out of their lives, and how much. Steger and his colleagues sum up this point of view as follows:

> The ability of the MLQ to measure search and presence independently allows for greater theoretical and empirical flexibility. It is now possible to identify those who feel great meaningfulness yet still seek to further their understanding of life's meaning and compare them with those who feel their life is meaningful and are not engaged in any further search for meaning. For instance, Dietrich Bonhoeffer, Malcolm X, or Mahatma Gandhi may all exemplify lives in which great purpose and meaning did not foreclose the active and open pursuit for greater understanding of their meaning and purpose in the world. (p. 89)[12]

Meaning in Life Questionnaire (MLQ)

Please take a moment to think about what makes your life and existence feel important and significant to you. Please respond to the following statements as truthfully and accurately as you can, and also please remember that these are very subjective questions and that there are no right or wrong answers. Please answer according to the scale below:

1	2	3	4	5	6	7
absolutely untrue	mostly untrue	somewhat untrue	can't say true or false	somewhat true	mostly true	absolutely true

1. _____ I understand my life's meaning.
2. _____ I am looking for something that makes my life feel meaningful.
3. _____ I am always looking to find my life's purpose.
4. _____ My life has a clear sense of purpose.
5. _____ I have a good sense of what makes my life meaningful.
6. _____ I have discovered a satisfying life purpose.

7. _____ I am always searching for something that makes my life feel significant.

8. _____ I am seeking a purpose or mission for my life.

9. _____ My life has no clear purpose.

10. _____ I am searching for meaning in my life.

Note: You can create two subscales from this measure; one on the "Presence" of meaning and the other on the "Search" for meaning.

Presence: 1, 4, 5, 6, & 9—reverse-coded

Search: 2, 3, 7, 8, & 10

Steger, who spent his early career studying what makes life meaningful for individuals, has recently shifted his research interests to the influence that leaders, managers, and organizations can have on the well-being of their employees through helping to create meaningful work. His research with colleagues in the United States, Canada, United Kingdom, and Israel has followed the progression from meaningful work to personal well-being and happiness, and from there even further to pro-social desires to make a positive difference in the world. His work with a wide range of people, including college students, volunteers for medical and public safety organizations, daycare providers, university employees, and people working at all levels in hospitals and financial services corporations, tells the same story: People who feel like they've found their true calling or vocation—that is, people who've found meaningful work—are happier, more engaged in their work, and feel life in general is more meaningful. The results of Steger's research also suggest that organizations should look to either hire or cultivate "high-meaning" workers because they are more committed to their organizations, more motivated at work, and more satisfied with their jobs. While acknowledging that meaningful work is generally desirable as an integral part of the "good life," he also points out one aspect of purposeful work that is likely to appeal to "bottom line executives." Dr. Steger says that workers high in meaning appear to be "cost-effective."[13] They are less likely to quit or take sick days. In addition, they report less hostility and depression, which may alleviate the productivity costs associated with hostile work environments and battling depression. In order to spread the possibilities of meaningful work as far and wide as he can, Steger has developed a theoretical model of the individual and organizational initiatives that should tip the scales in favor of meaningful work. With his fellow Colorado State University colleague, Bryan Dik, he founded Vocé Consulting to partner with leaders and organizations to foster meaning at work. Steger also sees great promise in helping adolescents begin to consider meaningful work and is conducting a series of interventions in a middle school. He reasons that if meaningful work is good work, and meaningful workers are good workers, then people should learn how to find work that is more than just another way to earn a paycheck. Meaningful work can be an enormous part of what makes life worth living.

▶ Assessment #5: Work-Life Questionnaire

Amy Wrzesniewski, a researcher at Yale University, has conducted a collection of studies that rank among my favorites. Following on the work of sociologist Robert Bellah, Amy was curious about how people relate to their own work. According to Bellah, people generally fall into one of three conceptual categories: They feel they are in a job, a career, or a calling.[14] People in a job orientation are primarily motivated by money. They do not necessarily like the work they do and often fantasize about getting away from work and look forward to the end of their shifts. People in a career, by contrast, are primarily motivated by advancement. These are the people who work hard and who see their work as a stepping-stone to ever-improving circumstances. They are interested in pay raises, increased supervisory responsibility, more status, or more perks related to work. They often throw themselves into their work but still look forward to vacations. People in the last group, those with a calling orientation, believe the work they do makes a meaningful and substantive contribution to the world. They love their work and view it as a kind of mission through which they can live their values. They are not workaholics, but they still think about their work, even while on vacation, because it is such an integrated part of their identity and values. Amy and her colleagues have found that people can fall into any of these three orientations regardless of their actual occupation. A bus driver could have a calling, for example, and a surgeon could feel she is in a job.

Work-Life Questionnaire[15]

Please read the following three paragraphs. After you have read all three, indicate how much each category of people is like you by circling one of the choices provided.

1. Category A people work primarily enough to earn enough money to support their lives outside of their jobs. If they were financially secure, they would no longer continue with their current line of work, but would really rather do something else instead. To these people, their jobs are basically a necessity of life, a lot like breathing or sleeping. They often wish the time would pass more quickly at work. They greatly anticipate weekends and vacations. If these people lived their lives over again, they probably would not go into the same line of work. They would not encourage their friends and children to enter their line of work. Category A people are very eager to retire.

2. Category B people basically enjoy their work, but do not expect to be in their current jobs five years from now. Instead, they plan to move on to better, higher-level jobs. They have several goals for their futures pertaining to the positions they would eventually like to hold. Sometimes their work seems a waste of time, but they know that they must do sufficiently well in their current positions to move on. Category B people can't wait to get a promotion. For them, a promotion means recognition of their good work, and is a sign of their success in competition with coworkers.

3. For Category C people, work is one of the most important parts of life. They are very pleased that they are in their line of work. Because what they do for a living is a vital part of who they are, it is one of the first things they tell people about

themselves. They tend to take their work home with them and on vacations, too. The majority of their friends are from their places of employment, and they belong to several organizations and clubs relating to their work. They feel good about their work because they love it, and because they think it makes the world a better place. They would encourage their friends and children to enter their line of work. Category C people would be pretty upset if they were forced to stop working, and they are not particularly looking forward to retirement.

Category A people are:

(a) very much like me   (b) somewhat like me   (c) a little like me   (d) not at all like me

Category B people are:

(a) very much like me   (b) somewhat like me   (c) a little like me   (d) not at all like me

Category C people are:

(a) very much like me   (b) somewhat like me   (c) a little like me   (d) not at all like me

Part 2:

How much do the following statements describe how you feel about the work you usually do?
4 = A lot
3 = Somewhat
2 = A little
1 = Not at all

1. _____ I enjoy talking about my work to others.
2. _____ My work is one of the most important things in my life.
3. _____ My main reason for working is financial—to support my family and life-style.
4. _____ I am eager to retire.
5. _____ If I was financially secure, I would continue my current work even if I stopped getting paid.
6. _____ My work makes the world a better place.
7. _____ I would choose my current work life again if I had the chance.
8. _____ I expect to be in a higher-level job in five years.
9. _____ I view my job as a stepping-stone to other jobs.
10. _____ I expect to be doing the same work in five years.

Job and calling are both represented by items 1, 2, 3, 4, 5, 6, and 7. They typically load onto a single factor in data analyses. Career is represented by 8, 9, and 10, and loads consistently together on a separate factor. You may choose to mix the career items with the other ones, rather than have them all appear at the end.

Note: To score this scale simply look at the highest score from the three vignettes. Vignette A describes a job orientation, vignette B describes a career orientation, and vignette C describes a calling orientation. Strong endorsement of one vignette and relatively weak endorsement of the other two will indicate a strong leaning for one of the types of work orientation.

Work orientation has a number of important ramifications for your work with your clients. Having a shared vocabulary for discussing how your client views his or her work can be helpful when discussing motivation, goals, and other work-related issues. In addition, it can be helpful to know which orientation best describes your client. This is particularly true because people in a calling orientation tend to engage in a set of behaviors that Amy calls "job crafting" that helps to make work more meaningful.[16] Calling-oriented individuals are far more likely than their job or career counterparts to work right at the edge of their actual job description—to bend the rules, as it were, and engage in activities that help provide more meaning. Take the simple example of a hair stylist. People who cut hair—by the terms of their job descriptions—are supposed to do exactly that, cut hair. However, you have almost undoubtedly had long, in-depth discussions with your stylist. The social interaction, advice and counseling, and self-disclosure that are typical of many stylists is a way in which they craft their jobs, adding additional rewarding activities to their basic duties. Where your clients are concerned, the idea of job crafting is a great starting point for breathing new passion and meaning into work. You can explore opportunities to create small modifications to the workload without compromising the basic obligations of your client's job. Amy and her colleagues point to three specific ways in which people craft their jobs. You can use these as a launching point for exploration and creating experiments for clients to engage in as homework:

1. *Change the amount or quality of social interactions at work:* This simply means that the interactions you engage in at work influence your sense of enjoyment and meaning. If you or your clients can find ways to make interactions with customers, supervisors, or colleagues more rewarding, then the work will feel better. Consider commutes, lunch breaks, e-mails, and other common hotbeds of potential interaction.

2. *Change the type of activities at work:* This simply means, in addition to your client's regular duties, he or she adopts some small rewarding tasks. I knew a parking lot attendant in a major city who created an organizational chart for parking the cars and "filing" the car keys. This task was not assigned to him by a supervisor, but his system helped his coworkers immeasurably.

3. *Change the cognitive boundaries of work:* This simply means that people often find more meaning when they view their concrete daily tasks in terms of larger, more abstract values. For instance, a janitor in a hospital might think of his job as being about emptying the wastebasket (concrete task) or as about promoting health by keeping the hospital clean (abstract). One of the shuttle drivers at my local airport told me he feels like his job is about keeping families together because he ferries people to the airport where they then take flights to see their relatives.

The Purposeful Work Scale is related to the Work-Life Questionnaire in that it is specifically about exploring your client's sense of purpose at work.[17] Unlike Wrzesniewski's measure, the Purposeful Work Scale does not divide people into one of multiple possible work-related categories. Instead, it provides a broad overview of your client's sense of purposeful engagement at work on a dimensional scale where low scores represent lower amounts of purpose and higher scores represent higher amounts of purpose. The items were created based on research into aspects of work that have been shown in other research to be related to high well-being, the experience of flow, and a sense of meaning. You can use your client responses on specific items to open conversations about specific aspects of work that might be modified to produce more meaning and more rewarding experiences.

Purposeful Work Scale

Copyright © 2009 Robert Biswas-Diener and Alex Linley

Following are eight statements with which you may agree or disagree. Using the 1–7 scale, indicate your agreement with each item by placing the appropriate number on the line preceding that item.

7 = Strongly agree
6 = Agree
5 = Slightly agree
4 = Mixed or neither agree nor disagree
3 = Slightly disagree
2 = Disagree
1 = Strongly disagree

1. _____ I learned something new at work today.
2. _____ I often feel "in flow" at work.
3. _____ My work is meaningful.
4. _____ I get along with others at work.
5. _____ My supervisor supports me.
6. _____ I look forward to going to work.
7. _____ I hope to have my same employer in five years.
8. _____ The amount of work I have is optimal.

▶ **Assessment # 7: Curiosity and Exploration Inventory**

Curiosity has a bit of a mixed reputation among most people. On the one hand, curiosity has obviously driven exploration and scientific inquiry, largely to the benefit of us all. On the other hand, people don't want neighbors who are nosy and admonish us that "curiosity killed the cat." Some children are scolded for their incessant questioning, while others are encouraged to explore the world around them to their heart's content. There is, as it turns out, a growing scientific literature on curiosity, and the news is both promising and interesting. Researchers Paul Silva and Todd Kashdan argue that curiosity is a vital psychological mechanism for intrinsic motivation.[18] Our natural tendency to be lured by the siren song of interest is what makes pursuits inherently rewarding. But curiosity means seeking out uncertain answers and facing unknown life events, both of which can be quite anxiety provoking. Curious people, then, have to be able to withstand a little stress. Curiosity has been linked to health and social benefits.

The Curiosity and Exploration Inventory was created by researcher Todd Kashdan and his colleagues.[19] These scientists tested a group of 36 items, which were later reduced to 10 items that form two separate factors: five items load onto a "stretching" factor that represents people's natural tendency to seek out novel experiences, and five items load onto an "embracing" factor that represents people's ability to face novel and uncertain events. While the personality dimension of "openness to experience" is, as you might imagine, correlated with both stretching and embracing, "mindfulness" is more heavily associated with embracing. It could be that more mindful individuals engage in thinking strategies or other habits that prepare them to withstand the unpleasantness of uncertain experiences. You can use this scale to identify your client's overall level of curiosity and open a discussion about topics such as facing uncertain situations, taking risks, hunger for knowledge, need for closure, openness to experience, personal comfort zones, and many others.

Trait Curiosity and Exploration Inventory-II

Rate the following statements for how accurately they reflect the way you generally feel and behave. Do not rate what you think you should do, or wish you do, or things you no longer do. Please be as honest as possible.

1	2	3	4	5
very slightly	a little	moderately	quite a bit	extremely or not at all

1. _____ I actively seek as much information as I can in new situations.
2. _____ I am the type of person who really enjoys the uncertainty of everyday life.
3. _____ I am at my best when doing something that is complex or challenging.
4. _____ Everywhere I go, I am looking out for new things or experiences.
5. _____ I view challenging situations as an opportunity to grow and learn.
6. _____ I like to do things that are a little frightening.
7. _____ I am always looking for experiences that challenge how I think about myself and the world.
8. _____ I prefer jobs that are excitingly unpredictable.
9. _____ I frequently seek out opportunities to challenge myself and grow as a person.
10. _____ I am the kind of person who embraces unfamiliar people, events, and places.

Note:

Items 1, 3, 5, 7, and 9 reflect Stretching.

Items 2, 4, 6, 8, and 10 reflect Embracing.

▶ Assessment #8: Savoring Beliefs Inventory

Another area of research that I love is on the concept of savoring. Savoring is the act of mentally stretching out a positive event. We savor, for example, when we share fond memories with friends, effectively plumbing pleasant past experiences for even more positivity in the present moment. Similarly, we draw out wonderful experiences at meals when we slowly chew delicious food, allowing the taste to be experienced longer and more fully than we normally would. University of Chicago researcher Fred Bryant and his colleagues have scientifically examined the act of savoring for years.[20] They have found, for example, that positively reminiscing about the past by either visualizing past successes or focusing on pieces of memorabilia such as a sports trophy can make people happier (and don't forget about all those benefits associated with feeling happy!).

The following is how to use the savoring beliefs scale.

Savoring Beliefs Inventory[21]

Instructions: For each statement listed, please circle the one number that best indicates how true the particular statement is for you. There are no right or wrong answers. Please be as honest as you can.

		strongly disagree					strongly agree	
1.	Before a good thing happens, I look forward to it in ways that give me pleasure in the present.	1	2	3	4	5	6	7
2.	It's hard for me to hang onto a good feeling for very long.	1	2	3	4	5	6	7
3.	I enjoy looking back on happy times from my past.	1	2	3	4	5	6	7
4.	I don't like to look forward to good times too much before they happen.	1	2	3	4	5	6	7
5.	I know how to make the most of a good time.	1	2	3	4	5	6	7
6.	I don't like to look back at good times too much after they've taken place.	1	2	3	4	5	6	7
7.	I feel a joy of anticipation when I think about upcoming good things.	1	2	3	4	5	6	7
8.	When it comes to enjoying myself, I'm my own "worst enemy."	1	2	3	4	5	6	7
9.	I can make myself feel good by remembering pleasant events from my past.	1	2	3	4	5	6	7

10. For me, anticipating what upcoming good
events will be like is basically a waste of time.   1 2 3 4 5 6 7

11. When something good happens, I can
make my enjoyment of it last longer by thinking
or doing certain things.   1 2 3 4 5 6 7

12. When I reminisce about pleasant memories,
I often start to feel sad or disappointed.   1 2 3 4 5 6 7

13. I can enjoy pleasant events in my mind
before they actually occur.   1 2 3 4 5 6 7

14. I can't seem to capture the joy of happy moments.   1 2 3 4 5 6 7

15. I like to store memories of fun times that I
go through so that I can recall them later.   1 2 3 4 5 6 7

16. It's hard for me to get very excited about
fun times before they actually take place.   1 2 3 4 5 6 7

17. I feel fully able to appreciate
good things that happen to me.   1 2 3 4 5 6 7

18. I find that thinking about good times from
the past is basically a waste of time.   1 2 3 4 5 6 7

19. I can make myself feel good by imagining what
a happy time that is about to happen will be like.   1 2 3 4 5 6 7

20. I don't enjoy things as much as I should.   1 2 3 4 5 6 7

21. It's easy for me to rekindle
the joy from pleasant memories.   1 2 3 4 5 6 7

22. When I think about a pleasant event before it happens,
I often start to feel uneasy or uncomfortable.   1 2 3 4 5 6 7

23. It's easy for me to enjoy myself when I want to.   1 2 3 4 5 6 7

24. For me, once a fun time is over and gone,
it's best not to think about it.   1 2 3 4 5 6 7

You can think of savoring as an act that can be directed toward the past, present, or future. When we page through a photo album of our wedding we are savoring a past experience. When we luxuriate in a relaxing hot tub we are savoring the present moment. And when we find we are excited about an upcoming trip and fantasize about what fun we will have, we are savoring the future (called anticipating). The Savoring Beliefs Inventory is designed around the idea that different types of savoring focus on the past, present, and future. When you score the test for your clients you can use one of the following scoring strategies to identify the type of savoring to which your client is naturally drawn.

Instructions for Scoring the Savoring Beliefs Inventory (SBI)

Note: This information originally appeared in a slightly modified form in Fred Bryant and Joseph Veroff's book *Savoring: A new model of positive experience.*

Four scale-scores can be derived from the SBI:

(1) *Anticipating* subscale score

(2) *Savoring the Moment* subscale score

(3) *Reminiscing* subscale score

(4) *SBI Total* score

Bryant and his colleagues recommend two different scoring methods for the SBI. In the original scoring method he used to create this scale, positively anchored items are summed, negatively anchored items are summed, and then the sum of the negatively anchored items is subtracted from the sum of the positively anchored items. This produces an average score and is used both for each subscale and for the SBI Total score. With this scoring method, scores on each SBI subscale can range from −24 to +24, and SBI Total score can range from −72 to +72.

The other scoring method converts scale-scores back into the 1–7 "metric" of the response scale for the SBI by summing the positively anchored items, reverse-scoring the negatively anchored items, adding together these two sums, and dividing the resulting total by the number of constituent items. This scoring method provides average scores for the *Anticipating, Savoring the Moment*, and *Reminiscing* subscales, as well as an average score for SBI Total. With this scoring method, scores on the three SBI subscales and SBI Total score can range from 1 to 7. This scoring method makes it easy for researchers to interpret SBI scores in the "absolute" terms of the original 1–7 response scale. With this scoring method, 1 is the lowest possible "absolute" score (0th percentile); 2 lies at the 16.67th percentile on the absolute scale; 3 lies at the 33.33rd percentile on the absolute scale; 4 is the midpoint on the absolute scale (50th percentile); 5 lies at the 66.67th percentile on the absolute scale; 6 lies at the 83.33rd percentile on the absolute scale; and 7 is the highest possible "absolute" score (100th percentile).

The two scoring methods provide equivalent sets of scores that are perfectly correlated with each other. However, the two scoring methods provide different "metrics" for evaluating SBI scores—the first scoring method yields summed scores, whereas the second scoring method yields averaged scores. Researchers may choose one or the other scoring method, depending on their purpose or preference.

Scoring the SBI Using the Original "Summed Score" Method

I. *Anticipating subscale score*

    A. Sum up responses to the following four items: 1, 7, 13, 19.

    B. Sum up responses to the following four items: 4, 10, 16, and 22.

    C. Subtract the total obtained in Step B from the total obtained in Step A, to get a summed score for the *Anticipating* subscale.

II. *Savoring the Moment subscale score*

    A. Sum up responses to the following four items: 5, 11, 17, 23.

    B. Sum up responses to the following four items: 2, 8, 14, and 20.

    C. Subtract the total obtained in Step B from the total obtained in Step A, to get a summed score for the *Savoring the Moment* subscale.

III. *Reminiscing subscale score*

   A. Sum up responses to the following four items: 3, 9, 15, and 21.

   B. Sum up responses to the following four items: 6, 12, 18, and 24.

   C. Subtract the total obtained in Step B from the total obtained in Step A, to get a summed score for the *Reminiscing* subscale.

IV. *Total SBI score*

   A. Sum up responses to the following 12 (odd-numbered) items:

   1, 3, 5, 7, 9, 11, 13, 15, 17, 19, 21, and 23.

   B. Sum up responses to the following 12 (even-numbered) items:

   2, 4, 6, 8, 10, 12, 14, 16, 18, 20, 22, and 24.

   C. Subtract the total obtained in Step B from the total obtained in Step A, to get a summed SBI Total score.

Scoring the SBI Using the "Average Score" Method

I. *Anticipating subscale score*

   A. Reverse-score the following items: 4, 10, 16, and 22.

   B. Sum up responses to these four items.

   C. Sum up responses to the following four items: 1, 7, 13, 19.

   D. Add together the sum obtained in Step B and the sum obtained in Step C.

   E. Divide the resulting total by 8, to get a mean *Anticipating* score.

II. *Savoring the Moment subscale score*

   A. Reverse-score the following items: 2, 8, 14, and 20.

   B. Sum up responses to these four items.

   C. Sum up responses to the following four items: 5, 11, 17, 23.

   D. Add together the sum obtained in Step B and the sum obtained in Step C.

   E. Divide the resulting total by 8, to get a mean *Savoring the Moment* score.

III. *Reminiscing subscale score*

   A. Reverse-score the following items: 6, 12, 18, and 24.

   B. Sum up responses to these four items.

   C. Sum up responses to the following four items: 3, 9, 15, and 21.

   D. Add together the sum obtained in Step B and the sum obtained in Step C.

   E. Divide the resulting total by 8, to get a mean *Reminiscing* score.

IV. *Total SBI score*

   A. Reverse-score the following 12 (even-numbered) items:

   2, 4, 6, 8, 10, 12, 14, 16, 18, 20, 22, and 24.

   B. Sum up responses to these 12 (even-numbered items) items.

   C. Sum up responses to the following 12 (odd-numbered) items:

   1, 3, 5, 7, 9, 11, 13, 15, 17, 19, 21, and 23.

   D. Add together the sum obtained in Step B and the sum obtained in Step C.

   E. Divide the resulting total by 24, to get a mean SBI Total score.

As I mentioned earlier in this chapter the "incubator" work-style is a new area of research and practice interest for me. Incubators are those creative, cool-headed people who work well under tight deadlines and pressure. They often put off work until the last minute and then move into action when "the time is right." Most incubators are greatly relieved to have this label attached to them as they typically have a lifelong habit of thinking of themselves as procrastinators. Unfortunately, many procrastinators are also relieved to hear the incubator label as it gives them a cloak of strength behind which they can hide. The Work-Style scale was created to distinguish between four distinct types of motivational approaches to work—procrastinators, incubators, planners, and triflers. Once you have identified your client's natural work tendencies you can work with him to understand when he is likely to work best, how his work-style will affect others, and how to best plan for projects.

Work-Style Scale[22]

4 = Perfectly describes me
3 = Describes me somewhat
2 = Does not really describe me
1 = Does not describe me at all

1. _____ I always get my work completed on time.
2. _____ The quality of my work is superior.
3. _____ It takes a looming deadline to motivate me.
4. _____ I do my best work under pressure.
5. _____ I like to get started on a project right away.

To score the Work-Style Scale use the following method, looking for the following constellations of high scores:

Planners: Planners are those who strategize their work and feel compelled to get to work on even long-term projects immediately. They tend to be self-motivated. Planners generally score high on items A, B, and E.

Incubators: Incubators are those who put work off until the last minute. They often need deadlines to motivate them, but they always complete projects and always create superior quality work. Incubators generally score high on items A, B, C, and D.

Triflers: Triflers are those who start work early but get distracted, bored, or lose interest easily. Triflers tend to score high on item E and low on items A and B.

Procrastinators: Procrastinators are those people who put off work until the last minute and then race to complete projects before deadlines. They often hand in shoddy, mediocre quality work. Procrastinators tend to score high on items C or D, and low on items A and B.

▶ **Assessment #10: Authenticity Scale**

British researcher Alex Wood is one of the leading figures in the scientific exploration of authenticity.[23] Authenticity is, essentially, being genuine or true. From a scientific point of view the idea that there is a "true self" and that this self can be reflected in actions and emotions is problematic. It is difficult, for example, to measure this genuine core and to gauge its distance from the daily experience of life. When you speak out in anger, do something unusually risky, or help another person, how are we to know whether these acts are "authentic?" One way of assessing this elusive concept would be to see how typical these acts are for an individual. From a psychological perspective, authenticity is principally about bringing one's beliefs and actions into harmony, a synthesis of a person's behaviors with their identity. Wood and his colleagues refer to three primary aspects of authenticity: "self-alienation" (knowledge of one's beliefs, emotions, and purpose), "authentic living" (the degree to which a person lives in accord with her values), and "accepting external influences" (being influenced by the beliefs and desires of others). Wood and his colleagues created the following authenticity scale.

Authenticity Scale[24]

1 -------- 2 -------- 3 -------- 4 -------- 5 -------- 6 -------- 7

does not describe me at all   describes me perfectly

1. _____ "I think it is better to be yourself, than to be popular."
2. _____ "I don't know how I really feel inside."
3. _____ "I am strongly influenced by the opinions of others."
4. _____ "I usually do what other people tell me to do."
5. _____ "I always feel I need to do what others expect me to do."
6. _____ "Other people influence me greatly."
7. _____ "I feel as if I don't know myself very well."
8. _____ "I always stand by what I believe in."
9. _____ "I am true to myself in most situations."
10. _____ "I feel out of touch with the 'real me.'"
11. _____ "I live in accordance with my values and beliefs."
12. _____ "I feel alienated from myself."

You can use these scoring instructions to derive scores for the three dimensions of authenticity: Total Items 1, 8, 9, and 11 for Authentic Living; Items 3, 4, 5, and 6 for Accepting External Influence; and Items 2, 7, 10, and 12 for Self-Alienation.

The Authenticity Scale can be useful in your work with your clients. It is recommended for new leaders who are just "finding their feet" as well as others who are entering periods of rapid growth or identity transition, such as those associated with career change. The scale can be used as a touch point for discussing personal values and a sense of identity. Further, the three subscales contained within this measure can illuminate ways in which your clients might be more or less authentic. It may be helpful to know that accepting external influence and self-alienation were both significantly associated with stress and lower happiness while authentic living was associated with higher happiness. For comparison purposes, Wood and his colleague reported the mean scores for these three dimensions in both a students and community sample:[25]

	Students	Community
Authentic Living	22.05	19.02
Self-Alienation	13.34	13.67
Accepting External Influence	10.84	12.46

▶ Assessment #11: Strengths Use Scale

One of the most interesting aspects of strengths science, to me, is the fact that we tend to focus on specific strengths. Over the last 10 years that positive psychologists have been examining strengths, they have attended primarily to measuring individual strengths such as gratitude, forgiveness, and curiosity. It also makes sense to back up and look at strengths use in general, rather than the use of a specific strength. This is exactly what Reena Govindji and Alex Linley, two of my colleagues at the Centre for Applied Positive Psychology, have done.[26] Instead of asking about courage or leadership or creativity, they created a measure that asked people to report on their knack for using strengths in general. Interestingly, they found that strengths use—in the general sense of the word—was associated with authenticity, vitality, and increased well-being.

Strengths Use Scale

The following questions ask you about your strengths, that is, the things that you are able to do well or do best. Please respond to each statement using the scale below:

1	2	3	4	5	6	7
strongly disagree						strongly agree

1. _____ I am regularly able to do what I do best.
2. _____ I always play to my strengths.
3. _____ I always try to use my strengths.
4. _____ I achieve what I want by using my strengths.
5. _____ I use my strengths every day.
6. _____ I am able to use my strengths in lots of different situations.
7. _____ I use my strengths to get what I want out of life.

8. _____ My work gives me lots of opportunities to use my strengths.

9. _____ My life presents me with lots of different ways to use my strengths.

10. _____ Using my strengths comes naturally to me.

11. _____ I find it easy to use my strengths in the things I do.

12. _____ Most of my time is spent doing things that I am good at doing.

13. _____ Using my strengths is something I am familiar with.

14. _____ I am able to use my strengths in lots of different ways.

You can use this assessment with your clients in a variety of ways. Not only will this measure provide a general gauge of strengths use, but the individual items can be used for in-depth discussion. The item "My life presents me with lots of different ways to use my strengths," for example, begs the client to list these, thereby increasing awareness of potential opportunities and resources. Govindji and Linley speak directly to this point:

> We believe it also bears note that in completing the scales, many participants commented that various questions, particularly about their strengths, prompted them to ponder upon aspects of their lives and experiences that they had not previously considered. A number of participants spontaneously commented that this was helpful to them in thinking about their future life directions, and as such could readily be linked to applications in career coaching (Bench, 2003), as well as those instances in the coaching relationship when a person is struggling with the consideration of what to do and where to go next. (pp. 151–152)[27]

One of the best aspects of positive psychology, what distinguishes it from other forms of self-help and from many types of coaching, is that it is, above all, a science. As such, positive psychology relies heavily on empirical methods for investigating the positive aspects of human nature, including excellence. Researchers have created a wide range of conceptually and statistically intriguing assessments. Many of these, such as the ones presented in this chapter, are directly relevant to coaching and can be used effectively to quantify clients' psychological resources or open the door on fruitful conversations between coaches and clients. These scales are not intended to be "swallowed whole" or used with every single coaching client. Instead, they are meant to be used as an adjunct to existing coaching practices, placed where they are most useful and avoided where they are not. I tried to include measures that were relatively easy to score and which do not require special training in statistics or research methods. As always, it is sensible to take the measures you are interested in yourself, or to practice a "dry run" with a colleague or friend before using it with actual clients.

▶ Related Articles

Bryant, F. B. (2003). Savoring Beliefs Inventory (SBI): A scale for measuring beliefs about savouring. *Journal of Mental Health, 12,* 175–196.

Diener, E., Emmons, R. A., Larsen, R. J., & Griffin, S. (1985). The Satisfaction with Life Scale. *Journal of Personality Assessment, 49,* 71–75.

Govindji, R., & Linley, A. (2007). Strengths use, self-concordance and well-being: Implications for strengths coaching and coaching psychologists. *International Coaching Psychology Review, 2*, 143–153.

Kashdan, T. B., Gallagher, M. W., Silvia, P. J., Winterstein, B. P., Breen, W. E., Terhar, D., & Steger, M. F. (2009). The Curiosity and Exploration Inventory-II: Development, factor structure, and initial psychometrics. *Journal of Research in Personality, 43*, 987–998.

Lyubomirsky, S., & Lepper, H. (1999). A measure of subjective happiness: Preliminary reliability and construct validation. *Social Indicators Research, 46*, 137–155.

Pavot, W. G., Diener, E., Colvin, C. R., & Sandvik, E. (1991). Further validation of the Satisfaction with Life Scale: Evidence for the cross-method convergence of well-being measures. *Journal of Personality Assessment, 57*, 149–161.

Wood, A., Linley, A., Maltby, J., Baliousis, M., & Joseph, S. (2008). The authentic personality: A theoretical and empirical conceptualization and the development of the authenticity scale. *Journal of Counseling Psychology, 55*, 385–399.

Wrzesniewski, A., McCauley, C. R., Rozin, P., & Schwartz, B. (1997). Jobs, careers, and callings: People's relations to their work. *Journal of Research in Personality, 31*, 21–33.

CHAPTER SEVEN

Gray Hairs and Gravestones: Positive Psychology Coaching Across the Lifespan

"Mid-life is not mid-death."

Anonymous

Call me a slow learner, but after I had been coaching for two or three years it occurred to me that I had clients of a particular type. The common wisdom around the business of coaching is that a person should develop his or her niche, both to ensure work about which he is passionate and to more strategically market to a segmented population. There are, as a result, coaches of nearly every professional stripe. There are academic coaches and creativity coaches and parenting coaches and executive coaches. Each of these coaches has a clear sense of who their clientele is. Executive coaches work with executives and managers, and small business coaches work with entrepreneurs. The area I developed—positive psychology coaching—by contrast, had no discernable homogenous group of potential clients. People were walking in my door to decide on what to do after graduating college, to switch to a new career, and to find out how to donate the millions they made before retirement. The only thing they seemed to have in common is that they all had a natural desire to focus on the positive and a hankering to see what science had on offer. As it turns out, they also happened to be middle aged, broadly defined. This is a natural by-product of the fact that folks who can afford to pay for coaching are more likely to be older. I had a few clients in their mid-30s who were eager to ramp up their business success, and I had a few clients who were in their mid-50s and eager to find a rewarding second career. But they all seemed to be in that 30 to 50 (or occasionally early 60s) range.

Once I realized that my clientele was defined, in part, by their age I began reflecting on the types of issues with which they presented. Not unexpectedly, they sought my help regarding issues that were typical of their age bracket: They wanted to create a legacy, they wanted to rekindle their passion, they wanted to work on that dream that they had put on the back burner for so long. Interestingly, what motivates very many of these clients is middle age itself. We all know the cliché of the "mid-life crisis," the way in which our aging bodies betray us and fill us with a kind of existential dread that motivates dramatic change. Although not very many of my clients could be said to be "in crisis," they were all wrestling with these same basic thematic issues. Over time, I began working more explicitly with these issues, especially in the context of positive psychology topics such as passion and strengths. This chapter is my distillation of much of this experience. In the pages that immediately follow I want to share my insights and methods for working with people who could broadly be considered in mid-life. This includes people seeking career, life, and business coaching. This chapter is not necessarily for all coaches, confined as it is to a particular—albeit large—segment of clients. If you only work with the 30 or younger crowd, please accept my humble apologies for not writing you a tailor-made chapter!

▶ Welcome to Middle Age

At some point we all reach that stage where we get out of bed and find that our legs are sore or our back won't seem to cooperate or that we have a pain in a body part we never even knew existed. It often starts with physical symptoms: We bruise more easily, we have more joint pain, and we take longer to recover from injuries. Or, for that matter, we become injured inexplicably. My wife recently said to me, "Since when did I have to start warming up and stretching out just to check the rearview mirror on the highway?" Apparently a lack of proper physical preparation while driving left her with something like whiplash as she checked for a possible car in the adjacent lane. Of course, I am not talking about the day-to-day ailments of octogenarians or older retirees. I am talking about some of the physical transitions that occur for most of us as early as our thirties. These physical harbingers announce that period we all know as "middle age." For many people those two words conjure images of physical collapse, psychological turmoil, and the inescapability of time. For many people the prospect of entering those middle years is about as much fun as entering a prison cell, and with the same sense of finality.

Of course middle age is a cultural fiction.[1] We have, in fact, entirely made it up as an abstract concept. That mid-life period has occurred in later and later decades over the years. These days we generally think of the 40th birthday as the precise moment of middle age. With average life expectancies in most Western countries hovering around 80 this makes sense. Ages 1 through 39 are the slow clink-clink-clink as the roller coaster rides to the top of that terrible drop, and ages 40 and after, well, they are often seen as being that terrible drop. In the 1250s, however, the 40th birthday would have been a ripe old age. In 2,500 BC a 40-year-old would have been a revered community elder. And, as people live longer, stay healthier longer, and work later in life, the concept of middle age is shifting again. It is likely that, in many ways, the decade of the 50s will supplant the 40s as middle age, and the trend will continue in this fashion. In fact, we have already seen many recent changes in our concept of middle age. Not only have advances in health care extended the period we consider to be middle age, but changes in society have shifted the meaning of middle age. Some folks at age 40 are wondering what to do now that the kids have left home and others are just having their first baby. Mid-life no longer means the exact same thing to everyone. One thing, however, is certain: This middle period of life usually presents a series of psychological hurdles for even the healthiest of us.

To some extent, it doesn't matter if we are talking about a 34-year-old, a 40-year-old, or a 52-year-old, there is an idea about "middle age" that transcends both chronological advancement or physical maladies. Middle age, culturally speaking, is about a period in time when most of us face a daunting psychological transformation. Like puberty, middle age is a natural phase that requires some self-examination and an accounting of "who you are" whether at work, at home, or in relationships. It is because of the themes inherent in middle age—identity, legacy, success, health, and so forth—that this time period is so uniquely suited to coaching interventions. In many ways middle age is a period where people naturally "check in with themselves," rediscovering or reaffirming their values and dreams. Middle age is, centrally, about transformation, and keen readers will realize where I am headed: Coaching is fundamentally about transformation as well.

Everyone who ages has an implicit sense of transformation, but all too often this sense is one of "decline" rather than "improvement." People approaching or experiencing middle age frequently become anxious as they notice the first signs of physical decline. That first gray hair, that first hot flash, or that first time you had to sit and rest rather than finish that basketball game with your son. The middle of life is undeniably about a series of physical changes, and many of these seem to be changes in a direction we would not prefer: We seem to slow, gain weight, and lose muscle. In fact, in the 1990s, as the baby boomer generation experienced their middle-of-life stage, there was a groundswell in attention to all that could go wrong with an older body. Books, seminars, and experts were suddenly talking about menopause, male sexual decline, memory loss, and prostate cancer. It is precisely because there are some tangible physical declines at middle age that lead to a much broader psychological phenomenon that most people think of as "the mid-life crisis."

We have all either experienced this psychological topsy-turvy or seen people who have. The logic here is that, aware of our approaching deaths for the first time, we grasp about for feelings of youth. There are clichés about men growing ponytails and buying motorcycles, women having affairs with college boys and rushing to cosmetic surgeons. All too often the mid-life crisis is presented as an inevitable cultural narrative, a kind of unpleasant middle-aged puberty, where we must regress a bit psychologically before getting on with the serious business of living.

Nothing could be further from the truth. Although we must all confront some of the realities of aging bodies, we do not necessarily need to approach the *psychological* transitions of this period with anything other than grace. Perhaps even more important, we can rely on the vast experience of those who have endured this period before us as well as tap the enormous scientific resources on this stage of life. As coaches we can be influential in supporting our clients through a smooth, growth-filled mid-life experience.

Take Home Message #1:

Most people overlook the fact that people in middle life are typically in the best position to be effective. They have wisdom, respect, position, skill, social connections, resources, and acquired knowledge on their side. All of these can be harnessed to make middle life an exciting opportunity.

For those of you who can recall your high school or college psychology classes you will likely remember the "developmental stages," a theory by the esteemed Erik Erikson.[2] Middle adulthood, according to Erikson, was characterized, thematically, by a balancing act between "generativity" on the one hand and "stagnation" on the other. By this, Erikson simply was implying that people at this stage of life begin thinking about their legacies, about what they want to leave behind. Essentially, they want to be "generative," whether that is raising children, growing a business, or writing a book. One of the things that is so eloquent about Erikson's view is that he is not necessarily suggesting that people are bowled over by the threat of immediate decline—physical and mental—and rush to create a legacy for themselves. Instead, he suggests that people in mid-life happen to be in a uniquely privileged position: They are at the point where they are in the best position to be generative. They are at an age where they are the managers, the executives, the government leaders, the parents, the business owners, and so forth. Erikson's theory offers us the first glimpse into a major theme of this chapter: We can help our clients transform the idea of mid-life crisis to that of mid-life opportunity. Middle age need not be about anxiety, it can be about opportunity.

▶ How Do You Feel about Growing Older?

Everyone is different and not everyone shares the same view of aging. Many of our ideas about aging come from our cultures and personal experiences. Western culture tells us that 40-year-olds are expected to "freak out" as they contend with the uncertain chronological ground of mid-life. On the other hand, Western societies also send a clear message that people are staying healthier and more able later in life than at any other period in history. Some of our views come from our family histories. One woman I knew, who had a strong history of Alzheimer's disease in her family, was often worried about growing older. For her, the aging process was one fraught with intellectual peril. Each day brought her closer to the possibility of mental decline. A 55-year-old man I know, by contrast, seems more enthusiastic about his age every day. He often boasts about his own aged father—now in his late 80s—even when the stories concern the father being crotchety or getting confused. For this guy in his fifties, aging—even the negative aspects of aging—seems to be part of a larger comedy that he is greatly enjoying. He seems to have accepted ages as simply progressing from one stage to the next, and is able to take joy from the process. You also hold some ideas, both implicit and explicit, about the aging process. Take a moment and think about how you feel about getting older. Is it scary? Is it exciting? Is it a combination of feelings?

Measuring the Perception of Age

You or your clients can take the following measure to assess where you are in your own psychological journey related to aging. Next are a number of questions about aging. Use the following scale to indicate how much you agree or disagree with each of the items. Try to be as honest as possible when filling out this scale.

5 = Agree
4 = Slightly agree
3 = Neutral
2 = Slightly disagree
1 = Disagree

1. _____ I believe I am better now than I was 10 years ago.
2. _____ I am satisfied with my body.
3. _____ I am worried that I cannot learn new things.
4. _____ I feel as smart as I ever have.
5. _____ I am reasonably healthy.
6. _____ I believe I will be better in 10 years than I am now.
7. _____ I am fairly satisfied with the legacy I will leave behind.
8. _____ I wish I could live my youth over again.
9. _____ I think about dying regularly.
10. _____ I am satisfied with the work I do.

Scoring:

Now take a moment and add up your score. That is, simply tally the numbers and find a total score. However, and here is the tricky part, for item numbers 3, 8, and 9 you will need to "reverse" the score. That is, if you put a "1" you will need to transform it to a "5," a "2" would become a "4," and a "3" would just stay a three. So now, go ahead and find your total score. Here is how to interpret your score:

40–50 If you score in this range you seem to have some healthy attitudes about aging. You do not seem overly upset by the aging process and can see some redeeming value in it.

21–39 If you scored a 30, or very close to a 30, you are average. There are likely some aspects of aging that worry you and others you are comfortable with.

10–20 A score in this range indicates that you have some real concerns about aging and what it might bring for you.

Remember, these scores are benchmarks, and should be used only as very general indicators. If your score was lower than you hoped there is no cause for alarm; these are vague guidelines to give us a baseline reading, and you can take comfort in the fact that these scores can be raised. Regardless of your specific score, you will notice that there are some items related to physical health, some to a sense of "getting better or worse" over time, and some about focusing on the future versus on the past. In all likelihood, some of these are areas of strength for you or your clients while others are more troublesome. You can use these initial benchmark scores to open discussions, connecting them to issues that your clients bring to the table. For example, a client who wants to discuss "growing my business" might also be served by the insight that they generally believe they "are getting worse with age."

▶ **How to Make Mid-Life into an Opportunity**

I am often amazed by the playfulness, creativity, and resilience of children. My neighbor is an immigrant to the United States and, as a child, lived in the former Yugoslavia, growing up in the midst of the bloody war that raged for years in that place. His upbringing, naturally, was very different than my own. I can remember running through tall rows of corn on humid Midwestern nights. He can recall the sound of mortars on the front line, only miles from his house. I can remember my mother telling me to be home by dark. His mother sometimes cautioned him about snipers. When I first met my neighbor I could not imagine what it must have been like for him to grow up under such circumstances. I felt sorry for him, for the loss of his childhood. One day, when I mentioned this sentiment to him, he immediately corrected me. "But I did have a childhood," he told me, "I had a great childhood." Sure, he suffered without electricity sometimes, but he also sat on the porch with his friends and watched rockets hit the edge of town. He played in the ruins of bombed out buildings, he got to ride on a tank. The war, according to my neighbor, wasn't all about fighting every minute of every day. There were down periods, times of calm and—more important to a young boy—ample opportunity to explore the ruins around the town. Somehow, through some basic tenacity of the human spirit, my neighbor was able to turn the ugliest side of humanity into a playground. And—you can see where I am going with this—if he can do this with something as serious as "war," we can certainly do it with "middle age."

As coaches we can help our clients reframe common struggles as opportunities. I want to be clear, however, that I do not mean this in a naïve or unrealistic way. I am not of the mindset that every hardship is a "gift." I find it hard to believe that tough life experiences like dealing with cancer would be considered "the best thing that ever happened to me." I do, however, think that failure is a natural part of learning, that hardship can lead to resilience and growth, and that struggles generally can build character and meaning. Positive psychology is not about trying to convince clients that car accidents and lost jobs are really blessings in disguise. Rather, it is about looking at both sides of the issue. There are undeniable hardships associated with middle age, but it would be a mistake to reduce middle age only to these physical and psychological hurdles while overlooking all the blessing of mid-life. Because so much of coaching centers around workplace concerns and professional and financial goals and aspirations, I will center a large portion of the discussion of this chapter on these concerns.

What Have We Learned So Far?

1. The common cultural message tells us that middle age is the beginning of a long decline, both physical and mental. This is a fiction.

2. Middle age is a period of transition that often requires adjusting our sense of self and our expectancies for the future. There is, however, no need to adjust them downward. We can just as easily view our middle-aged selves as even better than we were in our 20s, and can believe that the future holds bright promise for us.

3. The truth is people at middle age have tremendous advantages over younger people. We are wiser, benefit from more life experience, typically have mastered more skills, are in a better position to teach and mentor others, are typically more financially secure, and hold positions at work and in the community that make us far more effective.

4. Middle age is an exciting time to think about legacies. Not because we fear death is just around the corner, but because we are—at last—in a position to create legacies (whether they be knowledge based, community impact, financial, etc.). These legacies are a unique way to imbue our lives with special meaning.

5. How we approach middle age—psychologically speaking—is a choice.

▶ Work at Mid-Life, or Has Anyone Seen My Passion?

One of the many things I love about coaches is that we come from so many different professional backgrounds. There are, of course, a few of us who went straight to coaching, but most of our ranks are filled with people who have jumped ship on a former profession. Remember when you were first starting out in your professional life? It doesn't matter if you were a grocery store checkout clerk, a bus driver, an apprentice lawyer, or a sales rep. Take a moment and think back to that time. Try to recall all that was good and not so good about it. The hours may have been long, your boss may have been a bully, or the pay may have been dreadful. But, chances are, there was also a sense of excitement about the work. A sense of learning new skills, "growing up," maybe even a sense of "going somewhere." I'll give you an even more concrete example of the type of thing I mean. Just the other day I asked my students at Portland State University about their career aspirations. They mentioned becoming counselors, owning their own businesses, becoming police officers, starting animal shelters, becoming researchers, and so forth. I then asked them *why* they wanted to be those things. That is, what values did they hold that made those jobs seem like a worthwhile way to spend the hours from 9 to 5 each day. As you might guess, their answers were highly idealistic. They said things like: I want to help people, I feel I can make a difference in the world, I want to make my community a better place, I feel strongly that I can help solve this pressing problem. None of them mentioned many of the very practical and highly positive aspects of day-to-day work: paychecks, the excitement of working on a new project, the rush of making a sale, or the deep sense of satisfaction that comes with learning a new skill. I found their idealism touching, and it reminded me of myself at their age.

Perhaps you see a bit of yourself in them as well. Perhaps when you were first starting out you looked forward to more than just a steady income. Maybe you thought about other values such as the respect of the community, providing for your family, creating a superior product, helping others, or gaining new skills. I'd be willing to bet that you experienced a palpable sense of excitement when you first entered the work world. My first job out of college was working with severely emotionally disturbed teenagers in a group home. There were times when they were truly violent: I was once kicked in the face, one of them tried to set another on fire, one of them tried to drink a bottle of bleach, a knife was pulled at one point. I made $9.07 an hour. Despite the tough work conditions and inadequate financial compensation, I loved it. I felt as if I had the opportunity to make a difference in the lives of these kids. I felt challenged. I felt like I was gaining skills and experience that would later help me get even better jobs or open further educational opportunities. Hopefully you can recall that same sense of enthusiasm from your own professional launching pad.

And then, for so many of us, somewhere along the way, that excitement seems to dull in its luster. For so many people that initial feeling of being a "rising star" changes into a sense of being a ho-hum dimly twinkling star. Those childhood dreams of being astronauts, professional baseball players, and movie stars end in the reality of positions as sales reps, structural engineers, and advertisers. As rewarding and realistic as these latter jobs can be, they can sometimes—especially mid-career—seem like life went horribly off-course. I spend a lot of my professional time as a coach and consultant dealing with mid-career professionals who suddenly "woke up" one day and realized that they had misplaced their passion. "I cannot understand it," I often hear. "I used to be so enthusiastic about work, but now it seems so dull." I also hear "I don't know if the job changed or if I changed, but one thing I am certain of is that I am not happy." This is a common phenomenon, and one to which people in middle age are particularly prone. Somewhere between "I want to help make the world a better place" and "What have I been doing with my life all these years," reality rained on the parade. Bills have to be paid, bosses are not always pleasant, businesses fail, careers change, co-workers are difficult, projects fall apart, and work stagnates. It is nobody's fault; work, like the weather, can just turn dreary.

The problem with losing your passion at work is obvious: The job isn't as fun or meaningful as it used to be. Energy sags, motivation lapses, quality plummets, general unhappiness sets in. But there are dangers that extend beyond personal malaise and lower productivity. When people lose their motivation on the job they often look for drastic change. They sometimes look to switch careers, which can be difficult and risky. A new career may mean loss of seniority, a return to school, lower pay, a geographic move, or the chance that the new job won't be any better. Disengaged employees can also bring their troubles home with them and marriages can suffer from it. Someone who doesn't feel like they do worthwhile work, who feels demoralized, can be depressed and difficult to live with. Their difficulties go deeper than just needing to be "cheered up." Disengaged workers can often feel angry, resentful, guilty, and despondent, and each of these emotions—in turn—can affect relationships outside of the office. And, perhaps worst of all, disengaged workers sometimes do nothing and are sentenced to a lifetime of work that—sadly—lacks purpose for them. They accept their lot in life—the commute, the cubicle, the copy machine—and resign themselves to redundancy, a lack of growth, and a lack of meaning.

The good news is that work can be fun, it can be invigorating, and it need not include a jump from one job to another. I would estimate the vast majority of the clients who come through my door—perhaps 75% of them—are mid-life, mid-career professionals who have lost their "oomph" and are considering a career switch. The idea of such a risky and ominous life decision is the only reason they haven't made the commitment. They nearly always have a "grass is greener" mentality, as if they are thinking, "If only I could get a new job with a better boss or a different project, then I would be happy." I nearly always caution them to take a look at themselves before making a drastic decision. Perhaps it isn't the overbearing supervisor that is the root of their problems. Perhaps the issue lies a bit closer to home. Maybe they have changed in some important way—their values, their view of the work, their expectations. I typically encourage—as a first step—that my clients look inward and examine what they can change within themselves to make their work more meaningful. If this process does not work, we always have the backdoor option of a new job. But before jumping ship, it makes sense to see if the boat can be salvaged! When I work with my clients there are several standard steps we can take to see if we can breathe new life into that old job, and I offer them to you here.

Take the dramatic example of my former client, Cliff. Cliff worked as a project manager for a software firm. More important, Cliff loathed his work. He dreaded dragging himself into the office every morning and he confided to me that he thought of it as "working in the mines." Cliff stated that he only stayed in the position because of the paycheck and because he was uncertain what else he might do. As you might expect, Cliff and I worked on an exit strategy. He wanted desperately to identify a new line of work and hunkered down to tolerate his current job in the meantime. And then one day Cliff had a heart attack. He sent me a message from the hospital telling me he was okay but that this event was a wake-up call. Naturally, I anticipated that the take-home message was "This workplace is toxic, and Cliff has to get out." I was shocked two weeks later to learn that Cliff was back at his desk. Rather than taking his health emergency as "the final straw," Cliff realized that his immediate problem was stress management. He wondered how he—rather than his job—could change to better tackle the world around him. It was a wake-up call for me as well: Clients do not necessarily need to "jump ship" on their hardships, even as tempting as this option sometimes is.

How Do You Feel about Your Work?

Each of us has a different relationship with his or her own job. Some folks drag themselves to the office on Monday morning and others can hardly tear themselves away from their desks on Friday evening. For people at the middle stage of life, and this usually means mid-career, there are often strong feelings about work. For some folks this stage is a professional highlight—they have more power and responsibility than ever before. Perhaps they have finally seen that start-up business take root and flourish. They feel effective, respected, and may enjoy some of the material rewards of their job. For many others, however, there is a sense of being lost. "How did I end up here?" these people ask themselves. Try taking the following survey to see how you relate to your work. You can also use an alternate form of this survey, the *Work-Life Questionnaire*,[3] found in the previous chapter. While the two assessments do not measure exactly the same things, there is some conceptual overlap between them.

Use the scale to indicate your agreement or disagreement with each statement. Try to be as honest as possible in your answering. Use the 1 to 5 scale to indicate your agreement with each of the following statements.

5 = Agree
4 = Slightly agree
3 = Neutral
2 = Slightly disagree
1 = Disagree

1. _____ I am satisfied with my job.

2. _____ I regularly learn something new at work.

3. _____ I feel my work contributes in some way to my community or to the world.

4. _____ I like my colleagues.

5. _____ There is someone at work who supports or encourages me.

6. _____ At work, I often have the opportunity to do what I do best.

7. _____ I look forward to going to work.

8. _____ I would recommend my line of work to a friend.

9. _____ I would like to stay in my current line of work.

10. _____ My work fulfills some of my personal values.

Now, simply tally your responses so that you end up with a final sore ranging from 10 to 50. There is no need to do any fancy reverse scoring. Simply add up all the numbers and there you have your total score. Use the following guide to help assess where you are in terms of your enthusiasm and engagement regarding your job.

40–50 If you scored in this range you likely find much about your job that is meaningful, likeable, and enjoyable.

21–39 This is the average range. Many people who score within this range have some complaints about work. Sometimes they feel disappointed with their jobs or just wish they could get more of a sense of purpose from work.

10–20 This is the lower range. Many people who score in this range are dissatisfied with their work. They often think about the weekend or other time away from the office, and wish they could find a more rewarding job.

■ Reconnecting with Work: Take Stock of Those Values

One of the potential pitfalls of middle age is a heightened awareness around a sense of meaning. At this stage of life, we want, according to the psychologist Erik Erikson, to be productive and generative.[4] Using yourself as a litmus test you can probably see this crop up in your own professional life. You probably want to help others, provide goods or services, make an impact on your community, and provide a comfortable existence for your family. Most of us also generally want to be successful, however it is we might define that term. Finally, we want to feel—where our jobs are concerned—worthwhile. No one wants to feel that their work is pointless or that their best attributes are being overlooked or misused. In this respect there is no difference between us and the students at the university who cling to high ideals. If your client has found that he is increasingly discouraged at work or has lost sight of the larger purpose in what he does, it is a perfect opportunity to take a step back and take stock of strengths and values. There is no need to rush to quit, complain all day, or suffer in silence. Why not use this as a wake-up call to reexamine where your client was—psychologically speaking—at the beginning of your career and where you are now.

Consider guiding your clients by asking questions such as: Do you remember how you ended up in your current line of work? Did you luck into it through a friend? Is it the subject you majored in at university? Did you follow in your father's footsteps? Was it a slow evolution from job to job? How did you arrive here? Try to recall what it was that led you to your current career. As a coach you can contrast this professional journey with a more internal process: "Now, try to remember what it was that attracted you to your current career." This is a very different notion altogether. Your client's friend, professor, or father may have landed him that first job, but what was it that made him accept the job? Consider questions such as these: What was it about the work that spoke to you? What excited you about the job? What did you expect to get out of the work? What were your career aspirations? What did you hope for? You may have your client reflect and write down a few of those core values by answering the following questions:

1. What was initially attractive about my job?
2. When I began working what did I expect or hope for out of my career?
3. What was exciting about my work when I first started out?
4. How are these seminal hopes and exciting job features similar to or different from my current work situation?

Often when I work with clients they are surprised by the answers to these questions. Either they had forgotten what they were initially so enthusiastic about, or surprised how these elements had disappeared from their work. I recently worked with a social worker from Chicago, for example, who entered the profession because she hoped to help poor people who were in crisis. Fifteen years later she was on the verge of quitting her job. Bureaucratic hassles, overwhelming caseloads, and a small salary had sapped all the excitement out of her work. When she reviewed the answers to the preceding questions she was surprised to recall the actual thrill of coming into the office. The million-dollar question for her, as it might be for you or for your clients, is this: How do you get that thrill back? For my social worker client we used three different steps: (a) we reminded her about her initial values, (b) we took a strengths approach to work, and (c) we created new values that fit with her new stage of life.

Three Steps to Finding Passion at Work:

1. Explore and identify values.
2. Identify and develop strengths.
3. Explore "fit" with who the client is at this stage of life.

■ Step One: The Ideals of Youth, or Revisiting Your Original Values

One of the things I envy most about the young is their idealism. I am not so cynical yet that I begrudge them their belief that the world can be a better place and that they can be instruments of that change. In fact, I think it can be healthy for people at every age to check in with their own youthful ideals. Too often at work we lose sight of the fact that it is our underlying values that are significant, not necessarily a paycheck. As in the case of the social worker I coached, she was so overwhelmed by her backlog of clients that she could hardly get a lunch break, let alone find the time to examine her underlying motives. But all too often it is exactly this type of time for reflection that is called for. When I asked her "When was the last time you felt like you really helped someone?" she nearly burst into tears. She had been so busy doing the work she had lost sight of the mission.

Let's conduct the same type of exercise here you might with a client: Take the time here to reflect on that original mission for yourself, the one that launched your career. What attracted you to coaching? Were you trying to help people? Beat the competition? Create a new product? Make money? Find a career that allowed you to work from home and with a flexible schedule? Now, let's look even deeper. Let's look at what I call the "line below the bottom line." What were the *values* that lay beneath these *motives*? Why would you want to help people? What do you believe leads you to want to beat the competition? What value is there in creating a new product? Go ahead and write down your mission, your value, someplace where you can refer to it or recall it easily. Perhaps tape it inside your desk drawer or carry it in your wallet. Whatever your idealistic value, try remembering it every time you walk into the office, every time you pick up the phone to chat with a client, and every time you do paperwork. Tell yourself, "This is what I am here for." Look for opportunities to fulfill your personal mission. This may not, by itself, be a magic pill that cures all the ills of your workplace complaints, but it has helped many people begin to feel reinvigorated.

When I was a little boy I liked to argue. I don't mean that I liked to talk back or that I was exceptionally naughty. I mean that I enjoyed the process of formulating a position and defending it, and of looking for ways to poke holes in the logic of others. I know, I probably don't sound like I was the most fun kid on the block to play with. Don't worry, I could ride a bike and do normal kid stuff as well. It's just that I was always pretty good at arguing. If I wanted to stay up past my bedtime I might come to my parents with a proposal: "I will give you three good reasons why I ought to have a one-time exception." As you might guess, from an early age people told me I should be a lawyer when I was finally at an age to enter the workforce. I seemed to have this trait—the ability to argue—and it seemed to fit hand in glove with the profession—courtroom litigation. Ultimately, I chose a different career path, but I have always thought about the idea that I was labeled with this particular trait when I was very young and, to this day, I believe it to be true about myself.

Your clients certainly have a similar experience in which their friends, teachers, or parents labeled them with some trait. Maybe they were the artistic kid, or the athlete, or the brains in the family, or the kid who seemed to be able to make friends with everyone. What most people don't realize is how culturally prescribed this notion is: that we have traits that are relatively immutable.[5] It is very Western—that is, typical of countries such as the United States, Canada, and the United Kingdom—to think of people in terms of constants. If a person is kind or courageous, we tend to think of him as kind and courageous across most, if not all, situations. We view the trait as living inside him, burning like an ember perhaps, ready to burst into flame when it is needed.

Not everyone thinks like this. Research from Eastern cultures, such as Japan, shows that people in those societies tend to put more emphasis on the power of the situation.[6] It is not necessarily that Sally is inherently courageous, they might think, but it is a given situation that makes her courageous. If you think about it, the Eastern view makes loads of sense: Even the people we perceive as being generous or forgiving are not *always* so. It is more of a propensity than an absolute. The difference between the Eastern and Western way of thinking about the self has some interesting and important implications. The Western view sees the "self" as relatively fixed, while the Eastern view tends to see the "self" as somewhat transitory and permeable. When I, as a Westerner, try to wrap my head around the Eastern way of thinking it actually scares me. I feel anchored and secure thinking of myself as fixed and as having immutable traits. To think that who I am might change from situation to situation makes me feel like an astronaut, floating free in space, and it is not entirely a pleasant sensation for me. I do not argue here that one view is superior to the other—they are simply the products of psychological geography. Instead, I want to point out how we might use the Eastern view to our advantage at work.

For the vast majority of us work is central to our identity. When we meet people for the first time we often ask them "What do you do?" The answer to this question betrays all kinds of information about skills, educational background, interests, economic class, and so forth. Because work takes up so much of our waking time, and because it provides us with so many of our goals and so much of our meaning, it only makes sense that it is central to our identities. The interesting notion, where middle age is concerned, is that it is centrally about a shift in identity. In Western cultures, where identity and traits are seen as relatively fixed, we often have a "crisis" during this time. Interestingly, anthropological research from India and Japan do not show evidence of "mid-life crises" in the Western sense. In these countries, people tend to view aging as part of a graduation of life stages, each with different status and responsibilities. That is, they give up a younger identity stage and trade it in for the new stage. In any case, there seems to be fewer crises associated with middle age in these places. Could it be that having a more fluid sense of identity could help us handle middle life transition more gracefully?

Possible Identities

One of the biggest challenges with growing older is that the realities—physical, mental, and social—of middle age are often not aligned with who we see ourselves as being. I can clearly remember the first time my wife referred to me as "a big guy." I thought she was joking. I'm not a big guy, I thought, I am a pretty lithe, pretty graceful guy. Impish and sprightly almost. And then I looked in the mirror, and it appeared that an ogre had eaten the sprite. It may be a defense mechanism, it may be a cultural phenomenon, and it may be our brains' laziness, but we are sometimes slow to update our identities. You will see this with your clients. Your clients develop a certain view of themselves and can—like the rest of us—be slow to update this picture to bring it in line with changing realities. The danger here is that pointing out discrepancies between an idealized sense of self and a more down-to-earth self can be quite unsettling for clients and the emotional upset can run counter to some of the goals of coaching. It takes a bit of mental gymnastics to come to terms with changes in our bodies, our social status, our cognitive functioning, and our values. Even so, these changes need not be for the worse.

Is Life Getting Better or Worse?

Try thinking about the person you are right now, at this stage of life. Consider every aspect of yourself. Do you have the tendency to see yourself as in decline or as getting better? Try taking the following survey to get a sense of which direction you see yourself traveling. As before, use the 1 to 5 scale to indicate your agreement with each item, and try to be as honest as possible in your responding.

5 = Agree
4 = Slightly agree
3 = Neutral
2 = Slightly disagree
1 = Disagree

1. _____ I enjoy more respect in my community than I did earlier in life.

2. _____ I feel more established than I did earlier in life.

3. _____ I am proud of my work accomplishments.

4. _____ I am proud of my family accomplishments.

5. _____ I am healthy.

6. _____ I am getting more attractive as I get older.

7. _____ I have more opportunities available to me these days.

8. _____ I feel I have mastered a skill or acquired important knowledge.

9. _____ I look forward to learning more in the future.

10. _____ I am smarter now than when I was younger.

> **40–50** This is the high range. People who score in this range are generally satisfied with their station in life. They view themselves as improving, and look forward to the future.
>
> **21–39** This is the middle range. People who score in this range typically see some gains associated with aging, but they might also have some complaints.
>
> **10–20** This is the lower range. People who score in this range typically think of the aging process as a decline.

As you look over your answers you might be surprised to see in how many ways middle age is associated with positive outcomes. Older people generally enjoy more respect, hold more positions of power, have more achievements at work and at home, and have acquired wisdom, skill, and knowledge. In fact, if there is one common complaint among the middle-aged, it is related to physical health. Interesting, isn't it, that small declines in our bodies can color our outlook on this stage of life that is, arguably, replete with benefits! Try thinking about the person you are, your identity, what makes you "you." How has this sense of self shifted from when you were younger? Is this shift generally for the better? Feel free to write down notes about your sense of self (and you can, of course, use this method with your clients as well):

1. Who am I?
2. How have I grown in the last decade?
3. To what extent would I want to trade places with "me" from 10 years ago?
4. How frequently do I spend time romanticizing my earlier days?
5. When I think about who I want to become, how close am I to that ideal relative to 10 years ago?

Possible Selves at Work

If work is so central to who we think we are, then part of getting new meaning out of work is testing the waters of who we could be.[7] This is especially relevant to clients who wrestle with career change, promotions, and other shifts in identity. Think about yourself, perhaps a year in the future, and everything has gone about as well as could be hoped (not perfectly but pretty well). You have generally gotten the things you want and generally behaved in the way you would prefer. What would that life look like? What would that person be like? How far away from being that idealized person are you? What is something small you can do to take a step toward that better life? This last question I think is especially important because it carries the implicit assumption that people can change in important ways. Although we all know the adage "you can't teach an old dog new tricks," we also all know this to be false. Just as Scrooge discovered generosity late in life, we can all think of folks who surprised us by making big life changes. The octogenarian who suddenly became a computer whiz, the guy with the hot temper who mellowed over time, the retiree who took up painting and became a master. People can change, and when they do it is typically a reflection of the way they see themselves, a change in their identity. You can play with your possible identities at work. Although you have a specific job title, you have flexibility in how you fulfill that role. If your client is a "shift manager," she could be a tyrant, a micromanager, a buddy, or absent. Each of these represents a different managerial style, and you have the freedom to redefine yourself in middle age to fit with your new values and the way you would like to work.

In the chapter on positive assessment I mentioned Amy Wrzesniewski's research on people's relation to their work.[8] This research on how people view their work shows that some folks are motivated by the prospect of advancement (promotions, pay raises, increased responsibility) while others are motivated by a sense that they are contributing something meaningful. The former are referred to as "career oriented," and the latter are thought of as having "callings." Interestingly, it doesn't matter if you are a bus driver or a corporate lawyer; you could have either of these orientations toward your work. Wrzesniewski and her colleagues were curious as to what the difference was between those who were in careers and those who were in callings. What they discovered was that those people who felt they were in a calling tended to engage in "job crafting." Job crafting just means doing small things, modifying your work to make it more rewarding. These people were still accomplishing their basic job descriptions, but they were also making little changes that made the job more enjoyable. They would, for example, change the amount or type of social interactions they had at work. Hairdressers are a perfect example of this. Technically, hairdressers are supposed to cut hair, and the business arrangement between hairdresser and client revolves solely around cutting hair. But, chances are, most hairdressers you have been to have been chatty, wanting to talk while they work. For hairdressers, getting to know their clients, hearing stories, dispensing advice, and other social interactions make the job feel more rewarding.

If you are looking for more meaning at work, and you are open to the possibility of change, try taking the "who/what/when/where" approach to crafting your job. With each of these questions, write down how you could make a small change that would make the work feel more engaging to you.

1. *Who:* How could I change my social interactions so that they are more rewarding? Who are my most rewarding interactions with these days? Are there particular times that lend themselves to rewarding interactions? Who am I not interacting with that I might like?

2. *What:* What are the tasks of my job that I like, and which don't I like? What are the ways I can increase the former and decrease the latter? How might I modify those less likeable tasks to make them more palatable? What is it I really like about the enjoyable tasks? How can I get more of that?

3. *When:* When I consider my workday, when is it that I do my best work? Am I best in the morning? Do I come alive in the afternoons? Is it when I am alone or when I am working in groups? How can I harness my best time to get the most done and set realistic expectations for myself?

4. *Where:* Think about the actual physical location of your job and workspace. How do you feel about your commute? How do you feel about the architecture and decor of your office? How do you feel about your desk, office, or space that you consider distinctly "yours"? What changes could you make so that your workspace was more pleasant or reflected you in a better way?

Again, thinking in terms of experimenting with possible selves, looking at ways to engage in job crafting, and considering the "who-what-when-why" of work are not magic pills that will transform your work life overnight. They are, however, potentially effective strategies that have worked with many people to help them feel more engaged at work.

The Specter of Death

It has long been part of the popular consciousness that turning 40 is mid-life, and that this means each day takes us further from birth and closer to death. Everyone knows stories of people who panic around this age, who desperately want to be young again. These are people who pick up dangerous thrill-seeking hobbies or start dating people half their age. The popular idea is that the physical signs of aging—those gray hairs, early wrinkles, and extra cellulite—send us into a kind of existential tail-spin. Next comes age spots, broken hips, and, let's be honest, death. Whole philosophies have been developed around people's natural fear of the inevitable, so we might as well address it here. Are middle-age transition problems just difficulties adjusting to a new sense of self? Are mid-life crises just the honest struggles with the hardships that are endemic to that period of life such as raising money for children's college tuition? Or, ultimately, is it the fear of death that really startles us in middle age? Is the time period a psychological wake-up call that forces us to reexamine the choices we have made, the life we have lived, and the contribution we hope to make to the world?

As it turns out, there is a fascinating body of research on precisely this issue. Psychologists are a curious bunch, and they like to leave no intellectual stone unturned, the fear of death among them. This particular field of study has the fanciful, if somewhat ominous, name "Terror Management Theory."[9] The premise goes something like this: Although none of us likes to spend even one second thinking about it, we all know that we will one day die. Occasionally, we are reminded of this fact, and in these cases we are motivated to think or act in a way that helps us find meaning in life. That makes sense doesn't it? In a variety of studies experimenters have found that people who are reminded of their own mortality are more likely to endorse comforting beliefs, such as the belief in an afterlife, and more extreme behaviors that will ensure their safety. As an example of the latter, researchers reminded study participants about their own mortality by having these subjects write short descriptions about death and dying. Based on this "priming" of death, the researchers found that participants' political views changed. They were, for example, more likely to favor conservative candidates and endorse stronger military interventions, regardless of their own expressed political preferences. In this case it appears that just reminding folks of an emotionally charged tragedy was enough to make them act (endorsing a candidate, in this example) in a way that helped them address the problem.[10]

An even more compelling piece of research by the same scientists comes from a study conducted on a city sidewalk in Boulder, Colorado.[11] Pedestrians were surveyed about various charities and about certain virtuous qualities that were important to them. Here's the catch: Some of the people were interviewed in front of a funeral home with a large sign out front and others were interviewed on the same street, but a couple of blocks away. By rights, there should be no real difference between these two groups. On average, they should show the same variation in answers. They were just a random group of people stopped at two different points on the sidewalk. But, in this case, those folks interviewed in front of the funeral home were more positive about charitable donations, said that kindness and generosity were more important to them, and were more likely to endorse the importance of spirituality. All of this just because of a subtle reminder of death.

Bringing Terror Management Theory into the idea of aging, it is easy to see why people might act out in extreme or defensive ways as they are reminded of their mortality. For some people, gray hair around the temples might be just the kick in the pants they need to donate money to charity—not just because it makes them feel good, but because it actually helps us psychologically to know that we can be good and make a positive difference. The defense mechanism at work here—if you want to call it that—is that we can take comfort in having lived a life well. For others, those same gray hairs might be a call-to-arms to try skydiving. For these people, their natural defense mechanism is to face their fear head on and show that although they might die someday, it isn't going to be *this* day. Nobody likes the physical declines that accompany age, and nobody particularly cares for the idea that our time in the world is finite. But what you do with this knowledge is a choice. You can try to block it out and ignore it (that's what humans do 99% of the time, and it helps us get through each day). Or you can use this knowledge as a chance to rise to the occasion, rise to the challenge of living a worthwhile life. Confronting declining health, physical ability, and limited time can be a motivational kick in the pants for clients to take action and begin crafting their legacies. I sometimes use such discussions to introduce writing a personal life mission statement or suggest that my clients post a mantra that can serve to motivate them each day. Past mantras include simple but powerful statements such as "It is never too late to start a project," "Each day is a gift," and "How will my actions today be remembered?" In every case the mantras are generated by my clients and are couched in language that they find personally resonant.

The Three Other Fears

One of the interesting aspects of the fear of our own mortality is that it brings up the subject of how we are oriented in time. Traditionally, people have assumed that problems associated with the transitions of middle age are the result of a future focus. The common idea is that people dwell on the future: the decline in health, the slowing down, and ultimately death. Further reflection will show you, however, that the major fear related to mid-life is not necessarily fear of the future. There are three other common fears, none of them future focused.

Three Common Fears

1. *Fear of losing a brighter past:* The past was good, and life diminishes as we age. Once vital we are now slow.
2. *Fear of having "mis-lived" the past:* A worry that our litany of mistakes defines us, defines our legacy, and is irreversible.
3. *Fear of accepting the present:* The courage it takes to accept our limitations, mistakes, and the ways we have changed.

First, there is a fear related to the past. I call this the "fear of losing the past." By this I mean the fear of losing the person we used to be. If we once were active and vital and hopeful and fun, it can sometimes be tough to look in the mirror of middle age and see the changes that have occurred. Nobody wants to feel like the fun and vitality has been sucked out of them. One of the major alarming aspects of growing older is that we do not want to lose those great youthful qualities. There is a tendency to cling desperately to any chance of seeing ourselves as spontaneous, energetic, or any of the other traits we typically associate with youth. It may be helpful to keep in mind the fact that you likely have not lost many of these qualities. The surface of your life may have changed—you may not go out and see live music much any more or drink with your buddies until 2 A.M., but you probably have many of the same core characteristics. If you were a fun playful person at 20, you likely still are at 45, although how this trait manifests may have changed. Take the time to catalog the things you liked about yourself when you were younger, and see how many of those qualities you still have. Try not to focus on the surface-level details such as what time you went to bed or whether you liked spicy food. Instead, think about those core characteristics—your talents, strengths, skills, and virtues. In all likelihood, you are more similar to that person from the past than you give yourself credit for.

The second fear is also related to a focus on the past. I call this fear "the fear of having lived the past wrong." There are a number of ways this particular concern rears its ugly head. Many of us harbor regrets over poor decisions or missed opportunities. Others feel we have missed the boat on our potential. If our teens and twenties are characterized by hopes, dreams, and potential, then our thirties, forties, fifties, and beyond must contend with the realization of those hopes and the fulfillment of that potential. If you wanted to write a novel when you were 25 years old, chances are there seemed like there was plenty of time to do so, but at age 40 you may have to face up to the fact that this dream has gone too long on the back burner of life. If, at age 19, you wanted to marry Mister Right and start a loving family, you might, at age 39, have to face up to the fact that you divorced Mister Right five years ago. The mistakes and missed opportunities of the past weigh on everyone, and they have a way of coming into sharp focus as we hit middle age. Once again, how we deal with our past is largely a matter of choice. We can dwell on our mistakes, beat ourselves up for poor decisions, and lament not getting to that dream novel, or we can learn and move on. Part of failure, disappointment, and mistakes is that they are a necessary part of maturing, gaining wisdom, and—ultimately—being able to live a more effective life. Nobody is perfect, and for each of us, our trials, troubles, and failures were important chapters in our lives, one imbued with meaning and learning. For people who fear they lived the past wrong because they made poor choices, middle age is the ideal place to apply those lessons and start living the present right. For people who fear they lived the past wrong because they never fulfilled their dreams, or put their true passions on the shelf for years, middle age is a great opportunity to fulfill those dreams. One of the hallmark features of middle age is a sense of urgency, and you can harness this urgency where your dreams are concerned: Use this urgency to motivate yourself to start that charity, write that novel, or take that dream vacation!

The final fear is related to a focus on the present. I call this the "fear of accepting the present." By this I mean the anxiety we all feel in accepting our limitations and the difficulties in forming an honest accurate self-appraisal. Even smart, talented people make mistakes, but it can be hard to admit them. Accepting setbacks and failures can be instrumental in moving past them, especially if they can be used to learn important life lessons. But the negatives are really only half the picture. Many people also have trouble accepting the positive present. I have worked, for example, with several clients whose anxiety was raised by a promotion at work. The freedom and responsibility they were handed led directly to stress, and often to a feeling of "imposter syndrome." Coming to terms with one's ability to handle responsibility can be every bit as challenging as accepting personal limitations. As a coach, you can facilitate the process of self-acceptance through the use of honest feedback, championing, acknowledgment, and reframing.

The Three Fears and Your Client

Fear of losing the past: Listen carefully for stories and language that seem to romanticize the past. Gauge the motivational consequences of feeling that the best life has already been lived. Try shifting the focus to growth, advancement, and potential.

Fear of having mis-lived the past: Listen for signs of your client being mired in past mistakes. This can prevent people from taking appropriate risks and promote a self-critical attitude that can interfere with performance. In some cases therapy might be indicated, but in many cases an acknowledgment that mistakes are both inescapable and important to growth can be helpful.

Fear of accepting the present: People have a natural tendency to believe in their own ability to control outcomes. Because of this they sometimes have a hard time coping with setbacks or successes. Try to coach them through these periods by helping them understand that setbacks and successes are part of life, and not the whole of life.

In many ways this chapter is quite different from the others. Instead of presenting a broad topic such as happiness or strengths and discussing the research and coaching relevant to the application of these topics, I have chosen to discuss a more philosophical, more psychological topic that affects us all. I recognize that both stylistically and contentwise this chapter has a different tone from the others, and I make no apology for that. Whether your clients are entrepreneurs, executives, or managers at nonprofit organizations, they are likely to wrestle with some of the issues presented in the chapter. In my own coaching practice I have seen these basic issues present themselves time and again, even if they were not the main thrust of the coaching agenda. It is my hope that articulating some of these issues and providing a brief overview of research and a few suggestions for intervention will be as helpful to your clients as they have been to mine.

▶ Further Reading

Ibarra, H. (2003). *Working identity: Unconventional strategies for reinventing your career.* Cambridge, MA: Harvard Business School Press.

Shweder, R. (1998). *Welcome to middle age! And other cultural fictions.* University of Chicago Press.

CHAPTER EIGHT

The Practice of Positive Psychology Coaching

Up to this point I have talked about the tools of positive psychology coaching—the assessments, the underlying research, questions, and activities that might be used with clients. But positive psychology coaching is also a professional endeavor, not simply a toolbox. This means, as I mentioned way back in Chapter 1, that the practice of positive psychology coaching needs to be discussed in terms of issues like ethics, credentialing, continuing education, and setting up client expectations and measuring satisfaction. In this final chapter I would like to shift away from the nuts and bolts of coaching technique and broaden the focus to coaching as a professional endeavor.

If you are, like me, the proprietor of a private or group coaching practice, you have likely fielded countless questions from prospective clients such as "What is coaching?" "How is coaching different from therapy?" and "Does coaching work?" One of the most common queries I receive relates specifically to positive psychology coaching. Often, I come across people who have been coach shopping, and when they land at my metaphorical doorstep they all want to know the same thing: "How does positive psychology coaching look different than any other type of coaching?" This is a wonderful question, and I am thrilled to receive it. In part, I like hearing it because it forces me to articulate an answer. I believe that clients are pretty sophisticated, and lame responses like "positive psychology is based on science" or "positive psychology coaching focuses on the positive" just do not cut it with the discerning public. They want more, and—frankly—they deserve better.

Positive psychology coaching looks like other forms of coaching in a great many ways. Both are co-created relationships. Both assume that clients are functional and resourceful. Both are professional relationships that require attention to contracts, fees, and ethical behavior. And both draw heavily from the same toolbox, including asking open-ended questions, the use of acknowledgment, intruding, asking permission, championing, tracking client energy, reframing, and creating structures for accountability.[1] I think these tools are the basic building blocks of any good coaching practice—including a positive psychology coaching practice—and are amazingly effective when artfully applied. In fact, I am so enchanted with the artfulness and effectiveness of traditional coaching, such that it can be defined, that I do not make any claims about positive psychology coaching being better than other forms of coaching. I am not in a contest with other coaches, have no personal axe to grind about the rightness of my own method, and am not threatened by the clever interventions of other forms of coaching.

Positive psychology coaching practices have unique features as well. By its very definition these coaching practices are (or should be) deeply rooted in the science of positive psychology. This means that the knowledge base underlying the coaching is dynamic and that coaches are required to be active consumers of research to continually update their interventions and approaches. You may have noticed that I have resisted creating a model for positive psychology coaching even as a pioneer in the field. While I believe models are useful pieces of shorthand with which to communicate complex ideas, I also think they have a few downsides. There is, for example, a temptation to believe that a model is, itself, the truth. This makes it difficult to update and revise the model, to dispense with the model, and to modify the model so that it fits with other models. Because we are so early in our professional life, positive psychologists are not ready to create comprehensive models of how flourishing happens, how change works, and how strengths relate to weaknesses. To be sure, we know much about these things. But the ancient astronomers knew much about the stars without having fully realized theories of gravity, relativity, or black holes. Similarly, I think positive psychology coaching is best framed as having basic tenets, rather than a complex functional model of its inner workings:

1. Humans have an innate drive to grow, change, and overcome.

2. Focusing on strengths is as powerful, or more powerful, than focusing on weaknesses to achieve success.

3. Positivity—whether in the form of emotion or hope—is a powerful resource for facilitating change and achieving success.

4. Attention must be paid to both positive and negative aspects of life in order to address the complete client.

5. Scientifically derived knowledge and assessments give us unique ways of understanding clients and coaching.

Positive psychology coaching differs, if only subtly, from other forms of coaching in its focus on strengths. Without question seasoned coaches of all orientations focus on personal assets, talents, and other sources of success. But positive psychology offers a specific and sophisticated means for doing so that includes empirically validated assessments, theory about the origins and benefits of strengths use, and stratagems and language for identifying, developing, and employing strengths. So, to those prospective clients who ask about the unique features of positive psychology coaching, this is one of the first places I start. I say, "If you coach with me, or someone who uses my approach, you can expect to use a formal assessment of strengths, and for the theme of strengths use and development to crop up in our conversations." The other distinctive feature of positive psychology coaching is attention to positive affect. To be sure, many coaches track client energy, try to keep sessions light, and recognize that good moods facilitate forward progress. Positive psychology does the same, but with scientifically informed twists.[2] Researchers know a bit about the specific types of benefits of positive emotion, the limits of positive emotion and the complex relation of positive emotion to goals and motivation. These nuanced topics are brought to bear on positive psychology coaching sessions when and where such things are appropriate. In the end, positive psychology coaching is a set of tools and skills based in an empirical body of knowledge that can constitute its own distinctive brand of coaching or be used as an adjunct to existing practices.

▶ How to Talk about a PPC Practice

A simple tour around the Internet will reveal that there are a number of people who hang their shingles and advertise as being positive psychology coaches. It should come as no surprise that there is an enormous range of training and quality represented among this group. Some of these folks have certificates gained through coursework, some have doctorate degrees but no coach training, some are certified coaches. Savvy clients will be able to ask smart questions about the credentials of coaches including:

1. How long have you been practicing?
2. What type of coach training do you have?
3. What type of positive psychology training do you have?
4. What types of assessments do you use?

But positive psychology coaches should be equally prepared to articulate the specific nature of their services. In every introductory session I conduct with a client I outline the difference between coaching and therapy, between coaching and positive psychology coaching, and what they can expect from coaching with me. Specifically, I talk about positive psychology as a tool and not as an outcome. There are those who advertise as "happiness coaches" with the implicit (or explicit) promise to clients of being happy. I am somewhat skeptical of this approach. While I would stop well short of calling these people charlatans, I do find an advertised promise of happiness to be problematic for several reasons. First, at least some of happiness happens from within. Whether it is genetically determined or a state of mind, there are limits to how much happiness can be facilitated. Second, happiness is not something we can deliver on an ongoing basis. People adapt to circumstances and occasionally feel upset, frustrated, angry or sad, and I believe we should feel these emotions; they are functional, and the promise of enduring happiness is unrealistic at best, and irresponsible at worst. Third, promising happiness presents—to my mind— interesting ethical implications for coaching. Just consider these two examples of coaching practice, the first of which comes from the ICF ethical guidelines:[3]

1. I will not knowingly make any public statement that is untrue or misleading about what I offer as a coach, or make false claims in any written documents relating to the coaching profession or my credentials or the ICF.

Within the context of happiness coaching the best an ethical coach can do is promise to work toward happiness, to help educate about research on happiness within the limits of his or her expertise, or to employ techniques that will temporarily boost mood. Interestingly, this is no different from virtually every other form of coaching—the product of which is almost always more enthusiasm, a feeling of progress and optimism, satisfaction, and other happiness-related outcomes. Similarly, the idea of happiness coaching has interesting implications for commonly accepted standards of practice, such as those outlined by *Co-Active Coaching* pioneer Laura Whitworth and her colleagues:[5]

2. The agenda comes from the client.

The idea that the coach provides the ultimate framework for assessing success in the relationship—the delivery from happiness—risks stepping on the toes of clients whose agendas might include making more money, getting a promotion, recording an album, or exercising three times a week. I suppose it could be argued that the clients who hire such coaches know what they are getting into, and might even want increased happiness as their primary goal. Even so, it lacks nuance. It is like a personal trainer at a gym promising to make someone healthy or to make them physically fit. I believe what we can responsibly offer is support, encouragement, and accountability; we might even reasonably be able to promise progress, but cannot ensure the final product.

Returning to the idea that positive psychology is a tool and not an outcome, I believe the most responsible way of talking about positive psychology coaching is in these terms. Telling prospective clients that you will be working with them on traditional issues of their choice—skills building, work-life balance, developing a sense of meaning, completing a project—is an important part of honestly framing your services. To this you can reasonably add the idea that it is through positive psychology-influenced tools and interventions that you hope to work on these issues. For instance, I often tell clients, "What you choose to talk about and work on is entirely up to you. I am here to support you in getting where you want to go. What makes my approach to coaching somewhat distinct is that I draw heavily upon scientific research to inform my thinking about human nature, emotion, motivation, and other concerns that might tangentially relate to our work together. In addition, I sometimes talk about strengths or happiness—both positive psychology topics—as a means of facilitating forward momentum. It is not my mission to make you happy. Instead, it is my job to help you with the issues you care about, and it is possible that happiness will be a natural by-product of any progress we make."

▶ Certification

This brings me back, one final and brief time, to the idea of certification for positive psychology coaching. I believe it is in the best interests of both positive psychology and coaching for professionals to be credentialed in positive psychology coaching. To some extent ICF certification protects clients and establishes standards for practice. Unfortunately, ICF standards are neither universally recognized nor adopted. I am not so presumptive as to think that a positive psychology coaching credential would fare better. I do, however, think that a standardized positive psychology coaching credential would offer additional protection for clients who gravitate toward the life-coaching end of the professional spectrum.

Certification in positive psychology coaching must meet the twin benchmarks of coaching competency and positive psychology competency. It is possible, for example, that an ICF certified coach would know next to nothing about positive psychology or that a graduate of a master's in applied positive psychology program would not have specific coach training. My strong recommendation for certification in positive psychology coaching is as follows:

1. The portfolio approach

   Just as the ICF accepts portfolios from people who have received training at multiple programs, I believe that positive psychology coaching certification must, in its preliminary stage, accept that there is no unified training program for professionals. As such, candidates for certification would need to provide evidence that they have received adequate coach training, such as a certificate or degree from a recognized training institution. In addition, they would have to provide evidence that they have training specific to positive psychology, such as a certificate or degree from the University of Pennsylvania, the University of East London, the Centre for Applied Positive Psychology, or other reputable institutions.

2. All-in-one training

   As positive psychology and coaching become better integrated and as institutions become better at delivering both basic coaching skills and expert knowledge in positive psychology, a certificate from a single learning institution should suffice for credentialing.

The question remains: Who would oversee and regulate this credentialing process? To whom would applications for credentialing be submitted, and who would endorse these credentials? The natural answer is that the best entities to promote these types of policies already exist. They are the professional bodies that form the governing structure for coaching. The International Coach Federation is a natural candidate, but it is not the single authoritative world body for coaching. The Special Group on Coaching of the British Psychological Society is another likely candidate.[5] It could be that universities serve as a third form of credentialing body, since this is already part of their existing mission. Ultimately, a blue ribbon panel of experts should be convened to discuss these issues. Until progress toward credentialing is made, positive psychology coaching will remain a "buyer beware" market.

▶ How to Prepare for a PPC Session

One other interesting aspect of the actual practice of positive psychology coaching remains to be discussed: how the coach actually approaches and prepares for a session. All coaches have their own pet practices and rituals for approaching a coaching session. Some review the previous week's notes, others take a couple of minutes to meditate and clear their own worries and problems, and still others launch right in with little preparation. Positive psychology coaching is one of those instances in which the medicine is good for the doctor also. Just as we encourage our clients to take stock of their strengths, be mindful, promote hope, and increase joy, these are also strategies that can help us prepare for and engage in sessions with our clients. For example, before every session I take a couple of minutes to review my client's strengths. This helps me refresh my knowledge of their personal psychological assets. It also helps remind me of what I like about my client and to be particularly favorably predisposed toward him or her. Just as a person can look at a mission statement to remind herself of the meaning behind her work, I look at strengths lists to remember what gets me so excited about working with individuals. I feel roused by the sense that my clients have readily identifiable strengths. I recommend that you also take a few minutes to mentally prepare for upcoming sessions as a way of focusing yourself on the impending work and making that focus positive.

Take the clever example of my friend and colleague Sunny Kotecha, from Silver Lining Coaching.[6] Like most coaches Sunny spends a few minutes before each session immersing herself in client notes. It helps her remember the specific details of the earlier conversation and, more importantly, reminds her of action points that might need follow-up. This is pretty standard fare, but Sunny quickly shifts into positive psychology territory once the session begins. She recently told me, "I begin each session with a positive highlight from the past week and have 2 minutes reflection after this, to clarify and integrate in the client's mind what they want to get out of this session." Even coaches who are not specifically oriented in positive psychology might engage in similar activities, but I think it is worth noting that this is, fundamentally, a positive thing to do and one with positive psychological consequences specifically. Sunny also comes prepared to break client negative states by having them move around or play with Legos or Silly Putty. Once again, this is an example of novel, humorous, and fun interventions designed to promote positivity.

Sunny's example is illustrative of a larger issue in positive psychology coaching: creating structures for positivity. To the extent that you, the coach, can design a positive architecture for the coaching session you will be better able to promote a positive mood and harness the many benefits of happiness. Here is an incomplete list of the types of activities you might consider. Note that these are not just interventions to be tried in the moment; they require advanced planning and preparation or, at times, advanced discussion with clients.

1. Keep a stash of small gifts to give clients.

2. Keep a record of client successes, strengths, and learning moments. More importantly, keep it in bullet-point format so that it can be easily shared when the moment calls.

3. Create a culture in which humor and silliness are appropriate. While I can be very serious with clients, they also know that they can expect occasional joking and silliness from me, when circumstances call for such things.

4. Take a break. Many people assume that a coaching call or in-person session has to be a continuous event because that is how virtually all of our professional relationships are structured. What would happen if you designed sessions with an escape hatch or other 10-minute break in the middle? Would it disrupt forward momentum? How might you best use the break?

▶ The Future

In the end, the future of positive psychology coaching is, I believe, bright. The field of positive psychology itself is growing. There are more conferences, more publications, more learning programs, and more people interested in the field than ever before. The momentum is clearly on the upswing, and this bodes well for positive psychology coaches. This means that there will be a larger body of research and theoretical knowledge upon which to draw for interventions and assessments. It means that there will be more popular media articles that will put your practice in an attractive light. It means that there will be increasing numbers of potential clients who will turn to this field for answers and, ultimately, for coaching. In addition, coaching itself is on the rise. Increasing professionalization is helping people take coaching more seriously as an effective helping profession. Indeed, even the growing numbers of coaches serve our collective interest; instead of being our professional competition, the people joining our ranks act as marketers. They explain our services and reach more people with the promise of coaching than any of us could individually.

All that said, we have not yet fully arrived. Positive psychology coaching, like the science it is based on, is a dynamic, evolving organism. Our knowledge, interventions, marketing, and services will all become better and more sophisticated as time goes on. In 2007 my colleague Ben Dean and I wrote an introductory book to the field: *Positive Psychology Coaching: Putting the science of happiness to work for your clients.*[7] The book, as I mentioned in Chapter 1, was largely an overview of the exciting new field of positive psychology. It presented the latest findings, made a few preliminary suggestions for coaches, and discussed a bit about professional service and ethics. Fast forward three years and we have come a long way. This volume, I hope you will agree, contains a much broader and more contemporary range of research and theory and assessment. More importantly, I have taken more initiative to suggest specific ways in which this knowledge and these tools might be effectively used by coaches. The past three years have seen a marked growth in our ability to actually apply positive psychology to coaching. For all these gains there are more on the horizon. If I were to write a book in three years' time, I would hope to be able to report on the gains in credentialing, innovative new uses of positive technology, exciting new studies, and other advances in positive psychology. Fortunately, we don't have to wait to enjoy the fruits of progress. There is much contained between the covers of this book that you can use today, right now, in your own life and in your own coaching practice. You get to be a pioneer, testing and trying a robust new set of tools and knowledge even as you get to hold out for an even brighter professional future.

Endnotes

▶ Chapter One Notes

1. Biswas-Diener, R., & Dean, B. (2007). *Positive psychology coaching: Putting the science of happiness to work for your clients*. Hoboken, NJ: John & Wiley Sons.

2. Haidt, J. (2003). Elevation and the positive psychology of morality. In C. L. M. Keyes & J. Haidt (Eds.), *Flourishing: Positive psychology and the life well-lived* (pp. 275–289). Washington, DC: American Psychological Association.

3. Biswas-Diener, R. (2010, February). Coaching and positive psychology. *Choice*, 7(4).

4. Bryant, F. (2005). Using the past to enhance the present: Boosting happiness through positive reminiscence. *Journal of Happiness Studies, 6*(3), 227–260.

5. Gilbert, D. (2007). *Stumbling on happiness*. Toronto: Random House of Canada.

6. Oishi, S., Diener, E., & Lucas, R. (2007). The optimum level of well-being: Can people be too happy? *Perspectives on Psychological Science, 2*(4), 346–360.

7. Oettingten, G., & Stephens, E. (2009). Fantasies and motivationally intelligent goal setting. In G. Moskowitz, & H. Grant (Eds.), *The psychology of goals* (pp. 153–178). New York: Guilford Press.

8. Linley, A. (2008). *Average to A+: Realising strengths in yourself and others*. Coventry, UK: CAPP Press.

9. Grant, A., Curtayne, L., & Burton, G. (2009). Executive coaching enhances goal attainment, resilience and workplace well-being: A randomised controlled study. *Journal of Positive Psychology, 4*(5), 396–407.

10. Diener, E., & Biswas-Diener, R. (2002). Will money increase subjective well-being? A literature review and guide to needed research. *Social Indicators Research, 57*, 119–169.

11. Easterlin, R. A. (1974). Does economic growth improve the human lot? In Paul A. David & Melvin W. Reder (Eds.), *Nations and households in economic growth: Essays in honor of Moses Abramovitz*. New York: Academic Press.

12. Veenhoven, R., & Hagerty, M. (2006). Rising happiness in nations 1946–2004: A reply to Easterlin. *Social Indicators Research, 79*(3), 421–436.

13. Stevenson, B., & Wolfers, J. (2008). *Economic growth and subjective well-being: reassessing the Easterlin paradox* (NBER Working Papers 14282). Cambridge, MA: National Bureau of Economic Research, Inc.

14. Diener, E., & Kahneman, D. (2009). The Easterlin paradox explained. Social Indicators Network News (SINET). Blacksburg, VA: International Society for Quality-of-Life Studies.

15. Diener, E., Emmons, R. A., Larsen, R. J., & Griffin, S. (1985). The satisfaction with life scale. *Journal of Personality Assessment, 49*, 71–75.

16. Pavot, W., & Diener, E. (1993). Review of the satisfaction with life scale. *Psychological Assessment, 5,* 164–172.

17. Whitworth, L. (2007). *Co-active coaching: New skills for coaching people toward success in work and life.* Mountain View, CA: Davis-Black.

▶ Chapter Two Notes

1. Drucker, P. F. (2002). *The effective executive.* New York: HarperCollins.

2. Cameron, K. S., Dutton, J. E., & Quinn, R. E. (2003). *Positive organizational scholarship: Foundations of a new discipline.* San Francisco: Berrett-Koehler.

3. Linley, A. (2008). *Average to A+: Realizing strengths in yourself and others.* Conventry, UK: CAPP Press.

4. Biswas-Diener, R. (2010). *The 11th hour: How working under pressure can be a strength.* Retrieved from http://www.oprah.com/spirit/Working-Under-Pressure-Can-Be-a-Strength-Robert-Biswas-Diener.

5. Linley, A. (2008). *Average to A+: Realising strengths in yourself and others.* Conventry, UK: CAPP Press.

6. Linley, A., Willars, J., Stairs, M., Page, N., & Biswas-Diener, R. (2010). *The strengths book: What you can do, love to do, and find it hard to do—and why it matters.* Coventry, UK: CAPP Press.

7. Jones, E., Rock, L., Shaver, K., Goethals, G., & Ward, L. (1968). Pattern of performance and ability attribution: An unexpected primacy effect. *Journal of Personality & Social Psychology, 10,* 317–340.

8. Biswas-Diener, R., & Garcea, N. (2009). Strengths-based performance management. Human Capital Review. Johannesburg, South Africa: Knowledge Resources.

9. Seligman, M. (2004). *Authentic happiness.* New York: Simon & Schuster Adult Publishing Group.

10. Seligman, M., Steen, T., Park, N., & Peterson, C. (2005). Positive psychology progress: Empirical validation of interventions. *American Psychologist, 60*(5), 410–421.

11. Ibid.

12. Arakawa, D., & Greenburg, M. (2007). Optimistic managers and their influence on productivity and employee engagement in a technology organization: Implications for coaching psychologists. *International Coaching Psychology Review, 2,* 78–89.

13. Wood, A. M., Maltby, J., Gillett, R., Linley, A., & Joseph, S. (2008). The role of gratitude in the development of social support, stress, and depression: Two longitudinal studies. *Journal of Research in Personality, 4,* 854–871.

14. Kashdan, T. B., Julian, T., Merritt, K., & Uswatte, G. (2006). Social anxiety and posttraumatic stress in combat veterans: Relations to well-being and character strengths. *Behaviour Research and Therapy, 44,* 561–583.

15. Peterson, C., Park, N., & Seligman, M. (2006). Greater strengths of character and recovery from illness. *Journal of Positive Psychology, 1*(1), 17–26.

16. Cameron, K. S., Dutton, J. E., & Quinn, R. E. (Eds.). (2003). *Positive organizational scholarship: Foundations of a new discipline.* San Francisco: Berrett-Koehler.

17. Seligman, M., Rashid, T., & Parks, A. (2006). Positive psychotherapy. *American Psychologist, 61*(8), 774–788.

18. Rath, T., & Clifton, D. O. (2004). *How full is your bucket?* Washington, DC: Gallup Press.

19. Linley, A., Willars, J., Stairs, M., Page, N., & Biswas-Diener, R. (2010). *The strengths book: What you can do, love to do, and find it hard to do—and why it matters.* Coventry, UK: CAPP Press.

20. Centre for Applied Positive Psychology (CAPP). Internal data.

21. Cameron, K. S., Dutton, J. E., & Quinn, R. E. (Eds.). (2003). *Positive organizational scholarship: Foundations of a new discipline.* San Francisco: Berrett-Koehler.

22. Buckingham, M., & Clifton, D. (2001). *Now discover your strengths.* New York: Simon & Schuster Adult Publishing Group.

▶ Chapter Three Notes

1. Lyubomirsky, S., King, L., & Diener, E. (2005). The benefits of frequent positive affect: Does happiness lead to success? *Psychological Bulletin, 131,* 803–855.

2. Diener, E., & Biswas-Diener, R. (2008). *Happiness: Unlocking the mysteries of psychological wealth.* Malden, MA: Wiley/Blackwell.

3. Isen, A., & Levin, P. (1972). The effect of feeling good on helping: Cookies and kindness. *Journal of Personality and Social Psychology, 17,* 107–112.

4. Isen, A., Daubman, K., & Nowicki, G. (1987). Positive affect facilitates creative problem solving. *Journal of Personality and Social Psychology, 21,* 384–388.

5. Fredrickson, B. (2001). The role of positive emotions in positive psychology: The Broaden and Build Theory of positive emotions. *American Psychologist, 56,* 218–226.

6. Lyubomirsky, S., King, L., & Diener, E. (2005). The benefits of frequent positive affect: Does happiness lead to success? *Psychological Bulletin, 131,* 803–855.

7. Fredrickson, B. L., & Levenson, R. W. (1998). Positive emotions speed recovery from the cardiovascular sequelae of negative emotions. *Cognition and Emotion, 12,* 191–220.

8. Fredrickson, B. L., Cohn, M. A., Coffey, K. A., Pek, J., & Finkel, S. M. Open hearts build lives: Positive emotions, induced through loving-kindness meditation, build consequential personal resources. *Journal of Personality and Social Psychology, 95,* 1045–1062.

9. Fredrickson, B., & Joiner, T. (2002). Positive emotions trigger upward spirals toward emotional well-being. *Psychological Science, 13,* 172–175. See also Burns, A. B., Brown, J. S., Sachs-Ericsson, N., Plant, E. A., Curtis, J. T., Fredrickson, B. L., & Joiner, T. E. (2008). Upward spirals of positive emotion and coping: Replication, extension, and initial exploration of neurochemical substrates. *Personality and Individuals Differences, 44,* 360–370.

10. Lyubomirsky, S., King, L., & Diener, E. (2005). The benefits of frequent positive affect: Does happiness lead to success? *Psychological Bulletin, 131,* 803–855.

11. Sander, T. (in press). Positive technology. In R. Biswas-Diener (Ed.), *Positive Psychology as Social Change* (in press). Dordrecht, Netherlands: Springer.

12. Seligman, M., Steen, T., Park, N., & Peterson, C. (2005). Positive psychology progress: Empirical validation of interventions. *American Psychologist, 60,* 410–421.

See also Emmons, R. A., & McCullough, M. E. (2003). Counting blessings versus burdens: Experimental studies of gratitude and subjective well-being in daily life. *Journal of Personality and Social Psychology, 84,* 377–389.

13. Lyubomirsky, S. (2008). *The how of happiness.* New York: Penguin.

14. Rath, T., & Clifton, D. (2004). *How full is your bucket? Positive strategies for work and life.* New York: Gallup Press.

15. King, L. (2001). The health benefits of writing about life goals. *Personality and Social Psychology Bulletin, 27,* 798–807.

16. Boyatzis, R. (2006). An overview of intentional change from a complexity perspective. *Journal of Management Development, 25,* 607–623.

17. Boyatzis, R., & Akrivou, K. (2006). The ideal self as the driver of change. *Journal of Management Development, 25,* 624–642.

18. For an overview of cognitive distortions about the self see David, D., Lynn, S., & Ellis, A. (Eds.). (2010). *Rational and irrational beliefs: Research, theory and clinical practice.* Oxford: Oxford University Press.

19. Boyatzis, R. (2006). An overview of intentional change from a complexity perspective. *Journal of Management Development, 25,* 607–623.

20. Boyatzis, R. (2008). Leadership development from a complexity perspective. *Consulting Psychology Journal: Practice and Research, 60,* 298–313.

21. Cooperrider, D., Whitney, D., Stavros, J., & Frey, R. (2008). *Appreciative inquiry handbook: For leaders of change.* San Francisco: Berrett-Koehler

22. The reflected best self exercise. You can purchase the exercise online: http://www .bus.umich.edu/Positive/POS-Teaching-and-Learning/ReflectedBestSelfExercise .htm.

23. No author. (2008). *2008 Zappos Culture Book.* Available at: http://www.zappos .com.

24. Oishi, S., Diener, E., & Lucas, R. E. (2007). Optimal level of well-being: Can people be too happy? *Perspectives on Psychological Science, 2,* 346–360.

25. Warr, P. (1999). Well-being and the workplace. In D. Kahneman, E. Diener, & N. Schwarz (Eds.), *Well-being: The foundations of hedonic psychology* (pp. 392–412). New York: Russell Sage Foundation.

26. Gostick, A., & Christopher, S. (2008). *The levity effect.* Hoboken, NJ: John Wiley & Sons.

27. An article on "optimal feedback" is available free at my Web site at http://www.intentionalhappiness.com

▶ Chapter Four Notes

1. Christie, P. (2009). *Every leader a storyteller.* South Africa: KnowRes Publishing.

2. Emmons, R. (1999). *The psychology of ultimate concerns: Motivation and spirituality in personality.* New York: Guilford Press.

3. Gilbert, D. (2006). *Stumbling on happiness.* New York: Knopf.

4. Gilbert, D. T., Pinel, E. C., Wilson, T. D., Blumberg, S. J., & Wheatley, T. P. (1998). Immune neglect: A source of durability bias in affective forecasting. *Journal of Personality and Social Psychology, 75,* 617–638.

5. Gilbert, D. T., Pinel, E. C., Wilson, T. D., Blumberg, S. J., & Wheatley, T. P. (1998). Immune neglect: A source of durability bias in affective forecasting. *Journal of Personality and Social Psychology, 75*, 617–638.

6. Pomerantz, E. M., Saxon, J. L., & Oishi, S. (2000). The psychological trade-offs of goal investment. *Journal of Personality and Social Psychology, 79*, 617–630.

7. Sheldon, K. (2009). *Positive motivation.* A workbook from Positive Psychology Servives, LLC: http://www.intentionalhappiness.com

8. Moskowitz, G. B., & Grant, H. (2008). *The psychology of goals.* New York: Guilford Press.

9. Ibid.

10. Langer, E. (2005). Unpublished data, In T. Kashdan (Ed.). *Curious? Discover the missing ingredients to a fulfilling life.* New York: William Morrow.

11. Kashdan, T. (2008). *Curious? Discover the missing ingredients to a fulfilling life.* New York: William Morrow.

12. Markus, H., & Nurius, P. (1986). Possible selves. *American Psychologist, 41*, 954–969.

13. Dweck, C. (2006). *Mindset: The new psychology of success.* New York: Ballantine Books.

▶ Chapter Five Notes

1. American Psychiatric Association. (1994). *Diagnostic and statistical manual of mental disorders* (4th ed). Washington, DC: Author.

2. Abraham, M. (1971). *The farther reaches of human nature.* New York: Penguin Compass.

3. Sheldon, K. (2009). *Positive Motivation.* A workbook published by Positive Psychology Services, LLC: http://www.intentionalhappiness.com

4. Biswas-Diener, R. (January, 2010). *The 11th hour: How working under pressure can be a strength.* http://www.oprah.com

5. Seligman, M. E. P. (2002). *Authentic happiness: Using the new positive psychology to realize your potential for lasting fulfillment.* New York: Free Press.

6. Peterson, C., & Seligman, M. (2004). *Character strengths and virtues.* Oxford, UK: Oxford/American Psychological Association.

7. American Psychiatric Association. (1994). *Diagnostic and statistical manual of mental disorders* (4th ed). Washington, DC: Author.

8. Levy, A. (2009). Personal communication: A pilot test of positive diagnosis. Unpublished.

9. Linley, A., Willars, J., Stairs, M., Page, N., & Biswas-Diener, R. (2010). *The strengths book: What you can do, love to do, and find it hard to do—and why it matters.* Coventry, UK: CAPP Press.

10. Clifton, D. O., Anderson, E., & Schreiner, L. A. (2006). *Strengths quest: Discover and develop your strengths in academics, career, and beyond* (2nd ed.). New York: Gallup Press.

11. Peterson, C., & Seligman, M. (2004). *Character strengths and virtues.* Oxford, UK: Oxford/American Psychological Association.

12. Holland, J. L. (1996). Exploring careers with a typology: What we have learned and some new directions. *American Psychologist, 51*, 397–406.

13. Lubinski, D., & Benbow, C. P. (2006). Study of mathematically precocious youth after 35 years: Uncovering antecedents for the development of math-science expertise. *Perspectives on Psychological Science, 1*, 316–345. See also Lubinski, D., Benbow, C. P., Webb, R. M., & Bleske-Rechek, A. (2006). Tracking exceptional human capital over two decades. *Psychological Science, 17*, 194–199.

14. Diener, E., Suh, E., Lucas, R., & Smith, H. (1999). Subjective well-being: Three decades of progress. *Psychological Bulletin, 125*, 276–302. See also Diener, E., & Fujita, F. (1995). Resources, personal strivings, and subjective well-being: A nomothetic and idiographic approach. *Journal of Personality and Social Psychology, 68*, 926–935.

15. Diener, E., Emmons, R., Larsen, R., & Griffen, S. (1985). The satisfaction with life scale. *Journal of Personality Assessment, 49*, 71–75.

16. Ryff, C. D., & Singer, B. (1998). The contours of positive human health. *Psychological Inquiry, 9*, 1–28.

17. Diener, E., Wirtz, D., Tov, W., Kim-Prieto, C., Choi. D., Oishi, S., & Biswas-Diener, R. (in press). New measures of well-being: Flourishing and positive and negative feelings. *Social Indicators Research.*

18. Boniwell, I., & Zimbardo, P. G. (2004). Balancing time perspective in pursuit of optimal functioning. In A. Linley & S. Joseph (Eds.), *Positive psychology in practice.* Hoboken, NJ: John Wiley & Sons.

19. Snyder, C. R. (2002). Hope theory: Rainbows of the mind. *Psychological Inquiry, 13*, 249–275.

20. Snyder, C. R., Harris, C., Anderson, J. R., Holleran, S. A., Irving, L. M., & Sigmon, S. T., et al. (1991). The will and the ways: Development and validation of an individual-differences measure of hope. *Journal of Personality and Social Psychology 60*, 570–585.

21. Schwartz, S. H., & Bilsky, W. (1990). Toward a theory of the universal content and structure of values: Extensions and cross cultural replications. *Journal of Personality and Social Psychology, 58*, 878–891.

▶ Chapter Six Notes

1. Tellegen, A., Ben-Porath, Y. S., McNulty, J. L., Arbisi, P. A., Graham, J. R., & Kaemmer, B. (2003). *The MMPI-2 restructured clinical scales: Development, validation, and interpretation.* Minneapolis, MN: University of Minnesota Press.

2. Peterson, C., & Seligman, M. E. P. (2004). *Character strengths and virtues: A handbook and classification.* Washington, DC: APA Press and Oxford University Press.

3. Linley, A., Willars, J., Stairs, M., Page, N., & Biswas-Diener, R. (2010). *The strengths book: What you can do, love to do, and find it hard to do—and why it matters.* Coventry, UK: CAPP Press.

4. Emmons, R. A., & McCullough, M. E. (2003). Counting blessings versus burdens: An experimental investigation of gratitude and subjective well-being in daily life. *Journal of Personality and Social Psychology, 84*, 377–389.

5. Dweck, C. (2006). *Mindset: The new psychology of success.* New York: Ballentine Books.

6. Diener, E., Emmons, R. A., Larsen, R. J., & Griffin, S. (1985). The satisfaction with life scale. *Journal of Personality Assessment, 49,* 71–75. See also Pavot, W. G., Diener, E., Colvin, C. R., & Sandvik, E. (1991). Further validation of the satisfaction with life scale: Evidence for the cross-method convergence of well-being measures. *Journal of Personality Assessment, 57,* 149–161.

7. Frisch, M. B. (2006). *Quality of life therapy: Applying a life satisfaction approach to positive psychology and cognitive therapy.* Hoboken, NJ: John Wiley & Sons.

8. Oishi, S., Diener, E., & Lucas, R. (2007). The optimum level of well-being: Can people be too happy? *Perspectives on Psychological Science, 2*(4), 346–360.

9. Diener, E., Wirtz, D., Tov, W., Kim-Prieto, C., Choi, D., Oishi, S., & Biswas-Diener, R. (in press). New measures of well-being: Flourishing and positive and negative feelings. *Social Indicators Research.*

10. Lyubomirsky, S., & Lepper, H. (1999). A measure of subjective happiness: Preliminary reliability and construct validation. *Social Indicators Research, 46,* 137–155.

11. Steger, M. F., Frazier, P., Oishi, S., & Kaler, M. (2006). The meaning in life questionnaire: Assessing the presence of and search for meaning in life. *Journal of Counseling Psychology, 53,* 80–93.

12. Steger, M. F., Frazier, P., Oishi, S., & Kaler, M. (2006). The meaning in life questionnaire: Assessing the presence of and search for meaning in life. *Journal of Counseling Psychology, 53,* 80–93.

13. Steger, M. (January, 2010). Personal communication.

14. Bellah, R. N., Madsen, R., Sullivan, W. M., Swidler, A., & Tipton, S. M. (1996). *Habits of the heart: Individualism and commitment in American life* (updated ed.) Berkeley, CA: University of California Press.

15. Wrzesniewski, A., McCauley, C. R., Rozin, P., & Schwartz, B. (1997). Jobs, careers, and callings: People's relations to their work. *Journal of Research in Personality, 31,* 21–33.

16. Wrzesniewski, A., & Dutton, J. E. (2001). Crafting a job: Revisioning employees as active crafters of their work. *Academy of Management Review, 26,* 179–201.

17. Biswas-Diener, R., & Linley, A. (2009). *Purposeful work scale.* Unpublished.

18. Kashdan, T. B., & Silvia, P. J. (2009). Curiosity and interest: The benefits of thriving on novelty and challenge. In C. R. Snyder & S. J. Lopez (Eds.), *Handbook of positive psychology* (2nd ed., pp. 367–374). New York: Oxford University Press.

19. Kashdan, T. B., Gallagher, M. W., Silvia, P. J., Winterstein, B. P., Breen, W. E., Terhar, D., & Steger, M. F. (2009). The Curiosity and Exploration Inventory-II: Development, factor structure, and initial psychometrics. *Journal of Research in Personality, 43,* 987–998.

20. Bryant, F. & Veroff, J. (2007). *Savoring: A new model of positive emotion.* Mahwah, NJ: Lawrence Erlbaum.

21. Bryant, F. B. (2003). Savoring Beliefs Inventory (SBI): A scale for measuring beliefs about savoring. *Journal of Mental Health, 12,* 175–196.

22. Biswas-Diener, R. (2009). *Work style scale.* Unpublished pilot data.

23. Wood, A., Linley, A., Maltby, J., Baliousis, M., & Joseph, S. (2008). The authentic personality: A theoretical and empirical conceptualization and the development of the authenticity scale. *Journal of Counseling Psychology, 55,* 385–399.

24. Wood, A., Linley, A., Maltby, J., Baliousis, M., & Joseph, S. (2008). The authentic personality: A theoretical and empirical conceptualization and the development of the authenticity scale. *Journal of Counseling Psychology, 55,* 385–399.

25. Wood, A., Linley, A., Maltby, J., Baliousis, M., & Joseph, S. (2008). The authentic personality: A theoretical and empirical conceptualization and the development of the authenticity scale. *Journal of Counseling Psychology, 55,* 385–399.

26. Govindji, R., & Linley, A. (2007). Strengths use, self-concordance and well-being: Implications for strengths coaching and coaching psychologists. *International Coaching Psychology Review, 2,* 143–153.

27. Govindji, R., & Linley, A. (2007). Strengths use, self-concordance, and well-being: Implications for strengths coaching and coaching psychologists. *International Coaching Psychology Review, 2,* 143–153.

▶ Chapter Seven Notes

1. Shweder, R. (1998). *Welcome to middle age! And other cultural fictions.* University of Chicago Press.

2. Erikson, E. (1994). *Identity and the life cycle.* New York: W. W. Norton.

3. Wrzesniewski, A., McCauley, C. R., Rozin, P., & Schwartz, B. (1997). Jobs, careers, and callings: People's relations to their work. *Journal of Research in Personality, 31,* 21–33.

4. Erikson, E. (1994). *Identity and the life cycle.* New York: W.W. Norton.

5. Kitiyama, S., & Markus, H. (2000). The pursuit of happiness and the realization of sympathy: Cultural patterns of self, social relations, and well-being. In E. Diener & E. M. Suh (Eds.), *Culture and subjective well-being* (pp. 113–161). Cambridge, MA: MIT Press.

6. Nisbett, R. (2003). *The geography of thought.* New York: Free Press. See also Suh, E. M. (2000). Self: The hyphen between culture and subjective well-being. In E. Diener & E. M. Suh (Eds.), *Culture and subjective well-being* (pp. 63–86). Cambridge, MA: MIT Press.

7. Ibarra, H. (2003). *Working identity: Unconventional strategies for reinventing your career.* Boston: Harvard Business School Press.

8. Wrzesniewski, A., McCauley, C. R., Rozin, P., & Schwartz, B. (1997). Jobs, careers, and callings: People's relations to their work. *Journal of Research in Personality, 31,* 21–33.

9. Strachan, E., Schimel, J., Arndt, J., Williams, T., Solomon, S., Pyszczynski, T., & Greenberg, J. (2007). Terror mismanagement: Evidence that mortality salience exacerbates phobic and compulsive behaviors. *Personality and Social Psychology Bulletin, 33,* 1137–1151.

10. Pyszczynski, T., Abdollahi, A., Solomon, S., Greenberg, J., Cohen, F., & Weise, D. (2006). Mortality salience, martyrdom, and military might: The Great Satan versus the Axis of Evil. *Personality and Social Psychology Bulletin, 32,* 525–537. See also Weise, T., Pyszczynski, C., Cox, J., Arndt, J., Greenberg, & Solomon, S.

(2008). Interpersonal politics: The role of terror management and attachment processes in shaping political preferences. *Psychological Science, 19,* 448–455.

11. Pyszczynski, T., Wicklund, R., Floresku, S., & Koch, H. (1996). Whistling in the dark: Exaggerated consensus estimates in response to incidental reminders of mortality. *Psychological Science, 7,* 332–336.

▶ Chapter Eight Notes

1. Biswas-Diener, R. (2009). Personal coaching as a positive intervention. *Journal of Clinical Psychology, 65,* 544–553.

2. Seligman, M. E. P. (2002). *Authentic happiness: Using the new positive psychology to realize your potential for lasting fulfillment.* New York: Free Press.

3. International Coach Federation: Code of ethics. http://www.coachfederation.org/about-icf/ethics-&-regulation/.

4. Whitworth, L., Kimsey-House, H., & Sandhal, P. (1998). *Co-active coaching: New skills for coaching people toward success in work and life.* Palo Alto, CA: Davies-Black.

5. Special Group in Coaching Psychology—British Psychological Society. http://www.bps.org.uk/sgcp/sgcp_home.cfm.

6. Kotecha, S. (May, 2009). Personal communication.

7. Biswas-Diener, R., & Dean, B. (2007). *Positive psychology coaching: Putting the science of happiness to work for your clients.* Hoboken, NJ: John Wiley & Sons.

Author Index

A

Akrivou, K., 45
Arakawa, D., 32

B

Bellah, R., 111
Boniwell, I., 90
Boyatzis, R., 15, 44, 45, 47–48
Bryant, F., 5, 116, 118
Buckingham, M., 38

C

Christie, P., 62
Christopher, S., 55
Clifton, D., 20
Clifton, D. O., 32
Cooperrider, D., 48
Covey, S., 1

D

Dean, B., 1, 151
Diener, E., 9, 106
Dik, B., 110
Drucker, P., 20
Dweck, C., 73, 103

E

Erikson, E., 128, 134

F

Fredrickson, B., 40–41
Frisch, M., 105

G

Gilbert, D., 64
Gillett, R., 32
Gostick, A., 55
Govindji, R., 122, 123
Grant, A., 6
Greenberg, M., 32

H

Harter, J. K., 32
Holland, J., 84
Hsieh, T., 49

J

Jordan, M., 73
Joseph, S., 32
Julian, T., 32

K

Kashdan, T., 72, 115
Kashdan, T. B., 32
King, L., 44
Kotecha, S., 150

L

Langer, E., 72
Levy, A., 81
Linley, A., 32, 122, 123
Lubinski, D., 84
Lyubomirsky, S., 15, 41, 43, 108

M

Maltby, J., 32
Markus, H., 72
Maslow, A., 78, 80
Merritt, K., 32

O

Oettingen, G., 71

P

Park, N., 32
Parks, A., 32
Peterson, C., 32, 80
Pomerantz, E., 66

R

Rashid, T., 32
Rath, T., 32, 43
Ryff, C., 89

S

Schwartz, S., 95
Seligman, M., 32, 63, 80
Silva, P., 115
Snyder, R., 91
Steen, T., 32
Steger, M., 109–110

U

Uswatte, G., 32

W

Warr, P., 15, 53–54
Whitworth, L., 12, 148
Wilson, T., 64
Wood, A., 121
Wood, A. M., 32
Wrzesniewski, A., 111, 139

Z

Zimbardo, P., 90

Subject Index

A

Accepting external influences, 121–122
Adult Hope Scale, 91–92
Affect, 68
Age, measuring perception of, 128–129.
   See also Lifespan, coaching across
Agency thinking, 91
All-in-one training (for certification),
   149
Appreciation, 43
Appreciative Inquiry, 48
Artistic interests, 84
Assessments, 16, 99–123
   Adult Hope Scale, 91–92
   advantages of, 99–100
   Authenticity Scale, 121–123
   criteria for, 101
   Curiosity and Exploration Inventory,
     114–116
   Domain Satisfaction Scales, 104–106
   empirically validated, 102–103
   Individual Strengths Assessment, 33
   labels, 103–104
   Meaning in Life Questionnaire,
     109–110
   personal development and, 76
   Psychological Well-Being Scale, 90
   Purposeful Work Scale, 114
   Satisfaction with Life Scale, 9, 88–89
   Savoring Beliefs Inventory, 116–119
   Scale of Positive and Negative
     Experience (SPANE), 106–107
   self-assessment, 101
   strengths assessments, 83
   Strengths Use Scale, 122–123
   Subjective Happiness Scale, 108
   using established positive psychology
     assessments, 9–10
   VIA assessment of strengths, 80–81
Work-Life Questionnaire, 111–113
Work-Style Scale, 120
Asset-based Thinking Focus, 81–82
Authenticity Scale, 121–123
Authentic living, 121–122
Autonomy, in psychological well-being, 89

B

Baby boomer generation, 127
Behavioral strengths, 33. *See also*
   Strengths
Brainstorming, 12–13
Bravery, 32
British Psychological Society, 149

C

Capacities (axis 1)
   coaching interests guide, 85
   interests, 84–86
   resources, 86–87
   strengths, 83
   strengths assessment guide, 83
CAPP (Centre for Applied Positive
   Psychology), 5
Career change, 132
Center for Positive Organizational
   Scholarship (U. of Michigan), 49
Centre for Applied Positive Psychology
   (CAPP), 5
Certification, 8, 11–12, 148–149
Clients
   capacities, 83–87
   client agenda, 63, 148
   communicating your approach with,
     10–11
   developing strengths of, 34–36
   identifying personal values, 49–51
   identifying strengths of, 26–28

Clients *(Continued)*
　introducing strengths to, 29–33
　reluctance of, to focus on strengths,
　　32–33
　reviewing strengths of, 149–150
Clifton StrengthsFinder, 83. *See also*
　StrengthsFinder
Coaching. *See* Positive psychology
　coaching
Co-Active Coaching (Whitworth),
　12, 148
Connectedness, in psychological well-
　being, 89
Construct validity, 102
Conventional interests, 84
Courage, 137
Crafting your job, 140. *See also* Job
　crafting
Credentialing, 7–8
Criterion validity, 102
Curiosity, 72, 114–115
Curiosity and Exploration Inventory,
　114–116
Customer satisfaction surveys, 88

D

Death, fear of, 140–142
Development stages, 128
Diagnosis, multiaxial, 81. *See also*
　Positive diagnosis
*Diagnostic and Statistical Manual of
　Mental Disorders* (DSM), 76–77
Direction, toward goal, 68, 69
Directories, of coaches, 13
Discrepancy, and goal, 68, 69
Docility, 68
Domain Satisfaction Scales, 104–106
Duration neglect, 64

E

Easterlin Paradox, 7
"Education to Empowerment" model, 4
Effort, 69
Elevation, 3
Emotion

assessment of (*See* Scale of Positive
　and Negative Experience [SPANE])
　in workplace, 54
Empirical keying, 99
Empirical validation, 102–103
Employment
　career change, 132
　conceptual categories (work-life),
　　111–113
　meaningful work and, 110
　middle age and passion for, 131–144
　personal values and, 131–133
　purposeful work, 114
Energy, and strength, 22, 26–27
Enterprising interests, 84
Equifinality, 67–68
Expectations, 71
Experience, openness to, 115
Extrinsic motivation, 79

F

Failure, 74, 130
Failure impact predictions, 66
Fantasies, 71
Fear
　of accepting the present, 143–144,
　　144
　of death, 140–142
　of having lived the past wrong, 143,
　　144
　of losing the past, 142–143, 144
Feedback, 55–56
Fixed mindsets, 73
Fun, in workplace, 55
Future, pull of, 63–74
Future orientation
　Adult Hope Scale, 91–92
　positive diagnosis, axis 3, 90–94

G

Generativity, 128
Goals
　client disconnect, 70
　coach disconnect, 70
　curiosity and, 72

dark side of, 66
focus and, 66
as future-oriented benchmarks, 63
motivation and, 68–69
optimism and, 69–70
outside forces on, 61
resource-goal match, 70
success criteria, establishing, 70–71
Gratitude, 32
Gratitude exercise, 42–43, 102, 103
Growth
in psychological well-being, 89
unrealized strengths and, 34
Growth mindsets, 73

H

Happiness, 15, 147–148
income and level of, 7
optimal happiness concept, 52
positivity and, 40–42
psychological well-being, 89
strength identification and, 32
Subjective Happiness Scale, 108
Hardship, 130
Hope, 15
agency thinking, 91
goals and, 61–62
hope theory, 91
pathways thinking, 91
How Full is Your Bucket? (Rath), 32–33
Humor, 32

I

Idealism, 136
Identified motivation, 79
Identity, work as key to, 137
Illness, recovery from, 32
Impact bias, 64
Imposter syndrome, 143
Incubators (work-style), 24, 79–80, 120
Individual Change Theory, 44–48
ideal self, 45–47
positive affect, 47–48

Individual Strengths Assessment, 33
Inspiration, 3
"Intellectual tilt," 85
Interests (positive diagnosis, axis 1), 84–86
International Coach Federation (ICF), 6, 7
positive psychology coaching certification, 148–149
Interventions, 5, 102–103
Intrinsic motivation, 79
Introjected motivation, 79
Investigative interests, 84

J

Job crafting, 140
Jobs
conceptual categories (work-life), 111–113
meaningful, 110
purposeful work, 114
Job satisfaction surveys, 88

K

Kilimanjaro climb, 59–61
Kindness, 32

L

Labels, 103–104
Language
coaching and language of client, 33
strengths vocabulary, 23–25, 33
Layoffs, 38
Legacies, 131, 142
The Levity Effect (Gostick and Christopher), 55
Lifespan, coaching across
measuring perception of age, 128–129
middle age, 126–144 (*See also* Middle age)

M

Management, strengths-based, 37–38
Mantra, 142

Master's degree, in positive psychology coaching, 8
Mastery, in psychological well-being, 89
Meaning in Life Questionnaire, 109–110
Memorabilia, 116
MentorCoach, 8
Middle age
    as "development stage," 128
    Eastern cultures and, 137
    fear of death, 140–142
    "Is Life Getting Better or Worse" survey, 138–139
    as opportunity, 130–131
    perception of aging, 128–129
    personal values and, 131–135
    physical transitions, 126, 127, 138–139, 141–142
    possible identities, 137–138
    psychological transformation, 127
    re-connecting with work, 134–135
    sense of urgency in, 143
    work and passion, 131–144
"Mid-life crisis," 125–126, 127, 137
Mindset, 73
Minnesota Multiphasic Personality Inventory-II, 99
Mission statement, 49–51, 142
MMPI 2, 99
Models, 146
Mortality. See Death, fear of
Motivation
    affect, 68–69
    curiosity and, 115
    docility, 68
    effort, 69
    equifinality, 67–68
    fantasies and, 71
    feedback and, 55–56
    goals and, 67–69
    markers of motivated behavior, 67–69
    persistence-until, 67
    positive diagnosis and, 79
    types of, 79
    values and, 136
    work-style and, 120

Mt. Kilimanjaro climb, 59–61
Multiaxial diagnosis, 81
Myers-Briggs Type Indicator, 76

N

Negative emotional attractors, 47
Norwich Union, 37

O

Openness, 115
Opportunity
    fear of having missed, 143
    middle age as, 130–131
Optimal happiness, 52
Optimism, 32, 91
    goals and, 69–70
    realism of, 70–72
Organizations, strength-based, 36–38
    recruitment and, 37
    strengths-based management, 37–38
Outplacement, 38

P

Panic attacks, diagnosing, 77
Paradigm shift, 11
Passion, for work, 135
Passive behavior, 67
Pathways thinking, 91
Performance recognition, 43
Persistence-Until, 67
Personal development, 49
Personal life mission statement, 142
Personal values, 49
Personal Values Survey, 95–96
Personal vision statement, 49
Planners (work-style), 120
Portfolio approach (to certification), 149
Positive diagnosis, 15, 75–96
    capacities (axis 1), 83–87
    client agendas, 75
    future orientation (axis 3), 90–94
    positive psychology and positive diagnosis, 76–78

Satisfaction with Life Scale, 88–89
self-actualization behaviors, 78–81
situational benefactors (axis 4), 92–94
suggestion for system for, 81–82
understanding *DSM* diagnosis, 77
values (axis 5), 95–96
well-being (axis 2), 87–90
Positive emotional attractors, 47
Positive fantasies, 71
Positive psychology. *See also* Positivity
marketing, 13–14
optimal happiness and, 52
as a science, 5
summarized, 5
Positive psychology coaching, 1–17, 145–
151. *See also* Lifespan, coaching across
advantages of, 5–7, 12–14
basic tools of, 145
certification, 148–149
compared to other forms of coaching,
10–11
comparison of types of, 146–147
credentialing, 7–8, 11–12, 147
defined, 90
developing client's strengths, 34–36
developing yourself as a strengths
coach, 22–28
"Education to Empowerment" model,
4
explaining, 147–148
goals and hopes for future, 59–74,
150–151
positivity and, 56–57
professionalism of, 7–12
session preparation, 149–150
with strengths vocabulary, 23–25, 33
summarized, 5
tenets of, 146
time orientation of, 90
training schools, 6
Positive Psychology Coaching (Biswas-
Diener and Dean), 151
negative review of, 1–2
writing and collaboration of, 1
"Positive reminiscence," 5–6
Positivity, 39–57
appreciation and, 43
benefits of, 41–42
best or better possible self, 51–53
coaching and, 56–57
creating structures for, 150
feedback and, 55–56
"gratitude exercise," 42–43
happiness and, 40–42
increasing, in workplace, 53–56
Individual Change Theory, 44–48
reflected best self, 48–49
satisfaction and, 52–53
updated, 44–53
"Possible selves," 72
Praise, 32–33
Pride, 20
Procrastinators (work-style), 79–80, 120
Professionalization, 151
Psychological Well-Being Scale, 90
Psychology, traditional, 80
Purposeful Work Scale, 114
Purpose in life, in psychological well-
being, 89

Q

Quality of Life Therapy, 105

R

Rate of progress, toward goal, 68, 69
Realise 2 Practitioner Programme, 9,
83, 99–100
Realistic interests, 84
"Recognition gap," 43
Recruitment, strengths-based, 37
Reflected best self, 48–49
"Resacralization," 78
Research, 8
Resilience trainings, 9
Resources, 86–87

S

Sailboat metaphor, 31
San Francisco State University
certificate coaching programs, 8

Satisfaction with Life Scale, 9, 88–89
Savoring Beliefs Inventory
   inventory, 116–117
   scoring, 117–119
Scale of Positive and Negative
     Experience (SPANE), 106–107
"Self"
   Eastern vs. Western views of, 137
   physical decline and, 138–139
   possible selves at work, 139–140
Self-acceptance, 144
Self-actualization behaviors, 78–81
Self-alienation, 121–122
Self-Directed Search, 84
Self-knowledge, situational benefactors,
   94
Sense of self, 72–74
Situational Benefactors, 92–94
SMART goals, 63
Social anxiety, 32
Social interactions, 113
Social interests, 84
Special Group on Coaching, 149
Spirituality, 141
Spontaneity, 72
Stagnation, 128
Stereotyping, 67
Storytelling, 62
Strengths, 15
   addressing weaknesses and, 30–31
   anticipation and, 28
   authentic and energizing, 21–22
   avoiding overuse of, 35
   behavioral, 33
   coaching, 22–28
   concept of, 20
   defined, 20–21
   developing client's strengths, 34–36
   identifying, 22, 26–28
   introducing, to clients, 29–33
   labeling, 25–26
   metaphors for, 26
   in organizations, 36–38
   positive diagnosis, axis 1, 83–87
   recruitment and, 37
   science of, 12
   scientific foundation for focus on, 31–32

   and success, 19–38
   tapping, 27
   "unrealized," 34
   VIA assessment of, 80–81
   vigilance in noting signs of, 9
   vocabulary, 23–25, 33
StrengthsFinder, Clifton, 83
Strengths introduction, 29–33
Strengths Training (VIA), 9
Strengths Use Scale, 122–123
Strengths x interests timeline activity, 86
"Strength tilt," 86
Strong Interest Inventory, 76
Subjective Happiness Scale, 108
Success, visualization of, 116

T

"Taking Stock of Your Positives," 81–82
Terror Management Theory, 141
Terry Levine Positive Psychology
     Coaching Program, 8
Time orientation, of coaching, 90
Training, 8–9
Trait Curiosity and Exploration
     Inventory-II, 115
Transitions, 16
Triflers (work-style), 120

U

Unemployment, 38
University of East London Master's
     degree program, 8
University of Michigan Center
     for Positive Organizational
     Scholarship, 49
University of Pennsylvania Master's
     degree program, 8, 13–14
Unrealized strengths, 34
Urgency, 143

V

Valence prediction, 64
Validity, 102–103

Values
    identifying personal, 49
    middle age careers and, 131–133
    motivation and, 136
    passion for work and, 134–135
    revisiting original values, 136–144
    Zappos.com and, 49–50
Values (axis 5), 95–96
Values in Action Institute (VIA), 99
    assessment of strengths, 80–81, 83
    strengths training, 9
VIA. *See* Values in Action Institute
        (VIA)
Visioning, 5, 62
Vision statement, 49
Visualization, 71, 116

W

Weaknesses, addressing, 30–31
Well-being
    positive diagnosis, axis 2, 87–90
    Psychological Well-Being Scale, 90

Satisfaction with Life Scale, 88–89
    in workplace, 53–54
Work issues
    conceptual categories (work-life), 111
    disengagement, 132
    feelings about work, 133–134
    "fun" in workplace, 55
    identifying employee strengths, 38
    increasing positivity, 53–56
    meaningful work, 110
    possible "selves" at work, 139–140
    purposeful work, 114
    "recognition gap," 43
    re-connecting with work, 134–135
    work and passion, 131–144
Work-Life Questionnaire, 111–113, 133
Work-Style Scale, 120

Z

Zappos.com, 49–50, 55

STUDY PACKAGE
CONTINUING EDUCATION
CREDIT INFORMATION

Practicing Positive Psychology Coaching: Assessment, Activities & Strategies for Success

Our goal is to provide you with current, accurate, and practical information from the most experienced and knowledgeable speakers and authors.

Listed below are the continuing education credit(s) currently available for this self-study package. *Please note: Your state licensing board dictates whether self study is an acceptable form of continuing education. Please refer to your state rules and regulations.*

COUNSELORS: PESI, LLC is recognized by the National Board for Certified Counselors to offer continuing education for National Certified Counselors. Provider #: 5896. We adhere to NBCC Continuing Education Guidelines. This self-study package qualifies for **3.0** contact hours.

SOCIAL WORKERS: PESI, LLC, 1030, is approved as a provider for continuing education by the Association of Social Work Boards, 400 South Ridge Parkway, Suite B, Culpeper, VA 22701. www.aswb.org. Social workers should contact their regulatory board to determine course approval. Course Level: All Levels. Social Workers will receive **3.0** (Clinical) continuing education clock hours for completing this self-study package.

PSYCHOLOGISTS: PESI, LLC is approved by the American Psychological Association to sponsor continuing education for psychologists. PESI, LLC maintains responsibility for these materials and their content. PESI is offering these self-study materials for **3.0** hours of continuing education credit.

ADDICTION COUNSELORS: PESI, LLC is a provider approved by NAADAC Approved Education Provider Program. Provider #: 366. This self-study package qualifies for **3.5** contact hours.

Procedures:

1. Review the material and read the book.

2. If seeking credit, complete the post-test/evaluation form:

   -Complete post-test/evaluation in entirety; include your e-mail address to receive your certificate much faster versus by mail.

   -Upon completion, mail to the address listed on the form along with the CE fee stated on the test. Tests will not be processed without the CE fee included.

   -Completed post-tests must be received 6 months from the date printed on the packing slip.

Your completed post-test/evaluation will be graded. If you receive a passing score (70% and above), you will be e-mailed/faxed/mailed a certificate of successful completion with earned continuing education credits. (Please write your e-mail address on the post-test/evaluation form for fastest response.) If you do not pass the post-test, you will be sent a letter indicating areas of deficiency, and another post-test to complete. The post-test must be resubmitted and receive a passing grade before credit can be awarded. We will allow you to retake as many times as necessary to receive a certificate.

If you have any questions, please feel free to contact our customer service department at 1.800.844.8260.

PESI LLC
PO BOX 1000
Eau Claire, WI 54702-1000

Practicing Positive Psychology Coaching: Assessment, Activities & Strategies for Success

PO BOX 1000
Eau Claire, WI 54702
800-844-8260

Any persons interested in receiving credit may photocopy this form, complete and return with a payment of $15.00 per person CE fee. A certificate of successful completion will be sent to you. To receive your certificate sooner than two weeks, rush processing is available for a fee of $10. Please attach check or include credit card information below.

Mail to: PESI, PO Box 1000, Eau Claire, WI 54702 or fax to PESI (800) 554-9775 (both sides)

CE Fee: $15: (Rush processing fee: $10)   **Total to be charged** _____

Credit Card #: _____   **Exp Date:** _____   **V-Code*:** _____
(*MC/VISA/Discover: last 3-digit # on signature panel on back of card.) (*American Express: 4-digit # above account # on face of card.)

	LAST	FIRST	M.I.

Name (please print): _____   _____   _____

Address: _____   Daytime Phone: _____

City: _____   State: _____   Zip Code: _____

Signature: _____   E-mail: _____

Date Completed: _____ Actual time (# of hours) taken to complete this offering: _____ hours

Program Objectives After completing this publication, I have been able to achieve these objectives:

Articulate the ways in which positive psychology coaching and clinical psychology can influence one another	Yes	No
Define Strengths and Happiness	Yes	No
Identify the components of Hope Theory and apply them to client situations	Yes	No
Identify and use positive psychology assessments	Yes	No
Explain the concept of positive diagnosis	Yes	No
Spot strengths in clients using the hallmark features of strengths	Yes	No

PESI LLC
PO BOX 1000
Eau Claire, WI 54702-1000

Participant Profile:

1. Job Title: _____ Employment setting: _____

1. Which of the following is the best definition of a "strength"?
a. A personality trait that is relatively fixed across time and situations.
b. A personal value that is the product of culture and personal experience.
c. A preexisting capacity that is energizing and which leads to success when used.
d. A talent that is developed through hard work and practice.

2. Which of the following is the best description of research on happiness?
a. Happiness has been found to be widely beneficial to health and relationships.
b. Happiness cannot be effectively studied because it is so subjective.
c. Happiness has been found to be associated with selfishness, distrust, and destructive pleasure-seeking behaviors.
d. Happiness has been found to exist in Western cultures, such as that of the United States, but not in Eastern cultures, such as that of Japan.

3. What are the two parts of "Hope Theory"?
a. Idea generation and idea implementation.
b. Positivity and the "rose-colored glasses" phenomenon.
c. Agency thinking and pathways thinking.
d. Savoring and optimism.

4. Which of the following is the distinguishing feature of the "positive diagnosis" system presented in the book?
a. It integrates positive and negative information.
b. It measures a person's strengths.
c. It is multiaxial, using information from many sources.
d. It is more valid than the traditional "medical model" system.

5. Which of the following is the best definition of "positive psychology coaching"?
a. Coaching which focuses on positive aspects of functioning while overlooking the negative.
b. Coaching which is informed by the science of positive psychology research and assessment.
c. Coaching which is practiced by someone who is a certified positive psychologist.
d. All coaching is positive psychology coaching.

6. Which of the following is most accurate about coaching during mid-life issues?
a. Mid-life has traditionally been viewed as a period of existential crisis, but the truth is people in mid-life have many advantages such as being—on average—wealthier, better respected, and more powerful than young people.
b. Mid-life is a period of crisis because of health problems associated with growing older. Only by addressing health issues first can practitioners effectively work with psychological and social issues.
c. Mid-life is a period of crisis for many people. The most effective way to deal with this transitional stage is to teach people resilience strategies such as "accepting their lot in life."
d. Mid-life is a period of unparalleled opportunity, and people who miss this fact may suffer from a lack of accurate self-knowledge.

7. Which of the following is true of positive assessment?
a. Positive assessment does not work because of the "Barnum Effect," in which people are likely to agree with flattering feedback regardless of its accuracy.
b. Positive assessment does not work because it describes only half of the human condition and overlooks important problems.
c. Positive assessment works by using validated measures to gauge mental health and psychological flourishing.
d. Positive assessment works by integrating a person's self-assessment with an empirically validated measure.

8. Which of the following best describes the current state of positive psychology coaching?
a. Positive psychology coaching is a successful business model because positive feedback and encouragement are attractive to potential clients.
b. Positive psychology coaching is not well regulated, and the author advocates for better standards for training and practice.
c. Positive psychology coaching is well regulated, and the author applauds the major accrediting bodies for the field.
d. Positive psychology coaching is indistinguishable from solutions-focused therapy.

9. Which of the following best describes the concept of "optimal happiness"?
a. Because it is subjectively defined, each individual is the best judge of how happy he or she should be.
b. Because happiness is so widely associated with health benefits, there is no such thing as "too much happiness."
c. Because happiness leads to a focus on the self, people should avoid being "too happy" because they will be less likely to help others.
d. Research shows that in achievement-oriented domains such as work and school performance, those who score an 8 out of 10 on satisfaction tend to outperform those who score a 9 or 10.

10. Which of the following is NOT a marker of client strengths?
a. The increased use of metaphor.
b. More rapid speech.
c. Increased deliberation before action.
d. More animated hand gestures.

PESI LLC
PO BOX 1000
Eau Claire, WI 54702-1000